PERL AND CGI

FOR THE WORLD WIDE WEB

VISUAL QUICKSTART GUIDE

SECOND EDITION

by Elizabeth Castro

 Peachpit Press

Perl and CGI for the World Wide Web, Second Edition:
Visual QuickStart Guide
by Elizabeth Castro

Peachpit Press
1249 Eighth Street
Berkeley, CA 94710
(510) 524-2178
(510) 524-2221 (fax)

Find us on the World Wide Web at: *http://www.peachpit.com*
Liz's support site for this book is at *http://www.cookwood.com/perl2e/*

Peachpit Press is a division of Pearson Education

Copyright © 2001 by Elizabeth Castro

Cover design: The Visual Group

ISBN: 0-201-73568-7

0 9 8 7 6 5 4 3 2 1

Printed in the United States of America

For Andreu, Anna, Xavier, and this new one,
who bring incredible joy to my life.

Special thanks to:

Nancy Davis, *my wonderful friend and editor.*

Matisse Enzer, *for his technical eye and for answering endless questions.*

Dave Cross, *who not only pointed out the problems but also helped me fix them.*

My crew of **beta testers** *who helped get the kinks out of the scripts and the text:* **Alan Stoner**, **Kevin K. Smith**, **Dave Hirano**, *and* **Rhonda Fentem** *were especially amazing, and I was also lucky to have* **Jim Bitrick, Scott Offen**, **Dave Shardell**, **Kevin Thomas**, **Rob Wyatt**, **Daniel Gray**, *and* **Brian Foster**.

Lincoln Stein, *who created CGI.pm and still makes time to answer questions about it.*

Larry Wall, *for creating Perl and for sharing it with the rest of us.*

And to Andreu, *who makes it all worth it.*

TABLE OF CONTENTS

Table of Contents

Table of Contents

Table of Contents

Table of Contents

INTRODUCTION

So what does it mean to program, anyway? Is it dangerous? And I don't mean that facetiously. Many people have a glorified idea of programming as this complicated thing that only pocket-protector carrying, certified nerds are clever enough to do. And if the rest of us try it we'll probably screw something up, like erase our hard disks or something.

Maybe programmers like this mystique... certainly they don't seem to make it easy to break into the art of programming. Most books that you read about programming start off somewhere in the middle, assuming you've already done some programming somewhere, and that you're just learning a *new* language, with the basic concepts already under your belt.

This book starts at the very beginning. Even if you've never, ever programmed before, you'll be able to understand this book. At the same time, I won't bore you to tears with a lot of theory or lengthy explanations. And I won't treat you like an idiot. We'll get started right away, but we'll start at the beginning. You don't have to have any previous knowledge of Unix commands, you don't have to already know what a variable is, or what arrays are, or any of that incomprehensible programspeak: I'll teach you as we go along. Let's start!

What Is a Program?

If you've used a computer, you've used a program. Perhaps you've written a letter with Microsoft Word, played a game of Doom, or balanced your checkbook with Quicken. All of these programs were created by writing lines of commands, called *code*. Each line of code contains instructions that dictate what should happen given a certain kind of input. For example, somewhere in Word's code there is a line (or three) that says "if the user chooses Times 12 point, change the text so that it is displayed in Times 12 point".

Unfortunately, programs aren't written in English (or any other spoken language). Instead, they're written in languages that are easy for computers to understand. And since the computers are the ones that have to do most of the work, I suppose that makes sense. Some common programming languages are C, C++, Pascal, and, well, Perl.

Like spoken languages, computer languages have their own grammar, syntax, and even their own punctuation. Thankfully, computer languages are generally a lot easier to learn than, say, French or Japanese. Computer languages have few or no exceptions (no, "i before e *except* after c"), and the rules are generally straightforward and easy to follow. And, you don't have to worry about pronunciation!

And scripts?

Like a program, a *script* is a collection of lines of code that contain instructions for the computer. The basic difference is that programs are *compiled* so that they'll run more quickly on particular operating systems while scripts are just text files that are *interpreted* as necessary. Perl is a bit of a hybrid, since it is written in text format (like scripts) that are compiled each time you run them. The most important thing you need to know is that you don't have to do anything special to a Perl script before running it.

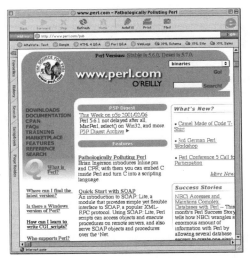

Figure 1.1 *This is Perl's home page, which you can find at* www.perl.com. *It contains a wealth of information and resources, as well as the history of Perl.*

Why Perl?

With so many languages from which to choose, why do so many people use Perl to make their Web pages interactive? Perl—which stands for *Practical Extraction and Report Language*—wasn't even designed for the Web. In fact, it was created by Larry Wall in 1986 to create reports for the company where he was working. Since then, he (and others) have added to it and made it into a powerful, full-featured (perhaps over-featured) programming language that does much more than provide the one solution for which it was created way back when.

In fact, nowadays, people use Perl to do a wide variety of things. But one of its most popular uses is to make Web pages interactive. There are Perl scripts for processing forms, creating guestbooks, creating Web-based bulletin boards, counting the number of times a Web page is visited, and much more.

Perl is particularly suited to Web-related tasks for three reasons. First, it is a powerful text-manipulation tool. You can take a long stream of characters (say, the information entered into a Web form) and quickly separate it into fields and data—that is, information that can be used, compiled, and stored. Second, Perl is easily moved *(ported)* from one platform to another. A script written on a Windows system can be easily copied to a Unix machine or Macintosh with few or no changes. Next, Perl has a reputation as a cool language—really! Perl programmers love to brag about how they can do anything with Perl, on one line, in several different ways. Finally, Perl is fun!

What about CGI?

If you already have a script written in Perl, what do you need CGI for? CGI—which stands for *Common Gateway Interface*—is a *protocol* (a way of doing things), not a programming language. That means that it's the usual way that servers talk to the programs that they interact with. Therefore, any script that sends or receives information from a server needs to follow the standards specified by CGI. When folks talk about *CGI scripts* (or if they're really cool, *CGIs*), they're talking about scripts written in a programming language—often, but not always, Perl—that follow the CGI protocol.

So, some Perl scripts are CGI scripts (the ones that follow the CGI protocol) and some are not. And some so-called CGI scripts are Perl scripts (the ones that are written in Perl), but some are not (they are also commonly found written in C, tcl, Visual Basic, and AppleScript).

In this book, you'll learn about creating Perl CGI scripts—specifically for getting, processing, and returning information through your Web pages. For information on learning more about non-Web related applications for Perl scripts, consult Appendix E, *Perl and CGI Resources.*

Security Issues

Letting complete strangers run programs on your server can constitute a security risk. When you give a CGI script access to files and directories on your server, you give the visitors that run those CGI scripts from their browsers access to those same files. Malicious computer crackers (*hacker* is considered a positive term in most programming circles) can take advantage of security holes to delete or modify files or to use your system to attack a third party. Even seemingly innocuous visitors can mess things up by unintentionally providing unexpected data.

It is extremely important that you take all of the necessary precautions (as discussed throughout this book) so that you don't leave your server vulnerable.

I discuss security in more detail in Chapter 18, *Security*, starting on page 237.

Security Issues

Perl and HTML

Because this book focuses on using Perl to enhance your Web pages, you should have at least a rudimentary familiarity with HTML—the language that most Web pages are written in. You don't need to know how to create tables, frames, or styles, or any of HTML's other advanced tags. You don't need to know JavaScript or DHTML. You don't even need to know how to create forms and links—the basic tools for getting data from visitors—since I'll show you how in Chapter 7, *Getting Data from Visitors*. Nevertheless, you *should* know what HTML tags are and how to use them to create a basic Web page.

Perl and HTML work harmoniously together. HTML lets you create links and forms that activate your Perl scripts. And Perl allows you to generate the HTML code behind the Web pages in which you'll display a script's results for your visitors.

If you would like to learn or brush up on HTML, you might try my (bestselling!) guide: *HTML 4 for the World Wide Web, Fourth Edition: Visual QuickStart Guide*, also published by Peachpit Press. For more details, check out *http://www.cookwood.com/html4_4e/* or *http://www.peachpit.com/vqs/html4/*.

Note: Since I'm focusing on Perl and CGI in this book, I have kept the HTML code to a bare minimum. While I keep to the standard HTML 4 specifications, you will notice that I often leave out optional tags like `<HTML>`, `<HEAD>`, and `<BODY>` to save space on the page and to keep the emphasis on the Perl code that we're discussing.

```
<HTML><HEAD><TITLE>Enviro-Web</TITLE>
</HEAD>
<BODY>
<H2>Figuring your tax deductions</H2>
<FORM METHOD=post ACTION=
"http://www.cookwood.com/cgi-bin/perl2e/
scalars/math.cgi">
Total value of contributions last year? <INPUT
TYPE=text NAME=donation SIZE=10>
 Number of contributions? <INPUT TYPE=text
NAME=times SIZE=5>
<BR>Value of premiums received? <INPUT
TYPE=text NAME=premium SIZE=10>
```

Figure 1.2 *Here is part of the HTML code for a form. When the visitor clicks the submit button, the browser sends the data that the visitor has typed in along with the contents of the NAME attributes to the Perl script referenced in the FORM tag's ACTION attribute.*

```
1   #!/usr/local/bin/perl -wT
2   use strict;
3   use CGI ':standard';
4   my ($total, $times, $premium, $average,
       $tax_deduction);
5
6   $total = param('donation');
7   $times = param('times');
8   $premium = param('premium');
9
10  $average = $total/$times;
11  $tax_deduction = $total - $premium;
12
13  print "Content-type: text/html\n\n";
14  print "<P>You donated $total dollars
       last year. Thank you.";
15  print "<P>Since you donated $times
       times, that works out to an average of
       $average dollars per donation.";
16  print "<P>Since your premium was worth
       $premium dollars, you can only take a
       tax deduction of $tax_deduction
       dollars.";
```

Figure 1.3 *This is the Perl script activated by the HTML page shown in Figure 1.2. Lines 13–16 create the Web page that will contain the results of the operations in the earlier part of the script. (For a complete explanation of this particular example, see page 112.)*

The Perl script is almost always displayed in its entirety. The particular functions being discussed are highlighted in red, while an explanation of those functions—in "plain English"—is offered in the shaded section below the script. The line numbers are for reference only—do not type them in!

Where space permits, the HTML code is displayed.

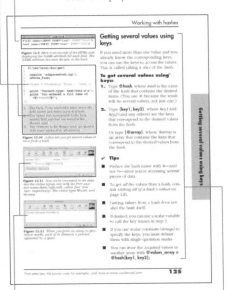

The HTML form used to access the script and the resulting output to the browser help you to understand exactly what the script does.

The step-by-step instructions tell you exactly what you need to type to use the Perl element in question. Tips remind you of important points and shortcuts.

Figure 1.4 *Because the main focus of the book is on Perl, the script itself is always displayed, together with a description of each of the lines being explained on the page. Where possible, the HTML code, the form as it appears in the browser with the visitor's input, and the output from the script are also displayed. You always have the option of going to the* Perl and CGI VQS Guide *Web site (see page 22) to see the source code for all the HTML and Perl documents.*

About This Book

One of the most difficult parts about writing this book was squeezing as much information as possible into each page. Counting the HTML code for the page that activates the Perl script, the way that Web page looks in a browser, the Perl script itself, the explanation for each of the pertinent lines in the Perl script, and the resulting output to the browser (and the HTML code behind it), it is simply impossible to display every step in the life of a Perl script in a column that measures 5 inches long and less than 2.5 inches wide.

Instead, I have focused on what I consider to be the two essential pieces of the puzzle: the Perl script itself—and what each line of code really does—and the way that script plays out in the browser. I have included additional pieces as space permits.

The blocks of Perl code that I display are numbered (in light gray) so that I can explain what each line does without having to repeat each line's contents. *You do not and should not number lines of Perl code in your scripts.*

To keep you from getting distracted, I have not always explained every line of code that is shown, but have focused on the functions being discussed on that page. If you find a line of code that you just don't get, ask about it on my Question & Answer board (*http://www.cookwood.com/perl/qanda/ indexqa.html*) and I, or someone else, will be happy to translate it into plain English for you.

In the step-by-step instructions, the things that you should type are set in **bold face**. Functions, operators, and code elsewhere in the book are offset with the `Andale font`. URLs and paths are set in *italics*.

What This Book Is Not

Perl is an incredibly rich and powerful programming language that is used in an almost infinite number of ways. You should know that this book is not—nor does it try to be—an exhaustive guide to Perl. Instead, it is a beginner's guide to using Perl for one particular purpose—making Web pages interactive.

This book won't teach you how to use Perl from the command line, how to take advantage of Perl's special report-generating functions, or how to incorporate Perl's advanced features in your scripts. Instead, you'll learn how to use a select group of Perl commands that are useful for making your Web pages interactive. All input is assumed to come from the Web and practically all output will go back to the Web. If you want to use Perl for some non-Web purpose, you'll need a different book *(see page 313)*.

I should probably also note that I have designed my examples to focus on and illustrate very specific, *individual* aspects of Perl. As such, the code is not always as elegant as it might be. My strategy is to help you understand Perl's components so that you can then construct your own masterpieces (or deconstruct someone else's). I'm not so interested in dazzling you with clever, complex code. Happily, there's plenty of it out there for you to explore, once you understand what you're looking at.

What's New

This new, second edition of *Perl and CGI for the World Wide Web: Visual QuickStart Guide* contains almost sixty brand new pages and has been thoroughly updated and tested throughout.

The largest new section includes information about how to set up and install a local server, so that you can learn Perl and test scripts without signing up with a commercial Web host.

The book also covers the basic use of Lincoln Stein's CGI.pm, the standard Perl module for analyzing incoming form data.

I have added a number of debugging and security details, including the use of warnings to catch errors, taint checking to catch bad input, and much more.

This new edition also explains how to create the HTML for file upload fields and how to use CGI.pm to parse and analyze those files once the visitor has submitted them.

Enjoy!

What's New

The Perl and CGI VQS Guide Web Site

On the *Perl and CGI Visual QuickStart Guide* Web site *(http://www.cookwood.com/perl/)*, you'll be able to find and download all of the Perl scripts from this book, along with all of the HTML pages that are used to activate those scripts. This will allow you to view the source code for the HTML pages, see which variables were used and how they work with the script, and test, test, test to your brain's content. You will also find updated links to the servers and other resources mentioned in this book.

The *Perl and CGI Visual QuickStart Guide* Web site also includes additional support material, including an online table of contents and index, a question and answer section, updates, and more.

Peachpit's companion site

Peachpit Press, the publisher of this book, also offers a companion Web site with the full table of contents, all of the example files, an excerpt from the book, and a list of errata and updates. You can find it at *http://www.peachpit.com/vqs/perlcgi/*.

Questions?

I encourage you to use my Web site's question and answer board *(http://www.cookwood.com/perl/qanda/indexqa.html)*, so that other readers can benefit from the discussion. You can also find information there for contacting me personally, should you be unable to find a solution elsewhere.

PERL BUILDING BLOCKS

Perl is designed to be a natural sounding language, as close to English as possible. In this chapter, I'll teach you about the basics of that language—the nouns and verbs as it were—as well as the grammar and syntax.

Once you're familiar with Perl's basic elements, we'll move on to the nuts and bolts of writing an actual script, creating output for a browser, and checking the script's syntax.

Then you'll be ready to move on with Chapters 3–6, which explain how to set up a server and install your scripts so that you can see Perl CGI in action.

Perl Data

Information in Perl, that is, what is operated on and processed, can be thought about in three ways. It will be either a number or a string, it will be either a constant or a variable, and it will be either a scalar, or part of an array or a hash.

Numbers and strings

Numbers are just what you'd expect: one or more digits representing a particular quantity. Numbers don't need very special treatment in Perl. Since it's hard to confuse them with other parts of the language, you don't have to set them aside or use special formatting.

A *string* is slightly more complicated—and flexible. It's simply a collection of characters: letters, numbers, or symbols—in fact any element from ASCII code 0 to 255. A word is a string, as is an entire sentence. Strings should be enclosed in straight single (') or double (") quotation marks. (For more on quotation marks, consult *Quotation Marks* on page 30.)

In other programming languages, you have to specify not only whether a particular value is a number or a string, but also what *kind* of number or string it is: integer, real number, floating-point integer, or whatever.

Perl, however, decides whether something is a string or a number by looking at what you're doing with it **(Figures 2.1 and 2.2)**. If you use a function that works on numbers, Perl assumes that the operands are numbers and treats them as such. Likewise, if you use a function that is for strings, Perl assumes the operands are strings.

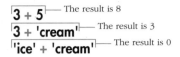

Figure 2.1 *In each of these expressions, there is a mathematical operator (+) that Perl assumes will be used only on numbers. It therefore treats any operands as numbers (and will convert any non-numerical values to 0, as necessary). (For more details about the addition operator, consult* Multiplying, Dividing, Adding, Subtracting *on page 112.)*

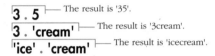

Figure 2.2 *In each of these expressions, Perl sees the concatenation operator (.) and assumes it will only be used on strings. It therefore treats any operands as strings (even ones that look like numbers). For more on the concatenation operator, consult* Connecting Strings Together *on page 117.*

Perl Data

Figure 2.3 *In this simple line of Perl code, the* print *function operates on the constant,* '3 Main Street'. *No matter when, where, or how often you use this line, it will always print out the same thing.*

Figure 2.4 *In this equally simple line of code, the* print *function operates on the* $address *variable. What actually prints out will depend on the contents of that variable at that time. The one thing that is sure is that whatever the content of the variable, that content will be printed.*

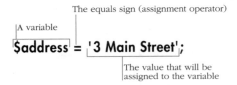

Figure 2.5 *You assign a value to a variable with the equals sign.*

Constants and variables

In Perl, you can either operate on a *specific piece of data* or you can build a process around a *placeholder*, which you will later replace with specific data.

Specific data is called a *constant* or *literal*. The name *constant* is appropriate because the data does not change. The word *literal* is also illustrative because what you see is what you get. There are no surprises **(Figure 2.3)**.

Placeholders are called *variables*. Instead of creating one operation for each piece of data, you can use variables for creating general processes that you can later apply to a whole set of data. As you might imagine, they are extremely useful **(Figure 2.4)**.

Variables look like labels. You can use any alphanumeric character and the underscore for the variable name—although the convention is to use only lowercase letters. It's a good idea to pick something descriptive and relatively short. Variable names always begin with either a dollar sign ($), an at sign (@) or a percent sign (%), depending on whether it's a scalar, array, or hash, respectively. You'll learn more about the three kinds of variables on page 26.

Specifying a variable's value is called *assigning* a value and is one of the most common Perl operations **(Figure 2.5)**. Although assignment is represented by an equals sign, it's better to translate it into English with something like "gets" or "is assigned the value of". This is particularly apparent when you have the same variable on both sides of the equals sign as in: $price = $price + 20, which translated means, "increase the current value of the price variable by twenty and assign the result to the price variable".

Perl Data

Scalars, arrays, and hashes

A *scalar* is any individual piece of data, such as a single number (though not necessarily a single digit) or a single string. Scalars can be constants or variables. Scalar constants look like familiar bits of information **(Figure 2.6)**. Remember that it's a good idea to enclose string constants in quotation marks.

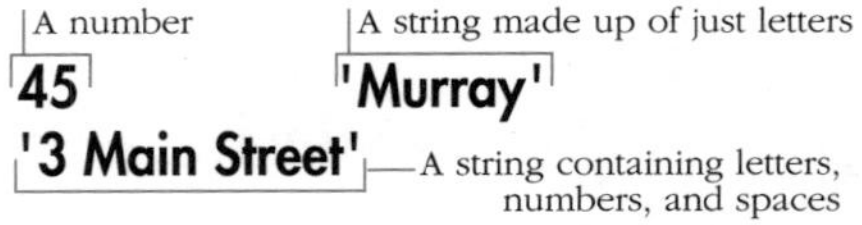

Scalar variables always begin with a dollar sign ($). The shape of the $ is supposed to remind you of the *S* in *scalar* **(Figure 2.7)**.

An *array* variable represents a *list* of scalars. Since scalars can be either constants or variables and either numbers or strings, an array is a collection of items that are either constants or variables and either numbers or strings. An array comprised completely of scalar constants is sometimes called a *list literal*.

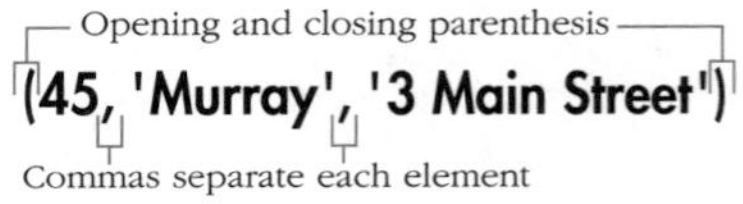

Technically, an array and a list are distinct concepts. A list is an ordered collection of scalars **(Figure 2.8)**; an array is a variable that *represents* such a collection **(Fig. 2.9)**. I (and many others) tend to use them interchangeably, though it's sometimes useful to remember the difference.

Although an array can seem to contain another array, it actually contains the *elements* of the second array. Arrays are always made up of scalars.

Array variables always begin with an at sign (@). The *a* in *at* is a mnemonic for *array*. You can also create variables that access individual members of the array, according to their position from left to right. We'll get into that in more detail in Chapter 12, *Working with Arrays*.

A number | A string made up of just letters

`45`   `'Murray'`
`'3 Main Street'`———A string containing letters, numbers, and spaces

Figure 2.6 *Scalar constants can be either numbers or strings. Strings should be enclosed in quotation marks (see page 30).*

A dollar sign

`$first_name`——The variable name

Figure 2.7 *Scalar variables always begin with a dollar sign ($). Their names can have up to 255 letters, numbers, and the underscore.*

——— Opening and closing parenthesis ———

Commas separate each element

Figure 2.8 *This list contains three elements. Lists are enclosed in parentheses with each element separated by a comma.*

An at sign

`@personal_info`——The variable name

Figure 2.9 *An array variable starts with an at sign. Its name can contain up to 255 characters, letters, and the underscore.*

Key
Value
Another pair
(age => 45, name => 'Murray',
One pair of elements
address => '3 Main Street')
Still another pair

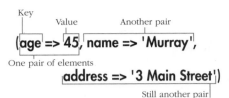

Figure 2.10 *A hash is made up of pairs of scalars. The first element in each pair is called the* key. *The second element is the* value. *Separate the keys from the values with the => operator. Separate one pair from another with a comma. As long as you use the => operator, you don't need to quote single-word keys.*

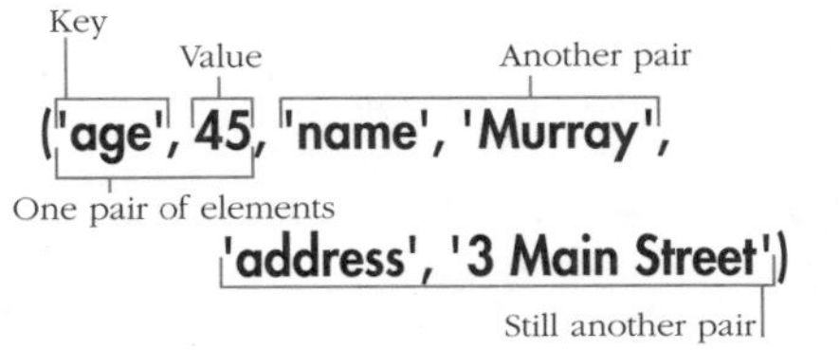

Key
Value
Another pair
('age', 45, 'name', 'Murray',
One pair of elements
'address', '3 Main Street')
Still another pair

Figure 2.11 *Another way to write a hash is by separating keys, values, and the pairs themselves with commas. With this system, keys must always be quoted.*

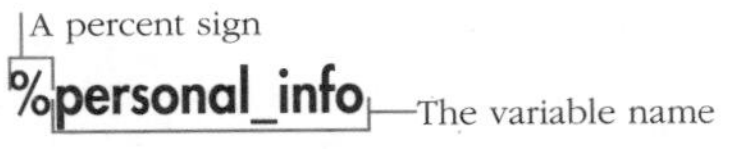

A percent sign
%personal_info
The variable name

Figure 2.12 *A hash variable begins with a percent sign and is followed by up to 255 characters, numbers, or the underscore.*

A *hash*, which is sometimes called an *associative array*, represents a collection of scalars in pairs. The first element in each pair is called the *key* and is a label for the second and ostensibly more important element, the *value*.

In contrast with an array, the order of a hash's pairs is completely irrelevant. There is no first pair. Instead of accessing data by its position in the list, you access a hash's data by referring to its keys.

Because the order of a hash's pairs cannot be ascertained, it is somewhat misleading to show a hash by listing its pairs **(Figures 2.10 and 2.11)**. You can think of those diagrams as one *possible* way to show the contents of a hash. Or you can think of them as lists that will be assigned to a hash.

Note that there are two separate methods for listing values that will be assigned to a hash. The easiest way is to separate keys from values with the => operator, and then each pair from the next with a comma. The first item in each pair is considered to be the key and the second is the value. With this system, the keys do not need to be enclosed in quotation marks unless they contain something besides alphanumeric characters and the underscore. Values are always quoted **(Figure 2.10)**.

You can also separate keys, values, and the pairs themselves with commas. In this case, you have to quote everything **(Figure 2.11)**.

Hash variables begin with a percent sign (%). One way to remember this symbol is to think of the two circles on each side of the slash as parts of a pair **(Figure 2.12)**.

Operators and Functions

If scalars, arrays, and hashes are the objects on which Perl actions are performed, the actors themselves are called *operators* or *functions*. Simple processes, like addition and multiplication, are represented by symbols and look pretty similar to how you see them in ordinary life. For example, to add 3 and 5 in Perl, you use the addition operator, which is (surprise!) the plus symbol (+), like this: 3 + 5. To divide the variable $distance by the variable $rate, you'd use $distance/$rate.

Functions are just operators with names—case-sensitive, and always in all lowercase letters—that generally perform slightly more complicated processes. For example, Perl has a function called print that sends the specified data to the specified output—which might be the browser or could be an external file.

Some functions operate on scalars, others on arrays or hashes, and still others work differently depending on where you aim them, that is, depending on the *context*. In general, a function's operands are enclosed in parentheses, and separated by commas if there are more than one. With single operands, you can generally leave parentheses out unless the resulting expression is ambiguous (**Figure 2.15**). White space is usually irrelevant. Use as much as you like (**Figure 2.16**).

The operators and functions in Perl that you need for making Web pages interactive are described throughout this book. In addition, they are listed in the index for quick reference. If there's a Perl function you're interested in that's not in the book, check out *http://www.perl.com/pub/v/documentation*.

You can also create your own functions to automate your most common operations. User-defined functions are called *subroutines* and are described in detail in Chapter 13, *Subroutines*.

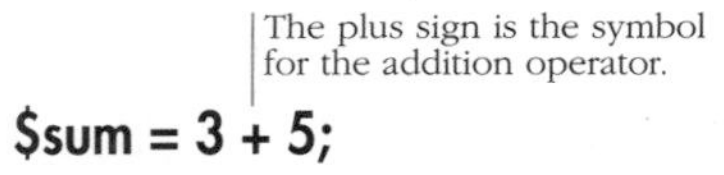

The plus sign is the symbol for the addition operator.

$sum = 3 + 5;

Figure 2.13 *Operators look like familiar everyday symbols. The addition operator (+) is used to add two numeric values together. The space around and between the different elements is unimportant.*

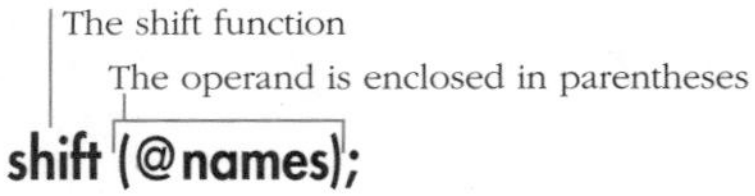

The shift function
The operand is enclosed in parentheses

shift (@names);

Figure 2.14 *A function's operands are usually enclosed in parentheses. Functions (which are just named operators) generally perform slightly more complicated tasks than operators.*

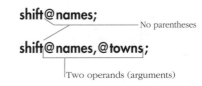

shift@names;   — No parentheses

shift@names, @towns;

Two operands (arguments)

Figure 2.15 *The top line is unambiguous, and thus equivalent to the one in Figure 2.14, despite having no parentheses. In the second line, however, it's not immediately clear whether the shift function should operate on only the @names array or also the @towns array. Thus, if you want the function to affect both, you have to enclose them in parentheses.*

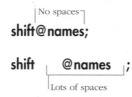

No spaces
shift@names;

shift   @names ;

Lots of spaces

Figure 2.16 *White space doesn't matter as long as Perl can figure out where the function ends and the argument begins—which is easy with variables because of their distinguishing symbols. Both of these statements are equivalent to the one in Figure 2.14.*

Result vs. return value

Functions and operators can affect the value of the data in your script in two ways. Some functions directly change the value of the operands on which they've operated. For example, the ++ operator in the expression `$n++;` *results* in the value of `$n` being increased by 1.

Other functions leave the variable unchanged and instead have a *return value* that can be analyzed. For example, `print $n;` does not affect the value of `$n`, it simply sends the contents of `$n` to output. The return value of any print statement is *1* if it is successful—that is, able to print—and *0* if not. This makes it easy to test if a particular function has been able to run correctly.

Still other functions change the variable *and* have a distinct return value. For example, the `shift` function changes the value of an array by removing its leftmost element and has a return value of the element that was removed. So if `@array` contains (`a, b, c`) the result of `shift(@array);` is (`b, c`) while the return value is `a`.

In this book, you'll learn whether a function or operator directly affects the variable, and if and why there is a return value that deserves your attention.

Operators and Functions

Quotation Marks

There are two kinds of straight quotation marks that you'll be using when writing Perl scripts: single and double. You won't need curly quotation marks at all.

Single quotation marks are for enclosing data that you want taken literally, exactly as it appears. Double quotation marks are for enclosing data that may need to be evaluated, or *interpolated*, before processing, like back-slashed character escapes and variables.

Backslashed character escapes let you include a newline, carriage return, tab or other special character in a string. As long as the string is interpolated, the special character (and not the backslashed code for the character) will be used **(Figure 2.17)**.

Likewise, if you want to include the *value* of a scalar or array variable in a string, the string must be enclosed in double quotes. If you want to include the *name* of the scalar or array variable—or in general are not interested in evaluating the contents—use single quotes **(Figure 2.18)**.

✔ Tips

- You can use double quotes to interpolate scalar and array variables, but not hash variables. You can, however, use double quotes to interpolate *slices* of both arrays and hashes—but we'll get to that later.

- Backslashes are also used in Perl to remove the special meaning from a symbol. For example, if you want to use double quotes *in* a double quoted string, you'd have to precede them with a backslash to remove their special meaning so that Perl would know where the end of the string was. You must always backslash the @ symbol in interpolated strings when it's not part of an array variable.

Single quotation marks take their contents literally, exactly as it appears.

```
print 'Print this on\ntwo lines';
```

The result would look like:
Print this on\ntwo lines

Double quotation marks evaluate and interpolate backslashed character escapes

```
print "Print this on\ntwo lines";
```

The result would look like:
Print this on
two lines

Figure 2.17 *If you need to include backslashed character escapes, use double quotes.*

Single quotation marks take their contents literally, exactly as it appears.

```
print 'You won $5';
```

The result would look like:
You won $5

Double quotation marks evaluate and interpolate scalar and array variables

```
print "You won $prize";
```

The result would depend on the value of $prize, and might look like:
You won a new car

Figure 2.18 *With single quotes, variables (or things that look like variables) are never evaluated, they're simply used as is. With double quotes, the current value of the variable is used.*

Quotation Marks

'the contestant\'s prize was $5.';

q (the contestant's prize was $5.)

The result in both cases looks like:
the contestant's prize was $5.

Figure 2.19 *Use the q function when you have a string that contains single quotes that you don't feel like backslashing, and you don't need interpolation.*

"<img src=\"prize.gif\" alt=\"$prize\">";

qq (<img src="prize.gif" alt="$prize">)

The result is identical (and interpolated) in both cases. Depending on the contents of $prize, it might look like:
<img src="prize.gif" alt="A new car!">

Figure 2.20 *These two expressions are equivalent. Notice in the top expression, since it is delimited by double quotes, any double quotes that it contains must be backslashed. Using parentheses for the delimiter in the bottom expression eliminates the need to backslash double quotes. (Instead you would need to backslash any parentheses in the content.)*

Without qw, each word must be enclosed in quotation marks and separated with a comma.

('cats', 'dogs', 'elephants')

qw(cats dogs elephants)

qw*cats dogs elephants*

Figure 2.21 *Each of these three expressions is equivalent.*

Quoting without Quotes

Perl lets you "quote" a string, either with interpolation or not, without actually using quotation marks. This makes it easy to quote strings that contain quotation marks since the marks no longer have special meaning and don't need to be backslashed.

To quote without quotes:

1. Type **q** if you want to quote without interpolation.

   Or type **qw** if you want to quote individual words without interpolation.

   Or type **qq** if you want to quote with interpolation.

2. Type **(**, where **(** is the symbol that will delimit what you're quoting. As long as there's a space after the function name in step 1, you can use any symbol or character that you want.

3. Type **string**, where *string* is the content that you want quoted. It may contain any symbol except the one used to delimit the string in step 2. (And it may even contain that symbol if you backslash it.)

4. Type **)**, where *)* matches the symbol used in step 2. If it has an obvious right and left version, use that, otherwise repeat the same symbol (as with, say #).

✔ Tips

- To include the delimiting character within the string, precede it with a backslash.

- The qw function is for single-quoting individual words—which should appear in the string separated by white space.

- The qq function is very useful for HTML code with both quoted attributes and variables that need to be interpolated *(see page 208)*.

Quoting without Quotes

Statements, Blocks, and Scope

A Perl script is made up of individual statements that may or may not be divided into blocks of code. A statement ends with a semicolon (;) and by convention, is generally placed on its own line **(Figure 2.22)**. However, since newlines and returns do not mark the end of a Perl statement and indeed, like white space, have no particularly special significance, you can write a statement across several lines if it makes it easier to understand **(Figure 2.23)**.

A *block* is one or more statements that go together, rather like a paragraph in English. An entire script might be made of a single block, or a script may be comprised of several "inner" blocks, in which case the individual blocks are enclosed in curly braces {}.

While blocks can be simply a way of grouping statements together, they also have two specific, specialized uses in Perl. First, a block might contain the action or actions that should occur given a particular condition **(Figure 2.24)**. We'll discuss conditional blocks in detail in Chapter 11, *Conditionals and Loops*.

A second kind of block identifies a series of Perl statements that together make up a subroutine **(Figure 2.25)**. You'll find more details in Chapter 13, *Subroutines*.

Another important feature of a block is that it controls the scope of variables.

Controlling a variable's scope

Imagine if everyone in the world were identified with only their first name. In small groups, there might not be any confusion, but with larger groups, chaos would reign. And the larger the group, and the more you combined it with other groups, the more likely it would be that there would be more than one person with the same name.

Figure 2.22 *A statement is like a Perl sentence—it usually contains a function (*print*, in this case) and something that function can work on (called an argument).*

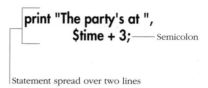

Figure 2.23 *A return or newline (like the one after the comma) does not mark the end of a Perl statement. Only the semicolon does that. (Note that I use double quotes even though there's nothing to interpolate so that I don't have to backslash the single quote.)*

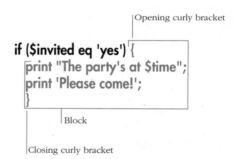

Figure 2.24 *Blocks are most often used to enclose the series of actions that will occur given a particular condition. Since white space is unimportant, you could put the opening curly bracket on the next line if you prefer.*

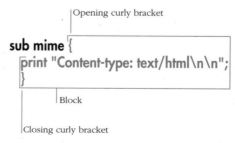

Figure 2.25 *Blocks are also used to contain the actions that define a subroutine.*

```
my $job = 'writer';

if ($alternate_universe) {
    my $job = 'Voyager editor';
}

print "I'm a $job";
```

Inner block

Figure 2.26 *The declaration of the* $job *variable in the inner scope temporarily hides the outer* $job *variable. When the inner block is finished, however, the inner* $job *variable disappears, and thus the statement "I'm a writer" is printed.*

One solution is to add additional names: no one, for example, would confuse Elizabeth *Castro* with Elizabeth *Taylor*. Another option is to identify the person with what they do: Elizabeth Castro, the *writer*, is not the same person (as many readers have asked) as Elizabeth Castro, the *editor* for television's *Star Trek Voyager*.

There is a similar difficulty with Perl variable names. If you should happen to use the same name for two different variables, or if you use someone else's script and some of their variable names are the same as yours, you will have big trouble. With Perl 4 and earlier, the solution was rather similar to surnames: variables belonged to families called *packages*. And while this generally solved the problem of unwittingly confusing one variable with another, it didn't allow programmers to protect their own variables as much as they wanted since package variables are still *global* and can be accessed and used absolutely anywhere (by calling their full name).

With Perl 5, instead of distinguishing variables with surnames (which is still allowed), the preferred method of keeping similarly named variables from being confused is by limiting where they can be used, that is, their *scope*. Variables limited in this way are called *lexical* or *private* variables (as opposed to global). I'll teach you how to declare private variables on page 34.

The scope of a private variable, by definition, is the block in which that variable is declared, including any subblocks contained within **(Figure 2.26)**. The variable may not be used outside of the block. If you try, you'll get an error message.

Statements, Blocks, and Scope

Declaring Private Variables

In order to protect the variables in your scripts from being confused with other variables with the same name, either in your script or someone else's, you should declare them as private variables.

To declare private variables:

1. Type **my**.

2. Type **$**, **@**, or **%**, depending on whether you're declaring a scalar, array, or hash variable.

3. Type **variable**, where *variable* is the name that you want to use for this particular variable **(Figure 2.27)**.

4. Type **;** to complete the line.

✔ Tips

■ If you don't declare your variables with my, they'll be considered global package variables *(see page 33)*. If you use use strict; *(see page 36))* such non-qualified variables will generate errors.

■ Declare multiple variables on the same line by enclosing them in parentheses and separating them with commas **(Figure 2.28)**.

■ You can declare variables and immediately start to work with them on the same line **(Figure 2.29)**.

■ Variable names declared with the my function can only be used in the same scope in which they were declared—this is why they're called *private (see page 32)*.

■ Private variables would be called *local variables* if it weren't for the existence of the badly named and little used local function.

my $address;

The my function creates a private variable.

Figure 2.27 *Declare a private variable with the my function. Be sure to declare the variable within the block in which it will be used.*

my ($street, $city, $state, $zip);

Enclose multiple variables in parentheses.

Figure 2.28 *Declare several variables at once by enclosing the variables in parentheses.*

my $address = '265 Buckminster Rd.';

Figure 2.29 *You can declare a private variable and assign it a value on the same line.*

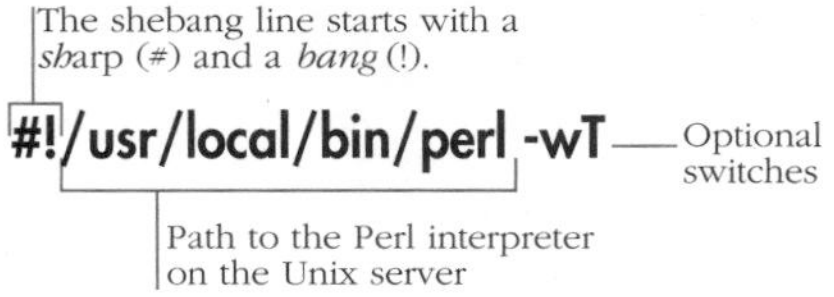

The shebang line starts with a *sh*arp (#) and a *bang* (!).

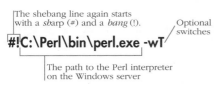

Figure 2.30 *A typical shebang line in a Perl script running on a Unix server starts with #! and is directly followed by the path to the Perl interpreter on the Unix server (starting with the root directory). Any switches (they're always optional) follow the path and a space.*

The shebang line again starts with a *sh*arp (#) and a *bang* (!).

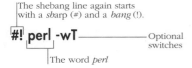

Figure 2.31 *On Windows systems, the shebang line is not strictly necessary, but often still used.*

The shebang line again starts with a *sh*arp (#) and a *bang* (!).

#! perl -wT ——— Optional switches

The word *perl*

Figure 2.32 *On Mac servers, the shebang line is used only to maintain portability or to use switches.*

The Shebang Line

When you double-click a file, your computer has to have a way to know which program it should use to open or execute that file. In fact, different computer platforms have different systems. On Windows, file extensions link files with appropriate programs. On a Mac, it is a file's TYPE and CREATOR that determine which program should be used to open the file. On Unix, there is the *shebang* line. The shebang line—so named because it starts with a *sh*arp (#) and a *bang* (!)—simply shows the path to the program that should be used to run the file **(Figure 2.30)**.

Since Perl was born on Unix, it has become customary to begin every script with a shebang line that pinpoints the location of the Perl interpreter on the Unix system.

The shebang line also houses *switches*, which should look familiar to command-line programmers, and which affect how the script is run. A few switches, including -c, -T, and -w are discussed in this book. (If you use more than one switch at a time, you can combine them with a single hyphen.) You can find the whole list at *http://www.perl.com/pub/doc/manual/html/pod/perlrun.html*.

So, while the shebang line should theoretically only be necessary on scripts that run on Unix servers, it's often seen in Perl scripts running on other platforms, including Windows and Macintosh. On Windows, use the shebang line as for Unix, in the same way I've described above—specifying the path to the Perl interpreter on the Windows system and adding any desired switches **(Figure 2.31)**. On Macintosh servers, the shebang line is really only necessary when you want to use switches—even then, the path part of the shebang line can be reduced to the word *perl* itself **(Figure 2.32)**.

Creating a Perl CGI Script

Perl CGI scripts are simple text documents with a few special characteristics that depend on the server on which they've been installed.

To create a Perl CGI script:

1. Open a new document in the text editor of your choice—any one will do, including WordPad or SimpleText **(Figure 2.33)**.

2. On the very, very first line of your file, type **#!path**, where *path* indicates the location on the server of the Perl interpreter that should be used to execute the script *(see page 35)*.

   (For scripts running on Macintosh servers only, use **#! perl**.)

3. At the end of that first line, type a space and then **-wT**. This tells the Perl interpreter to *w*arn you if it finds certain potential problems with your script and to return an error if you use unchecked, *t*ainted, outside data for modifying external files. While not required, both switches are highly recommended.

4. On the second line, type **use strict;** so that the Perl interpreter will require you to declare your variables, among other things. Again, this is not required, but is highly recommended.

5. Import the CGI.pm functions by typing **use CGI ':standard';** on the third line of the script **(Figure 2.34)**.

6. Write the body of your script. You'll learn how throughout the rest of this book **(Figure 2.35)**.

7. Choose File > Save As from your text editor **(Figure 2.36)**.

8. Choose the text-only format in the Save As dialog box.

Figure 2.33 *Open your favorite text editor. You can use any one that you like, from the simple—like Notepad or SimpleText, to the complicated—like Word or WordPerfect, or the specialized—like UltraEdit or BBEdit. The only requirement is that the editor be able to save documents as text only.*

Figure 2.34 *The first three lines of this script are standard fare for Perl CGI scripts in general.*

Figure 2.35 *After those first three lines, you're free to forge off in your own individual direction—which you'll explore as you go through this book.*

Figure 2.36 *Choose File > Save As to save your Perl CGI script.*

Figure 2.37 *Don't get hung up on the fact that this may not be your particular text editor—or even your platform. The important bits are all the same: you have to save the file with the proper extension (for your server), in text-only format, in the proper directory.*

9. Give the file a simple, but descriptive name and the appropriate extension for your server. (In general, *.pl* is used for Windows servers, *.cgi* is used on Mac servers, and both are popular on Unix servers. Ask your Web host to be sure.)

10. Save the file in the proper special directory, as required by your server (often the *cgi-bin* directory) **(Figure 2.37)**.

✔ Tips

- When naming your scripts, stick to numbers or lowercase letters, and if pushed, the underscore. Spaces and other symbols are more trouble than they're worth.

- The shebang line, extension, and directory vary from server to server. For specific instructions, check the chapter that pertains to the server you're going to use.

- Although you can use SimpleText and WordPad to write your scripts, there are several really robust text editors available. For more details, consult *Text Editors* on page 310.

- There are two general scenarios for writing scripts. First, you might write scripts on a local Windows or Macintosh computer, optionally test them on a local server, and finally upload them to a remote server (generally Unix, but sometimes Windows and more rarely Macintosh). Or, you can write scripts directly on the remote server on which you plan to run them.

- The -w switch and the use strict line (officially called a *pragma*) are designed to alert you to possible errors during compilation. The -T switch (combined here with -w) helps you avoid tainted data and is explained in more detail on page 244.

Creating a Perl CGI Script

Creating Output for a Browser

When running a Perl CGI script, you *must* output something to the browser. (Otherwise you'll get a dreaded Internal Server Error.) And to output something to the browser, you have to create a header that tells what kind of content is coming. Although I'll go into more detail about printing later *(see page 221)*, I'll start you off with the basics so you can actually use the examples as you progress through the book.

To create output for a browser:

1. Type **print "Content-type: text/html \n\n";**. There is a space after the colon but not between *html* and the first backslash or the first *n* and the second backslash. Those two backslashes and *n*'s denote newlines and are essential. This line tells the browser to expect MIME content of type *text/html*, that is, a Web page. The browser won't be able to display the output at all without this line.

2. On the next line, type **print**.

3. Then type **content**, where *content* is the material that you want to have appear on the Web page. The content can include HTML tags for formatting, strings of text, and variables that contain the processed output from the script (which you'll learn about soon).

4. Type **;** (a semicolon) to complete the print statement.

✔ Tips

- Any strings of text in the content, including HTML tags, must be enclosed in quotation marks *(see page 30)*.

- For more information about printing and using HTML in the output, consult Chapter 17, *Formatting, Printing, and HTML*.

```
1   #!/usr/local/bin/perl -wT
2   use strict;
3   use CGI ':standard';
4
5   my $animal;
6   $animal = param('animal');
7
8   print "Content-type: text/html\n\n";
9   print "Show me the $animal";
```

8: This line prints the all-important MIME content line that browsers require. Without it, browsers don't know what kind of output to expect and they refuse to do anything at all. Since the output in this particular example contains no actual HTML code, we could also use "text/plain", but it's not a crucial difference at this point, and I'd rather you get accustomed to typing "text/html".

9: This is a very simple example of something you might output in the browser. For real applications, you should output proper HTML headers (<HTML><HEAD>... etc.)

Figure 2.38 *Your output can range from something as simple as a sentence, as in this example, or as complicated as a full-blown Web page, with formatting, images, and even variables. It doesn't matter as long as you output something to the browser.*

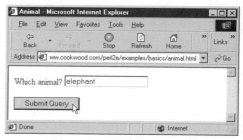

Figure 2.39 *Here is the simple form used to call our example script. We'll talk all about forms in Chapter 7, Getting Data from Visitors.*

Figure 2.40 *Both the content line (which is not shown in the browser) and the content itself (which can be as simple as a space) are required. Otherwise, you'll get an Internal Server Error.*

```
1   #!/usr/local/bin/perl -wT
2   use strict;
3   use CGI ':standard';
4
5   #Declare variable and then get data from
       form with CGI.pm
6   my $animal;
7   $animal = param('animal');
8
9   #Output MIME content line and something
       for the browser
10  print "Content-type: text/html\n\n";
11  print "Show me the $animal";
```

5: The comment line starts with a # sign and can contain anything you want. It does not need to end with a semicolon.

9: You can create as many comment lines as you like.

Figure 2.41 *Comments can be as long or as short as you need as long as each line is preceded with a #. Note that both lines 5 and 9 are single lines. They are shown with line breaks because of the width of the column in this book, not because they consist of two lines each.*

```
1   #!/usr/local/bin/perl -wT
2   use strict;
3   use CGI ':standard';
4
5.  my $animal; #Declare the variable
6   $animal = param('animal'); #use
       CGI.pm's param function to get form
       data
7
8   print "Content-type: text/html\n\n";
       #Tell the browser what to expect.
9   print "Show me the $animal"; #Give the
       browser something to do.
```

5: Lines 5-9 have comments that begin after each line's semi-colon.

Figure 2.42 *These are comments geared toward the total beginner. Note, however, that comments aren't much help if they just state the obvious.*

Figure 2.43 *Comments are completely invisible to your visitors. They are strictly for your benefit so you can remember what you were doing, and hopefully, why you were doing it.*

Documenting Your Script

Although you may live and breathe your script while you're writing it, a few months later you may not recognize your own handwriting, so to speak. It's a good idea to explain what you are doing in your script so that later, when you or someone else comes back to update the script, you can figure out why you did something a particular way and not have to invent that same wheel a second or third time.

To add comments on separate lines:

1. At the very beginning of the line, type **#** to begin the comment.

2. Type **comment**, where *comment* explains some part of the following block of code.

3. Repeat steps 1–2 for each line of comments **(Figure 2.41)**.

You can also add short comments at the end of a line of code.

To add comments on code lines:

1. Type your Perl statement. Make sure you don't forget the semicolon.

2. After the semicolon, type a space and then **#** to begin the comment.

3. Type **comment**, where *comment* explains some part of the line of code.

✔ Tips

■ Each individual line of comments must start with its own sharp sign (#). In other words, a comment ends with a return.

■ Comment lines do not need to end with a semicolon (or *anything* in particular, for that matter).

■ You can use comments to include copyright and author information.

Checking the Script's Syntax

The one thing about communicating with a computer is that you have to be very precise. Leave off a semicolon, and the computer gets very testy. Misspell a variable name and it may decide to hang up on you altogether. Perl has a handy command for finding typos and other minor syntax errors.

To test a script's syntax on Unix and Windows:

1. Open a command line interface, like MS-DOS Prompt in Windows, or konsole in Linux.

2. Navigate to the directory that contains the script in question (using **cd**, for example).

3. Type **perl -c scriptname**, where *script-name* is the full name of the script whose syntax you want to check. The Perl interpreter will advise you of any syntax problems in the script without actually running the script **(Figure 2.45)**.

To test a script's syntax on Macintosh:

1. In MacPerl, choose Script > Syntax Check **(Figure 2.46)**.

2. In the dialog box that appears, choose the script whose syntax you want to analyze and click OK. Errors are displayed in the MacPerl window **(Figure 2.47)**.

✔ Tips

■ If you're using the -T switch to avoid tainted data, you'll have to type **perl -cT scriptname** in step 3.

■ The -c is called a *switch* or *flag*. There are a whole slew of switches that you can use to configure how the Perl interpreter works. For the entire list, check out *http://www.perl.com/pub/doc/manual/html/pod/perlrun.html*.

```
1   #!/usr/local/bin/perl -wT
2   use strict;
3   use CGI ':standard';
4
5   my $animal;
6   $animal = param('animal');
7
8   print "Content-type: text/html\n\n";
9   print "Show me the $animal';
```

9: I've created an error by using a single quote to end the `print` statement that I had started with a double quote.

Figure 2.44 *Syntax errors are often hard to spot, even when they're circled and highlighted with a second color. (The error is at the end of line 9.)*

Figure 2.45 *Telnet to the directory on the Unix server (see page 296) that contains the script and then use the -c switch to see if there are any syntax errors. On Windows, use the MS-DOS Prompt to do the exact same operation.*

Figure 2.46 *On a Mac, choose Script > Syntax Check to find errors in a script.*

Figure 2.47 *Let MacPerl do the work finding syntax errors in your script.*

Figure 2.48 *If you test with the browser, you get a pretty generic, non-helpful error message.*

Checking the Script's Syntax

ABOUT SERVERS, PERL, AND CGI.PM

Before we get too deep into Perl itself, we'll need a place where we can install and run scripts. While Perl scripts work perfectly well without a server, Perl CGI scripts do not. Since CGI describes how servers talk to the programs they execute, it doesn't make sense to run a CGI script without a server.

There are two principal ways to get access to a server: sign up with a remote *Web host*—a company that runs servers for other people—or install a server on your own computer. I recommend that you do both. And I'll show you how.

In this chapter, I'll explain some basic platform-independent information about servers, Perl interpreters, and CGI.pm. In Chapter 4, you'll learn how to work with a remote Unix (or Linux) server. And in Chapters 5 and 6, I'll show you how to install and configure local Windows and Macintosh servers (respectively) so that you can test your scripts even without a remote Web host.

What Is a Server?

People are often confused and even intimidated by servers, thinking that a server is a big, huge computer that performs unimaginably complicated tasks. Part of the confusion comes from the fact that the word *server* is used in two related and overlapping ways. First, it's a software program that serves data (in our case Web pages), when requested to do so by a *client* (like a Web browser). But often, the machine on which that program is running is also called a server, even though it may run many other programs as well—even other servers.

That machine might be a Macintosh or Windows computer, but in most cases—about 65%—servers run on computers with the Unix operating system, prized for its networking capabilities. In the same way as with other kinds of software, there are distinct server programs for Macs, Windows, and Unix. While each server may have different features and interfaces, the basics are the same.

Using a remote Web host

Since most people use remote Unix-based (or Linux-based) servers, I'll explain the steps you'll need to get Perl CGI scripts running on such a system in Chapter 4, *Running Perl CGI on a Unix Server*. In addition, I've included an entire chapter on basic Unix techniques for the uninitiated (*see Appendix D*).

There are several factors you should keep in mind as you choose a prospective Web host. First, will they allow you to write and execute your own Perl CGI scripts? Since CGI can constitute a security risk, many Web hosts either restrict your CGI use to a set of prefabricated scripts or simply don't let you run any at all. Second, what server software and platform does your Web host use and does it have the Perl interpreter installed? You may want to set up your local server as similarly as possible to your future Web host (or choose a Web host that's similar to your local setup), in order to make the transition from one server to another as smooth as possible.

Third, what kind of support does your Web host offer? Some Web hosts offer round-the-clock technical support and are willing even to offer limited advice on Perl and CGI. Others limit their support to an outdated Web page. Your choice of Web hosts should depend on the answers to these questions.

Installing a personal server

Installing a server on your personal computer makes it easy to test your scripts, edit out the bugs, and test them again, until they're perfect—without having to deal with uploading files to a remote system. It's also great if you don't yet have a Web host, or if your current Web host doesn't allow CGI scripts (many don't). I explain the rudiments of installing a so-called personal server in Chapters 5 and 6.

Once your scripts are completed, and you want to use them out on the Internet, you'll have to upload them to your Web host's server. (While it is possible to serve a Web site from a personal Web server, I do not cover that in this book. I will teach you just enough about personal Web servers so that you can test Perl CGI scripts.) Thanks to Perl's portability from one operating system to another, the scripts should continue to work correctly, with minor adjustments (and often none at all). Those adjustments are discussed in Chapters 4, 5, and 6.

What Is a Server?

The Importance of Directories

A Web site, as you probably know, is mostly comprised of HTML files, GIF and JPEG images, and scripts. All of a site's files reside in a particular directory on the server. But it's important to remember that those files are not alone **(Figure 3.1)**. A server (remember that it's a computer system running server software, *among other things*) may contain files from hundreds of different sites. In addition, servers contain many files that have nothing at all to do with the server software (including the system software, other programs—like the Perl interpreter—and other unrelated files).

So, when a server gets a request for a particular file, it has to know where to find that file. It first looks carefully at the server name specified by the URL. This name might refer to an actual server, or more often these days, it is a virtual domain that is managed by an actual server. For example, my virtual domain—*www.cookwood.com*—is managed by a commercial Web host server called *crocker.com*. Regardless, the server checks an internal list and matches the server name with a particular directory on a particular hard drive somewhere on the server. That directory is called the site's *root Web directory*. It then constructs the actual location of the file by adding the rest of the URL—the path and the filename—to the root Web directory's location **(Figure 3.3)**. Once the server has established the location of the file, it can send it to the browser.

Every server is set up in its own way. So, in order to know which directory is your root Web directory, you either have to look at your server's configuration settings (or at the clues that I give you in the server installation chapters), or ask your commercial Web host.

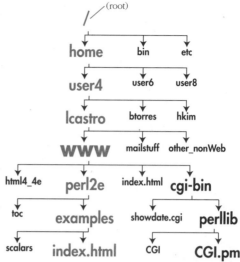

Figure 3.1 *Here's a peek at my Unix server. You can see the server's own files (in the* bin *and* etc *directories), the other sites' directories (*btorres *and* hkim*), and the only directory on the server to which I have access:* lcastro. *Within my directory, I have a root Web directory (*WWW*) where all the files that make up my Web site are stored, along with several other directories (like* mailstuff *and* other_nonWeb*) that are not accessible from the Web.*

The full path on my server from the root (/) to the index.html file

/home/user4/lcastro/WWW/perl2e/ examples/index.html

http://www.cookwood.com/perl2e/ examples/index.html

The URL for the index.html file

Figure 3.2 *The top line is the full path to the file, on the server. The bottom line is a URL to that same file. Note that they're not the same.*

Figure 3.3 *When you type a URL in a browser's Address box, the server looks at the specified server name* (www.cookwood.com) *and finds its corresponding root Web directory (which, in this case, is* /home/user4/lcastro/WWW/*). Next, it adds the path information* (perl2e/examples/ index.html) *to get the actual location of the desired file on the server:* /home/user4/lcastro/WWW/perl2e/examples/index.html.

The cgi-bin or Scripts directory

CGI scripts pose certain security risks to the server *(see page 237)*. While some servers will let you run scripts no matter where they are (within your corner of the server), others require that you place your CGI scripts in a special directory that has been pre-configured by the server administrator. If the script is located anywhere else, it simply won't run. This allows the server administrator to keep strict tabs on which CGI scripts are installed and where possible problems may lie.

In particular, on many Unix servers, CGI scripts must be enclosed in the special cgi-bin directory in order to work. That cgi-bin directory has a particular location on your server, just like your root Web directory. On Microsoft IIS servers, which we'll discuss in more detail in Chapter 5, the typical location for CGI scripts is *C:\Inetpub\scripts*.

To make it simple to type the URL for a script, many servers set up an alias or *virtual directory* name for the directory that contains the scripts. So, for example, on a standard IIS server, you'll type *http://www.yourserver.com/Scripts/* to access the contents of the *C:\Inetpub\scripts* directory. (For an example, see page 70.) Here, */Scripts* is an alias, or shortcut, that points to the *C:\Inetpub\scripts* directory.

You will have to ask your server administrator where CGI scripts must be stored and what the virtual name of their directory is. If you set up a personal server (as described in Chapters 5 and 6), you'll learn the typical configurations for both the scripts directories as well as their virtual names.

The Importance of Directories

Ask Your Web Host!

Since there are many different kinds of servers and many different configurations of even the same servers, in this book, I will sometimes advise you to "Ask your Web host". It's not a cop out. When I tell you to ask your Web host, it's because there's no way to tell from here what the answer will be. I'll usually give you an idea of what to expect, and perhaps something to try if you have a difficult relationship with your Web host, but it's often easiest and fastest to just ask them.

As long as they allow you to run CGI scripts, they have a *responsibility* to tell you certain things about the way the server is configured, including the name and version of the server, the platform (including version) the server is running on, the full location, from the root, of your Web directory, the full location, from the root, where CGI scripts need to be installed in order to run properly, the extension, if any, that CGI scripts must have to run properly, the full location, from the root, of the Perl interpreter, the version of perl they're running, including any modules, and finally, whether or not you can telnet to the server and any names and passwords you need to do so.

If a commercial Web host is not helpful with such requests, remind them that you are not asking for technical support. The information that you need to get from them simply cannot be obtained elsewhere. If they still won't help you, you may want to dump them and switch to a better host.

If you're testing scripts on a local server, your Web host is *you*. In that case, you may want to look over the configuration process in Chapters 5 and 6, or consult the server's documentation.

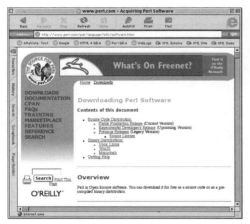

Figure 3.4 *For information about the most current versions of the Perl interpreter, point your browser to* http://www.perl.com/pub/language/info/software.html.

Perl vs. perl

Perl, with an uppercase *P*, is the programming language. *perl* with a lowercase *p* is the program that runs scripts in the Perl language. (Most, if not all programs born on Unix, are in all lowercase letters. Other examples are *pico*, *vi*, *grep*, and *cat*.) If that's not confusing enough, you also have the use of Perl as an adjective: the "Perl interpreter" interprets the Perl language, and so is spelled with a big *P*, even though it actually refers to the program (which should be spelled with a little *p*). So, you write *Perl scripts* (scripts in the Perl language) that are run with *perl* (the program, or Perl interpreter).

I almost always refer to the program as the "Perl interpreter" so that you won't be confused about what I'm talking about.

Getting a Perl Interpreter

In the same way that you need Microsoft Word to run Word documents and TurboTax to look at your tax records, the server needs a program called *perl*—with a lowercase *p* (see sidebar)—to run your Perl CGI scripts.

The perl program (or *interpreter* as it's more often referred) is Open Source software (which means that its source code is open to the public), and you can download and use it for free, with very few restrictions. There are versions (or *ports*) available for almost any platform, including Unix, Windows, and Macintosh, all of which can be found on the Perl Web site (*http://www.perl.com*).

You can usually download a Perl interpreter in one of two forms: source code and binary. The source code—which is the very latest version of the Perl interpreter—must be compiled so that it can run on your particular operating system; the binary versions are precompiled from a given, stable version of the source code in order to work only on a specific operating system. I heartily recommend that beginners take advantage of the appropriate binary version.

Almost all commercial Web hosts that allow CGI scripts will already have the Perl interpreter installed. If you've installed a local server on your personal computer, in most cases, you'll also have to install a Perl interpreter in order to execute Perl CGI scripts.

I explain how to locate an existing Perl interpreter on Unix machines on page 50. I explain how to install the Perl interpreter on Windows systems on page 67 and for Macs on page 78.

Getting a Perl Interpreter

Getting CGI.pm

The Perl community is renowned for its generosity and its reluctance to reinvent wheels (some call this *laziness*, and they mean it as a compliment). When one person writes a bit of script that might be useful to others, they often make it available to the general public (through a site called CPAN (Comprehensive Perl Archive Network): *http://www.cpan.org*). These scripts are usually called *modules*, since you can plug them into your own scripts and take advantage of the commands and instructions that they contain.

In the first edition of this book, I tried reinventing my own wheel for parsing the input from Perl CGI scripts, partly in a stab for independence, and partly to avoid object-oriented programming. Since then, however, I've taken a new look at the popular module CGI.pm (*pm* stands for *perl module*), written by Lincoln Stein (*http://stein.cshl.org/WWW/software/CGI/*) and I've found two things: CGI.pm offers a much better ride and you don't need to learn object-oriented programming in order to use it.

CGI.pm is so popular in fact that you generally don't even have to worry about installing it. If you've got perl version 5.004 or later (which you will once you set up your server), you've got CGI.pm.

Just because you have CGI.pm, however, doesn't mean you have the latest version. While the version is probably not crucial for learning Perl CGI scripting with this book, I'll teach you how to install the latest version in each platform's respective chapter (4, 5, and 6).

RUNNING PERL CGI ON A UNIX SERVER

According to Netcraft *(http://www.netcraft.com/survey/)* about 65% of the Web runs on Apache servers on the Unix platform. That's a lot. While Microsoft NT and IIS have consistently held about 20% of the market over the last few years, they don't seem to be gaining any ground.

This chapter will explain how to run Perl CGI scripts on a Unix server. While you can conceivably set up an Apache server on a personal computer (say, running Linux), I'm not going to go into the configuration details here. My guess is that if you're running Linux, you can work out installing Apache as well.

Instead, this chapter is geared towards those users whose *remote* Web host runs an Apache server on a Unix (or Linux) system. (You may or may not also decide to set up a local server on your personal computer—as described in Chapters 5 and 6.) This chapter will show you how to write (or upload) those scripts, how to word a shebang line, how to change the permissions, how to check the script's syntax, and finally, how to test and run the script.

If your Web host runs a Microsoft IIS server, your configuration instructions are basically the same as in Chapter 5, *Testing Scripts Locally on Windows*. If your Web host runs a Macintosh server, your configuration will closely mimic the instructions described in Chapter 6, *Testing Scripts Locally on the Mac*. If you have doubts, ask your Web host *(see page 46)*.

Which Perl Are They Running?

Any Web host that allows you to run CGI scripts will almost necessarily have the Perl interpreter already installed on their system. Apart from being convenient (you don't have to do the installation yourself), it's necessary: you probably don't have the access privileges you'd need to install it. You can and should, however, check out which version you have and where the Perl interpreter is located.

To find out which version of perl your Web host has:

1. Telnet to your Unix server *(see page 296)*.

2. Type **perl -v** at the prompt. You should be able to pick out the version number from the information that appears **(Figure 4.1)**.

To find out where perl is installed on your Web host's server:

1. Telnet to your Unix server *(see page 296)*.

2. Type either **which perl** or **whereis perl** at the prompt **(Figures 4.2 and 4.3)**. You'll need this information when constructing the shebang line (described on page 52).

✔ Tips

■ This book assumes you have version 5 (5.004 to be specific) or later of the Perl interpreter. If you don't, you'll have to ask your Web host to install a later version, or you'll have to switch Web hosts.

■ If your Web host doesn't allow you to telnet to the server, you still have several options. You can try one of the standard installation locations: /usr/bin/perl or /usr/local/bin/perl, you can check the PATH environment variable which sometimes contains the information *(see page 101)*, or you can simple ask your Web host.

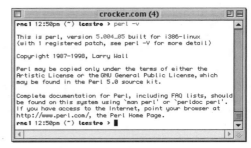

Figure 4.1 *As of version 5.6.0, the version of the Perl interpreter is displayed with three numbers: the first is the version, the second is the revision, and the third is the patch. Earlier versions (like mine shown above) have the syntax v.vvr_pp, where v is the version, r is the revision, and the optional pp gives the patch number.*

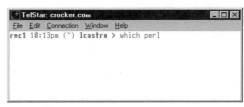

Figure 4.2 *To find out the location of the Perl interpreter on the server, type* **which perl** *at the prompt.*

Figure 4.3 *The server displays the full path to the Perl interpreter. This is the path that you should use in the shebang line.*

Figure 4.4 *This server has version 2.42 of CGI.pm installed.*

```
1   #!/usr/local/bin/perl -wT
2
3   use lib '/home/user4/lcastro/perllib';
4   use CGI ':standard';
5
6   my $version = $CGI::VERSION;
7
8   print "Content-type: text/html\n\n";
9   print "You're using version $version of
        CGI.pm";
```

3: If you have uploaded the latest version of CGI.pm to your personal directory on the Unix server, you'll have to tell the Perl interpreter where it is.

Figure 4.5 *If you decide to update your version of CGI.pm by copying it into one of your personal directories on the server, you'll have to tell the server's Perl interpreter about it. Otherwise, it'll keep using the one it already knows about.*

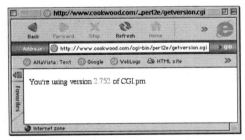

Figure 4.6 *When you run the script shown in Figure 4.5, you'll be able to see that the server is now using your updated version of CGI.pm.*

What About CGI.pm?

CGI.pm—the standard Perl module, or library used for parsing Perl CGI scripts—has been part of the standard Perl distribution since version 5.004 (of perl). That means that if you've got perl installed, you've got CGI.pm installed as well. While the version installed is probably not crucial for learning Perl CGI using this book, you still might want to know what you've got.

To find out what version of CGI.pm is installed on your Unix server:

1. Telnet to your Unix server *(see page 296)*.

2. At the prompt, type **perl -MCGI -e 'print $CGI::VERSION'**. You should be rewarded with the version of CGI.pm **(Figure 4.4)**.

✔ Tips

■ You can download the latest version of CGI.pm from Lincoln Stein's Web site: *http://stein.cshl.org/WWW/software/CGI/#installation*. You don't need to be the server administrator to update CGI.pm. You can copy CGI.pm to your private directory. Then add **use lib '/path_to_your_CGI.pm';** at the top of each of your scripts to direct the Perl interpreter to use your new version **(Figure 4.5)**.

■ CGI.pm doesn't work with versions prior to perl 5.004. If you're working with an older version of perl, you'll have to upgrade it—and CGI.pm will be automatically included.

■ For more details about how to use CGI.pm, consult Chapter 9, *Getting Data into the Script*.

What About CGI.pm?

Installing Scripts on Unix Servers

In order to run properly, Perl CGI scripts on a Unix server need to have the proper shebang line, extension, location, and permissions.

To install scripts on Unix servers:

1. Create your Perl CGI script as described on pages 36–39. Be sure to include the shebang line and save the script with a short, descriptive filename that ends with the proper extension. (Perl CGI scripts usually end with *.cgi* or *.pl* on Unix servers.)

2. Test the script's syntax *(see page 40)*.

3. Put the script in the proper directory (usually *cgi-bin*) on the Unix server. If you've created the file on Unix itself (say with pico or vi), you can complete this step while saving. If you've created the script on a Mac or Windows machine, you'll have to upload the file to the proper directory on the Unix server *(see pages 53–55)*.

4. Make the script executable by changing its permissions *(see pages 56–57)*.

✔ Tips

■ To find the path to perl on your server in order to construct the shebang line, consult *Which Perl Are They Running?* on page 50. For more about the shebang line itself, consult *The Shebang Line* on page 35.

■ You usually can't just save the script anywhere, and you can't create your own cgi-bin directory. Your Web host can tell you the proper location for your scripts.

■ For more about paths and Unix, consult *Dealing with Paths in Unix* on page 299.

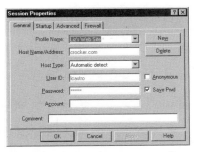

Figure 4.7 *In the Session Properties dialog box, type your server's name, your user ID, and your password. Then click OK.*

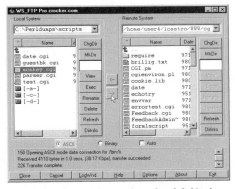

Figure 4.8 *In the left pane (your hard disk), choose the script you want to upload. On the right side (your server), choose the directory into which you wish to place the uploaded script. Click the ASCII option below the left list. Then click the Upload button (-->) between the frames.*

Uploading Your Script

If you create the script on a Mac or PC (which is perfectly fine), you'll have to upload it to the Unix server with an FTP program like WS_FTP (for Windows) or Fetch (for Mac). If you create the script directly on the server (say, with pico), you can skip this section.

To upload files from Windows (with WS_FTP Pro):

1. Launch WS_FTP Pro, or other FTP transfer program.

2. Click Connect at the bottom of the main WS_FTP window. The WS_FTP Sites dialog box appears.

3. Click Quick Connect (or New—as you prefer) and enter your server's name or IP address in the Name/IP Address box and your user ID and password in the corresponding boxes **(Figure 4.7)**.

4. Click OK to start the connection to the server and return to the main WS_FTP window.

5. On the left side of the window, navigate to the directory on your hard disk that contains the file you wish to upload and select the desired script **(Figure 4.8)**.

6. On the right side of the window, navigate to the directory on the server to which you wish to upload the script.

7. Click the ASCII option below the left list.

8. Click the Upload button (the right pointing arrow) between the panes. The file will be uploaded.

✔ Tip

■ Consult WS_FTP's documentation (and tutorials) at *http://www.ipswitch.com/products/ws_ftp/*.

Uploading Your Script

If you've created your scripts on a Mac, you can use Fetch to upload them to a Unix server. First you'll want to change your upload preferences, and then you can complete the actual file transfer.

To change your preferences for uploading CGI scripts from a Mac (with Fetch):

1. Launch Fetch, or other FTP program.

2. Choose Customize > Preferences **(Figure 4.9)**. The Preferences dialog box appears.

3. Click the Upload tab. The Upload preferences appear **(Figure 4.10)**.

4. Choose Text in the menu next to Default text format.

5. Be sure to *deselect* the Add .txt suffix in text files option.

6. Click OK to save your settings.

To upload your script to the server from a Mac (with Fetch):

1. Launch Fetch, or other FTP program.

2. If the New Connection window isn't already open, choose File > New Connection **(Figure 4.11)**.

3. In the New Connection window, type the server name (or IP address) in the Host box **(Figure 4.12)**.

4. Type your user name and password in the User ID and Password boxes.

5. Click OK. Fetch opens the connection with the server.

Figure 4.9 *In Fetch (on the Mac), choose Customize > Preferences.*

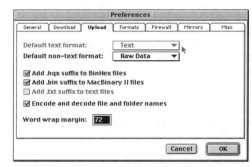

Figure 4.10 *Click the Upload tab at the top of the Preferences dialog box to see the Upload preferences. Then choose Text for the Default text format and make sure to deselect the Add .txt suffix to text files option.*

Figure 4.11 *In Fetch (on the Mac), choose File > New Connection to open a connection to your site for uploading files.*

Figure 4.12 *In the New Connection dialog box, type the name or IP address in the Host box, your user ID in the User ID box, and your password in the Password box. If you like, you can type the desired destination directory in the Directory box. Then click OK.*

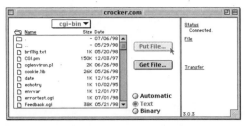

Figure 4.13 *Navigate to the directory into which you wish to upload your CGI scripts. On many servers, CGI scripts must be located in the cgi-bin directory in order to work properly. Ask your Web host to be sure. Then click Put File (or drag the file from the desktop).*

Figure 4.14 *After clicking Put File, choose the desired file from the dialog box that appears and click Open.*

Figure 4.15 *In the Put File dialog box, confirm that the name of the script is correct and that the format is Text.*

6. If necessary, navigate to the directory on the server into which you wish to upload the script **(Figure 4.13)**.

7. Make sure Text is selected (below the Get File button).

8. Click Put File, choose the file you wish to upload from the dialog box that appears, and then click Open **(Figure 4.14)**.

   Or, drag the desired script from your desktop to the Fetch window.

9. In the Put File dialog box that appears, confirm the name of the script you're uploading, make sure the Format is set to Text, and click OK **(Figure 4.15)**.

✔ Tips

■ Some Web hosts require that you upload your CGI scripts to the cgi-bin directory. Others let you run CGI scripts from wherever you like, as long as they have the .cgi extension. To be sure, ask your Web host administrator (*see page 46*).

■ Fetch was recently bought back from Dartmouth University by its principal engineer, Jim Matthews (thanks to winnings from a stint on the television show, *Who Wants to Be a Millionaire?*). You can find Fetch's new Web site, complete with new versions, documentation, and support at *http://fetchsoftworks.com/*.

Uploading Your Script

Changing Permissions

When you first upload a file to the Unix server, it is generally set so that only the owner can read and write to it, and everyone else can just read it. In order for others (and thus any browser) to be able to execute it, you have to change the permissions. You can either telnet to the server to change the permissions (described below) or often, you can use your FTP client for the job *(see page 57)*.

To change a file or directory's permissions directly on the server:

1. Telnet to the Unix server *(see page 296)*, and, if necessary, navigate to the directory that contains the file or directory whose permissions you want to change *(see page 302)*.

2. Type **chmod**.

3. If desired, type **-v** so that you'll get a message confirming the permissions.

4. Type a number in the format **oge**, where *o* is the number that indicates the *o*wner's permissions, *g* is the number that indicates the *g*roup's permissions, and *e* is the number that indicates *e*veryone else's permissions.

   Use *755* for files, like CGI scripts, that need to be executed. Use *644* for non-executables, including log files, configuration files, preferences files, external subroutines, libraries (like CGI.pm), and others.

5. Type **scriptname**, where *scriptname* is the full name of the script whose permissions you want to change.

6. Press Enter. The permissions are set. Unless you use **-v** there is no confirmation.

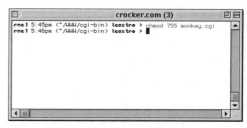

Figure 4.16 *Normally, the* chmod *function gives no feedback whatsoever. Still, as long as you're sure you typed the right permissions code, no news is probably good news.*

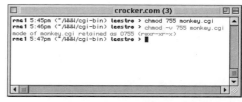

Figure 4.17 *If you use the* -v *flag with* chmod, *you'll get a message telling what permissions a file or directory has, and if they've changed or not.*

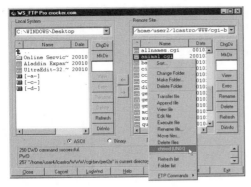

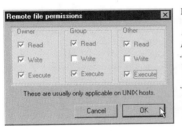

Figure 4.18 *In WS_FTP, right-click the desired file or directory and choose chmod (UNIX) in the pop-up menu.*

Figure 4.19 *Then choose the desired permissions for that file or directory in the Remote file permissions dialog box, and click OK.*

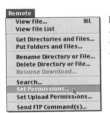

Figure 4.20 *In Fetch, select the desired file or directory and then choose Remote > Set Permissions.*

Figure 4.21 *Then choose the desired permissions for that file or directory in the Permissions dialog box, and click OK.*

Many FTP programs let you change a file or directory's permissions on a remote server.

To change permissions with WS_FTP:

1. Right-click the file or directory in the WS_FTP window whose permissions you want to change.

2. In the pop-up menu that appears, choose chmod (UNIX) **(Figure 4.18)**.

3. Check the desired permissions in the Remote file permissions dialog box and then click OK **(Figure 4.19)**.

To change permissions with Fetch:

1. In the Fetch window, select the file whose permissions you'd like to change.

2. Choose Remote > Set Permissions **(Figure 4.20)**.

3. In the dialog box that appears, choose the desired permissions and click OK **(Figure 4.21)**.

✔ Tips

■ For WS_FTP, display the permissions of a directory's files by clicking the DirInfo button in the main window.

■ With Fetch, set the default permissions for all files that you upload by choosing Remote > Set Upload Permissions.

■ In Fetch, view the current permissions of a directory's files by choosing Remote > View File List.

■ For more information about permissions, consult Appendix C, *Permissions on Unix*.

■ For more information about uploading files with WS_FTP, see page 53. For details about uploading files with Fetch, see pages 54–55.

Changing Permissions

Testing Your Unix Server

It's a good idea to test your server with a very, very simple Perl script to make sure everything is set up properly.

To test how your Unix server handles Perl scripts:

1. Write a very simple Perl script (like the one shown in Figure 4.22, name it *unixtest.cgi*, and install it as described on pages 52–56.

2. Open any Web browser.

3. In the Address box (it's called *Location* in Netscape), type **http://www.yourweb-host.com/virtual_scripts_directory/unixtest.cgi**, where *yourwebhost* is the name of your Web host's server (or your domain), *virtual_scripts_directory* is the name of the virtual directory that maps to the actual scripts directory where you installed the script—including any necessary path information—and *unixtest.cgi* is the file you created in step 1. The browser should display the results of the script **(Figure 4.23)**.

✔ Tips

■ Make sure you test the server with the *simplest possible* Perl script. That way, you can be sure that any problems that arise are due to the server and not the script. You'll have plenty of time to work with more complicated scripts once you're sure your server is functioning properly.

■ If you're not sure what your virtual scripts directory is, try *cgi-bin*. Or hey, ask your Web host *(see page 46)*!

```
1   #!/usr/local/bin/perl -wT
2
3   print "Content-type: text/html\n\n";
4   print "Show me the monkey with my new
        server!";
```

1: The shebang line for scripts running on Unix servers should show the path to the Perl interpreter that you found on page 50.

3: Even the simplest script requires a Content-type line that tells the server what kind of output to expect. Since the output (line 4) contains no actual HTML code, we could also use "text/plain", but it's not a crucial difference at this point, and I'd rather you get accustomed to typing "text/html".

4: Finally, we'll just output a simple line to make sure that the server's working.

Figure 4.22 *Be sure to use an excruciatingly simple script so that if you get an error, you can be sure the problem is with the server and not your script. You'll get to the complicated stuff soon enough.*

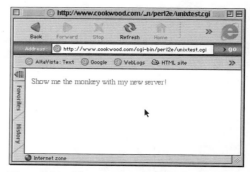

Figure 4.23 *If the server, Perl interpreter, and script have all been properly installed, the script will be processed and you'll see your message in the browser.*

TESTING SCRIPTS LOCALLY ON WINDOWS

As I described in Chapter 3, *About Servers, Perl, and CGI.pm*, the CGI part of Perl CGI requires that scripts be run on a server, not just through a local browser. If you don't have access to a server—perhaps you haven't signed up with a Web host yet, or your current Web host doesn't allow Perl CGI—you can install a server on your Windows machine so that you can test scripts locally. This is a great way to learn Perl from the comfort of your own home, without incurring start-up or monthly fees from a remote Web host.

This chapter describes how to install some of the most popular servers for Windows on your personal computer. The Microsoft servers are probably most like what you'd find at a Windows-based Web host; the Xitami and Sambar servers are much simpler to set up and to run, and are perfectly valid solutions. Of course, you only have to install *one* server—choose the one that suits you best.

Keep in mind that you can do a lot more with a server than just test Perl CGI scripts—including serving Web sites, FTP, and e-mail. Don't expect details on those other features here; I'll be sticking to testing Perl.

Regardless of the server you install, you should also install the latest version of the Perl interpreter. A company called ActiveState has made this process relatively painless for Windows users.

Finally, although the CGI.pm module for parsing Perl CGI scripts is included when you install perl, I'll also show you how to upgrade to the latest version, if you so desire.

Installing the Xitami or Sambar Server

There are several free servers available for Windows 32 systems (both 95/98 and NT/2000). The best that I have found are Samba and Xitami. They were easy to setup and easy to run and administer. Take your choice.

To install Xitami:

1. Download the latest version of Xitami for your particular version of Windows from *http://www.xitami.com*.

2. Run the server's install program by double-clicking the file you just downloaded. The file I downloaded was called *bw3224d7.exe*, though future versions will probably have slightly different—but perhaps equally oblique—names.

3. Accept the default configurations, including where the server is installed **(Figure 5.1)** and to which program manager group its icons are added.

4. Choose an administrator name and password and write them down somewhere you can find them again **(Figure 5.2)**. You'll need them if you decide to change the server's configurations.

5. Select a server profile (not shown). I recommend **Turbo** if you're just planning on running the server for testing Perl scripts and don't have to worry about other folks accessing your pages.

6. At the end of the installation, click Run to start up the Xitami server right away. When Xitami is running, you'll see a green icon with an X in the System Tray at the right (or bottom) end of the Taskbar **(Figure 5.3)**.

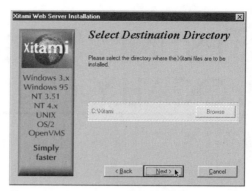

Figure 5.1 *You can accept the default directory for installing the Xitami server so that it's placed in C:\Xitami.*

Figure 5.2 *Choose an administrator name and password so that you can access the configuration settings.*

Figure 5.3 *Once Xitami's up and running, you'll see its icon in the System Tray (at the far end of the Taskbar).*

Installing the Xitami or Sambar Server

Figure 5.4 *First, download Sambar to your My Documents directory. Then, expand the zip document with Aladdin's Expander (or WinZip or whatever).*

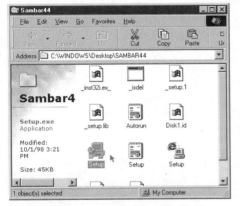

Figure 5.5 *Double-click the Setup.exe file (the extension may be hidden as shown here) that's inside the newly expanded directory in order to install Sambar.*

Figure 5.6 *Once the installation is completed and Sambar is running, you'll see its icon in the System Tray (at the far end of the Taskbar).*

To install Sambar:

1. Download the latest version of Sambar from *http://www.sambar.com* **(Figure 5.4)**.

2. Double-click the zip file you've just downloaded in order to expand it, using Aladdin's free Expander for Windows (*http://www.aladdinsys.com*) for example. A directory called *Sambar44* is created in the same directory as the zip file. (Future versions will probably have slightly different names.)

3. Double-click Setup.exe in the Sambar44 directory to begin the installation **(Figure 5.5)**.

4. Accept the default configuration values by clicking Next as necessary.

5. Once the server is installed, click Finish.

6. Start up the Sambar server, if it's not running already, by choosing it from the appropriate submenu of the Start menu. When it's running, you'll see a gray icon with an S on it in the System Tray at the right (or bottom) of the Taskbar **(Figure 5.6)**.

✔ Tips

- Turn off either Sambar or Xitami by right-clicking the icon in the System Tray and choosing Shutdown or Terminate, respectively. Turn one back on again by choosing its program name from the Start menu (its exact location will depend on how you installed it).

- By default, the Xitami server is installed to *C:\Xitami*. Sambar is installed to *C:\Sambar44*.

Installing the Xitami or Sambar Server

Installing Personal Web Server

The Windows 98 CD comes with Personal Web Server (or PWS) as an optional feature. While it's a bit harder to set up than Sambar and Xitami, it has the benefit of being from Microsoft, and is thus probably quite similar to what an NT-based Web host has.

To install Personal Web Server:

1. Close all open applications.

2. Insert your Windows 98 CD in your CD drive.

3. Choose Run from the Windows Start menu and then type **D:\add-ons\pws\ setup.exe** in the Open line, where *D* is the letter that corresponds to your CD drive (**Figure 5.7**).

4. Click OK to begin the installation.

5. Go through the installation, accepting the default settings and clicking Next, as necessary (**Figure 5.8**).

6. Restart your computer when you are prompted to do so. Be sure to boot from the hard disk if given the option (if you've left the CD in the drive). Once you've restarted, you'll see the PWS icon in the System Tray at the right end (or bottom) of the Taskbar (**Figure 5.9**).

✔ Tip

■ You can turn PWS off by right-clicking the icon in the System Tray and choosing Stop Service in the pop-up menu that appears. A little x in a red circle indicates the server is no longer running. Turn it back on by right-clicking and choosing Start Service from the pop-up menu.

Figure 5.7 *Choose Start > Run and then type* **D:\add-ons\pws\setup.exe**, *where D corresponds to your CD drive.*

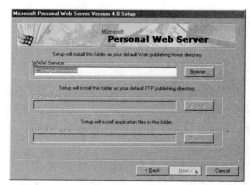

Figure 5.8 *Accept the default location for the root directory and server.*

Figure 5.9 *Once the installation is completed and PWS is running, you'll see its icon in the System Tray (at the far end of the Taskbar). If you point the cursor at it, you'll get a little pop-up message assuring you that PWS is running.*

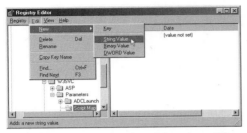

Figure 5.10 *Select Script Map and then choose Edit > New > String Value.*

Figure 5.11 *In the right pane, replace "New Value #1" by typing* **.pl**. *Then double-click the new value.*

Figure 5.12 *In the Edit String dialog box that appears, type the path to* perl.exe *followed by two sets of* **%s** *separated by a space.*

Figure 5.13 *When you're done, your new entry should look like this. Then close the Registry Editor window and restart both your computer and PWS.*

PWS also requires that you manually edit the registry so that it knows how to find the Perl interpreter.

Beware! Editing the registry is not something to do lightly. If you do it wrong, your computer may fail to boot up the next time. Be sure to do a full backup before editing the registry, and to follow these steps precisely.

To edit the registry for PWS and Perl:

1. Choose Start > Run.

2. Type **regedit** in the Open box and click OK.

3. In the Registry window, expand (by clicking the corresponding plus sign), in order, HKEY_Local_Machine, System, CurrentControlSet, Services, W3SVC, and Parameters.

4. Under Parameters, select Script Map.

5. Choose Edit > New > String Value **(Figure 5.10)**. A new entry appears in the right side of the window, labeled *New Value #1*.

6. Replace *New Value #1* with **.pl** **(Figure 5.11)**.

7. Double-click the new *.pl* entry.

8. In the Edit String dialog box that appears, on the Value data line, type **C:\Perl\bin\perl.exe %s %s**, where *C:\Perl\bin\perl.exe* is the path to your Perl interpreter *(see page 67)*.

9. Click OK **(Figure 5.12)**. Your Registry Editor window will show the new entry **(Figure 5.13)**.

10. Close the Registry (with the close box).

11. Restart the computer.

12. Start up PWS if it's not running already.

Installing Personal Web Server

Installing IIS on Windows 2000

If you have Windows 2000, you can install the Internet Information Server (IIS), which is probably identical to any Windows-based server your ISP will have.

To install IIS on Windows 2000 machines:

1. Choose Settings > Control Panel from the Windows Start menu.

2. Double-click the Add/Remove Programs icon in the Control Panel folder.

3. Click Add/Remove Windows Components in the left column **(Figure 5.14)**.

4. Select Internet Information Services (IIS) by making sure it has a checkmark in its box **(Figure 5.15)**.

5. Click Next to complete the installation.

✔ Tips

- To turn off just the IIS Web server, right-click the My Computer icon on the desktop and choose Manage. In the window that appears, expand Services and Applications and then Internet Information Services. Choose Default Web Site and finally choose Stop from the Action menu **(Figure 5.16)**. The Default Web Site item will now be labeled as "Stopped". To turn on IIS, choose Action > Start.

- To turn off *all* of your Internet services at once, including FTP and SMTP, choose Internet Information Services in the Computer Management window and then Action > Restart IIS.... Then choose Stop Internet Services on [server name] in the pop-up menu of the dialog box that appears.

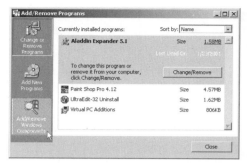

Figure 5.14 *In the Add/Remove Programs helper, choose Add/Remove Windows Components.*

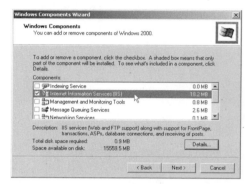

Figure 5.15 *Choose Internet Information Services in the list of Windows Components that appears.*

Figure 5.16 *IIS automatically turns on when you start up Windows 2000 and automatically turns off when you close Windows 2000. If you want to manually turn it off, right-click the My Computer icon to get to the window shown here, expand folders until you get to Default Web site, and then choose Action > Stop.*

Installing IIS on Windows 2000

Figure 5.17 *At first glance, you might think this Perl script has the right extension. However if you look more closely, you'll notice that it has a different icon than the Perl scripts around it—the same icon as most text files.*

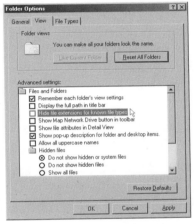

Figure 5.18 *Choose Start > Settings > Folder Options and in the dialog box that appears, make sure the* Hide file extensions for known file types *option is not checked.*

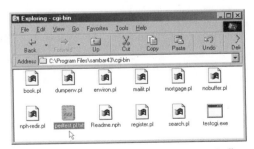

Figure 5.19 *The sneaky .txt extension, automatically and otherwise invisibly added by some text editors, is revealed. To get rid of it, select the name and delete those last four characters. You'll have to confirm that you want to change the extension and then you'll see the icon change. Then, and only then, will the script work properly.*

Displaying File Extensions

Windows has what I consider to be a pair of annoying habits. First, by default, it does not show file extensions on the desktop. The second, more insidious problem is that many Windows programs add extensions to filenames automatically—*in addition* to any file extension you've specified yourself. For example, if you use Notepad or Word to save a text file as "file.pl", it will actually be saved as "file.pl.txt". Not only will it not be recognized as a Perl file, you'll get a "file not found" error when you try to access it, since you'll be looking for "file.pl", which doesn't exist.

Your first recourse is to at least be able to see what extensions are being added.

To display and remove extensions on the Windows desktop:

1. Choose Start > Settings > Folder Options (Windows 9x) or Start Settings > Control Panel > Folder Options (Windows 2000).

2. Click the View tab.

3. Deselect the Hide file extensions for known file types option in the list **(Figure 5.18)**.

4. Click OK.

5. You can now see and manually remove any unwanted extensions on the Desktop.

To keep programs from adding extra, unwanted file extensions:

1. When you go to save your Perl or HTML files, choose the All Files (*.*) option in the Save Files of Type box.

2. Or, if that option is not available, which it often is not, save the file as a Text Document and also enclose the filename and desired file extension in double quotation marks.

Testing Your Server (Part 1)

Before you go too far, it's a good idea to test your server to make sure that it can serve simple Web pages. If it can, then it's properly installed and turned on, and we can move on to working with Perl scripts.

To test your Web server:

1. Create a simple test HTML file called *test.html* (**Figure 5.20**).

2. Save it in the server's root Web directory.

   By default, Sambar's root Web directory is *C:\Sambar44\docs*.

   Xitami's default root Web directory is *C:\Xitami\webpages*.

   PWS and IIS both use *C:\Inetpub\wwwroot* as their root Web directory.

3. Open a Web browser.

4. In the Address or Location box, type **http://localhost/test.html**. The result should match Figure 5.22 (assuming your HTML document matched Figure 5.20).

✔ Tips

- The root Web directory is a pre-mapped virtual directory. A virtual directory is one whose URL address doesn't match its actual location on your computer. So, when you type **http://localhost/somefile.html**, the *somefile.html* must be located in the root Web directory as specified above. (See also page 44.)

- If it doesn't work, check the easy stuff first. Is the server running? (Is the server's icon in the System Tray?) Did you save the HTML file in the proper directory with the proper extension? Did Notepad add that debilitating .txt extension *(see page 65)* to your HTML document?

```
<HTML><HEAD><TITLE>Is the Server
Working?</TITLE></HEAD>
<BODY>Yes, the server is working!</BODY>
</HTML>
```

Figure 5.20 *Use an excruciatingly simple HTML document so that you can be sure that any problems that may occur are due to your server and not your HTML coding.*

Figure 5.21 *Save your simple test HTML file in the proper directory for your server (Xitami's webpages directory is shown here). If you're using Notepad or WordPad, you may need to enclose the filename in double quotes to keep the program from appending the annoying and debilitating .txt extension to the filename (see page 65).*

Figure 5.22 *Type* http://localhost/test.html *in the Address box (the Location box if you're on Netscape) and then press Enter. Your HTML page should be displayed in the browser as shown here. (If you typed* C:\Xitami\webpages\test.html, *the page would also be shown, but it would not have gone through the server, which for Perl scripts is the whole point of the exercise.)*

Figure 5.23 *Download the ActivePerl file from ActiveState's site. You may also need to update your Windows installer to version 1.1 or higher.*

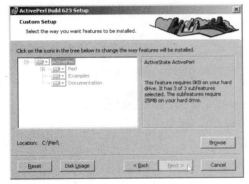

Figure 5.24 *I recommend accepting the default values unless you have a good reason not to. At the very least, your setup will match the one used in this book. Here, we're installing the Perl interpreter in C:\Perl.*

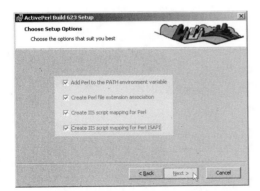

Figure 5.25 *The ActivePerl installer sets up the path variables for you so that the Perl interpreter is easily found for running scripts. The bottom two options are only activated when installing ActivePerl on a IIS server (i.e., on Windows 2000 if you're following this book).*

Installing the Perl Interpreter

In order for Perl scripts to run on your new server, you have to install a Perl interpreter that knows what to do with those scripts.

To install the Perl interpreter:

1. Download the latest version of ActivePerl: *http://www.activestate.com/Products/ ActivePerl/Download.html*.

2. If you're on Windows 95, 98, or NT, you will need to download the latest version of the Windows Installer (it's available on the ActiveState Perl download page) and then double-click it to install it.

3. Then double-click the ActivePerl file to install the Perl interpreter on your server.

4. Accept all the default settings by clicking Next to continue until you finally get to the Install button to complete the installation. By default, the Perl interpreter is installed to *C:\Perl\bin\perl.exe*.

✔ Tips

■ Although you can download and compile the very latest binary files from *http://www.perl.com*, it's much easier to download and install the pre-compiled ActivePerl from ActiveState.

■ ActivePerl is no more *active* than regular old perl. Its name comes from *ActiveState*, the company that compiles it and makes it easy to install on Windows systems. ActiveState does add some helpful features to its ActivePerl, but nothing crucial to running the examples in this book. For details, see *http://www.activestate.com*.

Installing the Perl Interpreter

Installing CGI.pm

When you install the Perl interpreter, CGI.pm, the standard module for parsing Perl CGI scripts, is automatically installed. However, that doesn't mean you have the latest version. If you'd like to make sure you're on the technological edge, you can install and download the most recent version of CGI.pm manually.

To find out what version of CGI.pm you have:

1. Choose Start > Accessories > MS-DOS Prompt (or Command Prompt on Windows 2000).

2. In the MS-DOS Prompt window that appears, type **perl -MCGI -e "print $CGI::VERSION"** (that's a dollar sign, $, preceding *CGI*).

To download the latest version of CGI.pm for Windows:

1. Point your browser to *http://stein.cshl.org/WWW/software/CGI/#installation* (**Figure 5.27**).

2. Download and unzip the Zip file containing CGI.pm for Windows.

3. Place both the CGI.pm file itself and the CGI directory (containing some auxiliary files) in the *C:\Perl\lib* directory (**Figures 5.28 and 5.29**).

✔ Tips

■ For the purposes of learning Perl CGI scripting with this book, any version of CGI.pm that comes with perl 5.004 or later is probably enough.

■ You don't have to make CGI.pm or any of its auxiliary files executable. While its functions are used by your executable scripts, it's not actually executed itself.

Figure 5.26 *At press time, the latest version of CGI.pm was 2.752.*

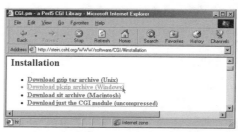

Figure 5.27 *You can download the latest version of CGI.pm from Lincoln Stein's site. Then unzip the contents and place them in the proper directories.*

Figure 5.28 *The CGI.pm module goes (loose) in the lib directory in the main Perl folder.*

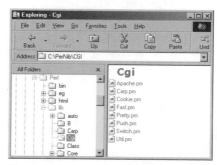

Figure 5.29 *The CGI folder (which contains auxiliary modules) should also be placed in the lib directory.*

```
1  #!C:\Perl\bin\perl.exe -wT
2
3  print "Content-type:text/html\n\n";
4  print "Show me the monkey with my new
        server!";
```

1: The shebang line for scripts running on Xitami or PWS must show the path to the Perl interpreter that you installed on page 67. While Sambar and IIS can run scripts without the shebang line, you still need to include it so that you can add the switches (-wT).

Figure 5.30 *Xitami and PWS require that you explicitly show where the Perl interpreter is. Sambar and IIS are indifferent to the shebang line.*

Figure 5.31 *Save the simple Perl script in the proper directory and with the proper extension. If you use Notepad or WordPad (or have trouble), enclose your filename in double-quotes so that no extra .txt extension gets tacked on.*

Installing Scripts on Windows Servers

The next step after installing a server and the Perl interpreter is to install your scripts. While each server is set up slightly differently, there are three main areas that you need to keep in mind for all servers: the shebang line, the file extension, and the location of the scripts.

To install scripts on your server:

1. Create your Perl CGI script as described on pages 36–39. Be sure to include the shebang line at the beginning of each script by typing **#!C:\Perl\bin\perl.exe -wT** where *C:\Perl\bin\perl.exe* is the path to the Perl interpreter you installed on page 67.

2. Check the script's syntax *(see page 40)*.

3. Make sure your script ends with the proper extension.

   In general, use the **.pl** extension. While Xitami doesn't care if you use it or not, most other servers do, so you might as well get into the habit of adding it.

4. Save the script to the proper directory.

   By default, scripts in Sambar should be saved to the *C:\Sambar44\cgi-bin* directory.

   Scripts in Xitami should be saved to the *C:\Xitami\cgi-bin* directory.

   Scripts in PWS and IIS should be saved to the *C:\Inetpub\scripts* directory.

✔ Tips

- Neither Sambar nor IIS cares much about the shebang line. However, you'll have to use it to use switches *(see page 36)*.

- Be sure and read *Displaying File Extensions* on page 65 before saving files.

Testing Your Server (Part II)

Now that you've got the Perl interpreter installed, it's a good idea to test your server with an achingly simple Perl script to make sure it can handle Perl scripts in general.

To test scripts on your server:

1. Install your server and test it as described on pages 60–66.

2. Install the Perl interpreter *(see page 67)*.

3. Write a very simple Perl script, name it *perltest.pl*, and install it as described on page 69 **(Figure 5.32)**.

4. Open any Web browser.

5. In the Address box (it's called *Location* in Netscape), type **http://localhost/ virtual_scripts_directory/perltest.pl**, where *virtual_scripts_directory* is the name of the virtual directory that maps to the actual scripts directory where you installed the script *(see page 69)* and *perltest.pl* is the file you created in step 3.

On Sambar and Xitami, the default virtual script directory is */cgi-bin*. On PWS and IIS, the virtual script directory is */Scripts*.

6. Press Enter. Your browser should display the results of the script **(Figure 5.33)**.

✔ Tips

■ Make sure you test the server with the *simplest possible* Perl script. That way, you can be sure that any problems that arise are due to the server and not the script. You'll have plenty of time to work with more complicated scripts once you're sure your server is functioning properly.

■ Do not save Perl Scripts as Unicode documents, at least not yet. Windows can't handle them.

```
1   #!C:\Perl\bin\perl.exe -wT
2
3   print "Content-type:text/html\n\n";
4   print "Show me the monkey with my new
        server!";
```

1: The shebang line for scripts running on Xitami or PWS should show the path to the Perl interpreter that you installed on page 67.
3: Even the simplest script requires a Content-type line that tells the server what kind of output to expect. Since the output contains no actual HTML code, we could also use "text/plain", but it's not a crucial difference at this point, and I'd rather you get accustomed to typing "text/html".
4: Finally, we'll just output a simple line to make sure that the server's working.

Figure 5.32 *Be sure to use an excruciatingly simple script so that if you get an error, you can be sure the problem is with the server and not your script. You'll get to the complicated stuff soon enough.*

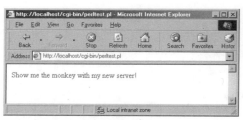

Figure 5.33 *If the server, Perl interpreter, and script have all been properly installed, the script will be processed and you'll see your print message in the browser.*

TESTING SCRIPTS LOCALLY ON THE MAC

6

While there are many fewer Macintosh servers than Unix or even Windows, the differences between Perl implementations on each of these systems are so slight, that testing on a Mac before uploading to a server—even to one with a different operating system—can be very worthwhile.

This chapter explains how to set up a Macintosh server, download MacPerl, create and install scripts, and then test them.

Installing Personal Web Sharing

Apple's Personal Web Sharing has been bundled with its system software since version 8.1 was released in January, 1998. It's made up of a control panel (aptly called Web Sharing) and an extension.

To install Personal Web Sharing:

1. Choose Control Panels > Extensions Manager from the Apple menu.

2. Check Web Sharing under Control Panels and then Web Sharing Extension under Extensions to make them active.

3. Click Restart to restart your computer.

✔ Tip

- If you don't have either the Web Sharing control panel or the Web Sharing Extension, you may have to re-install or upgrade your system software. (If you do so, you can use Custom Install with the Apple installer to add just the missing components, without having to redo your whole system.)

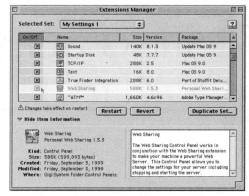

Figure 6.1 *Mark the checkboxes next to the Web Sharing control panel (as shown above) and the Web Sharing Extension (further down the list), in order to install the Personal Web Sharing Server. Then click Restart to restart your computer.*

The Root Web Directory

You need to choose one folder on your hard drive in which you will store all of the files you want to test, or more generally speaking, all of the files that will be served by Apple's Personal Web Server. This folder is called the "root Web directory".

To choose a root Web directory:

Decide which folder on your hard disk will contain the HTML and Perl CGI files that you'll be testing.

✔ Tips

■ The default root Web directory, called "Web Pages", is located at the top level of your hard disk. It contains a number of default files, supplied by Apple. It is a perfectly reasonable choice for the root Web directory.

■ While technically you are allowed to place aliases within the root Web directory that give access to other parts of your hard disk, I don't recommend it for security reasons. It's too easy to forget which files you're giving access to when they're all over your computer.

The Root Web Directory

Carefully Sharing the Root Web Directory

When you (or anyone else) run a CGI script on your Macintosh-based personal Web server, that CGI script has total access to every single file on your computer—and thus can conceivably create, modify, and even delete any file or folder. This is a huge security risk. While you will learn how to make your CGI scripts secure farther along in the book, you need to protect your Macintosh *right now*, during testing; as a beginner, your scripts may not be as secure as they need to be. Once you're confident that your scripts pose no security risk, you can choose to set up your Mac server differently.

Since you can't limit a CGI's access to your files and folders, I recommend limiting the access to your CGI scripts themselves. If you follow the instructions in this chapter, only you will be able to access your Web server; only you will be able to run CGI scripts on it. To do so, you have to make yourself the *owner* of your computer and then assign yourself the exclusive right to access your Web server, once it is online.

To create an Owner:

1. Choose Control Panels > File Sharing from the Apple menu **(Figure 6.2)**.

2. When the File Sharing dialog box finally appears (it takes a while), make sure the Start/Stop tab is showing. Then enter your name in the Owner Name box, and a password in the Owner Password box.

3. Click Start in the middle section of the dialog box, under File Sharing off. Your computer will pause a few minutes while file sharing is activated.

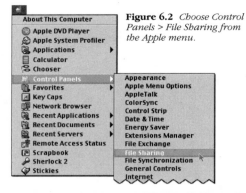

Figure 6.2 *Choose Control Panels > File Sharing from the Apple menu.*

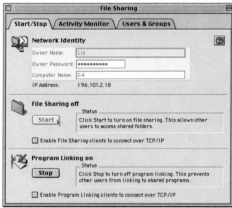

Figure 6.3 *Enter your name in the Owner Name box and a password in the Owner Password box. Make sure the password is hard to decipher. Then click the Start button in the second section, under File Sharing off.*

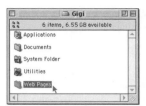

Figure 6.4 *Select the folder that you've decided will be the root Web directory.*

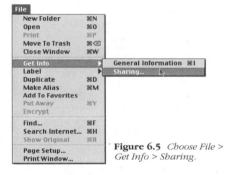

Figure 6.5 *Choose File > Get Info > Sharing.*

Figure 6.6 *Make sure to choose None (--) next to User/Group and Everyone so that no one but you can run your CGI scripts while you're learning Perl.*

 Web Pages

Figure 6.7 *Once you've shared the root Web directory, it'll sport this icon.*

To *carefully* share the root Web directory:

1. In the Finder, select the folder that you've chosen as your root Web directory.

2. Choose File > Get Info > Sharing. The [your root Web directory] Info dialog box appears.

3. First click the Share this item and its contents box to share the folder.

4. Then choose your name next to Owner and give yourself Read/Write privileges (the glasses and pencil icon) under the Privilege column.

5. Choose None (--) next to User/Group and None (--) again under Privilege for that category to deny access to any other user or group.

6. Choose None (--) next to Everyone to deny access to everyone else.

7. Finally, click Copy to ensure that all of the folders within your root Web directory have these same privileges. A dialog box will ask if you're sure you want to do this. Click Copy.

✔ Tips

■ You have to create an Owner, as described on the previous page, before you can limit access to the server to that owner.

■ If you decide to give someone else access to your Web server, be aware that they will be able to run your CGI scripts and thus will be able to create, modify, and even delete files and folders on your computer. Don't do it lightly.

Carefully Sharing the Root Web Directory

Starting the Web Sharing Server

Once you've made the root Web directory available to yourself and no one else, as described on pages 74–75, you're ready to safely start up the server.

To start the Web Sharing server:

1. Choose Control Panels > Web Sharing **(Figure 6.8)**. The Web Sharing dialog box will appear.

2. In the top half of the Web Sharing dialog box, next to Web Folder, you'll see the path to the folder that will serve as your root Web directory. Change the directory by clicking Select **(Figure 6.9)** and choosing the desired folder.

3. Likewise, you can choose the default homepage (for the root Web directory) by clicking the Select button next to Home Page.

4. In the lower half of the dialog box, choose Use File Sharing to control user access **(Figure 6.10)**. This limits access to the users with whom you've shared the folder (which is just you, if you've followed the instructions on pages 74–75).

5. Finally, click the Start button to start up the personal Web server. Your Mac may seem to hang. Be patient.

✔ Very Important!

■ Note that the Give everyone read-only access is a lie. If you mark this option, anyone out on the Internet can run your scripts, and those scripts have complete access to all of the files on your hard disk. I don't recommend it.

■ I recommend closing the Web server when you're not actively testing scripts.

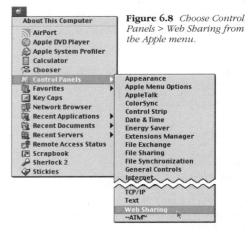

Figure 6.8 *Choose Control Panels > Web Sharing from the Apple menu.*

Figure 6.9 *Unless it is selected already, click the Select button next to Web Folder to designate the desired folder as the root Web directory.*

Figure 6.10 *Then choose the Use File Sharing to control user access radio button. Finally, click the Start button to start up the server. If you aren't currently connected to the Internet, a connection will be opened automatically.*

```
<HTML><HEAD><TITLE>Is the Server
Working?</TITLE></HEAD>
<BODY>Yes, the server is working!</BODY>
</HTML>
```

Figure 6.11 *Use an excruciatingly simple HTML document so that you can be sure that any problems that may occur are due to your server and not your HTML coding.*

Figure 6.12 *Save your simple test HTML file in the root Web directory (with the .html extension as usual).*

Figure 6.13 *When you type* **http://localhost/test.html** *in the browser's Address (or Location) box, you should see this dialog box asking for your User ID and Password (which you previously set in the File Sharing control panel—see page 74).*

Figure 6.14 *If the server is working properly, the Web page will be displayed in the browser, as shown here.*

Testing the Server (Part 1)

Before you go too far, it's a good idea to test your server to make sure that it can serve simple Web pages. If it can, then it's properly installed and turned on, and we can move on to working with Perl scripts.

To test your Web server:

1. Create a simple test HTML file called *test.html* **(Figure 6.11)**.

2. Save it in the server's root Web directory that you chose on page 73 and designated on page 76 **(Figure 6.12)**.

3. Open a Web browser.

4. In the Address or Location box, type **http://localhost/test.html**.

5. When prompted, enter your User ID (the Owner's name) and Password **(Figure 6.13)**.

6. Click OK. The Web page will be displayed in the browser **(Figure 6.14)**.

✔ Tips

■ The root Web directory is a pre-mapped virtual directory. A virtual directory is one whose URL address doesn't match its actual location on your computer. So, when you type **http://localhost/ somefile.html**, the *somefile.html* must be located in the root Web directory as specified above. (See also *The Importance of Directories* on page 44.)

■ If it doesn't work, check the easy stuff first. Did you start up File Sharing? Did you share the root Web directory? Did you start up Personal Web Sharing? Did you enter the proper password? Did you save the HTML file to the proper directory (the root Web directory)? Did you type the URL correctly?

Testing the Server (Part 1)

Installing MacPerl

In order for Perl CGI scripts to run on your new server, you have to have MacPerl—the Perl interpreter for the Macintosh operating system—installed on your computer.

To install MacPerl:

1. Download the latest version of MacPerl from *http://www.perl.com/CPAN/ports/index.html#mac*.

2. Expand the stuffed file, if necessary, and then double-click the installer (currently called "Mac_Perl_520r4_appl" and sporting a blue Vise icon).

3. Accept the licensing agreement and then click Install in the Easy Install window to install MacPerl on your computer **(Figures 6.15 and 6.16)**.

✔ Tips

■ You can thank Matthias Neeracher for MacPerl.

■ You can get all sorts of information about MacPerl at *http://www.macperl.com*.

■ It doesn't matter where you install MacPerl.

■ The MacPerl CGI folder is not much use to us. It's principally about using an extension to add CGI functionality to an older version of MacPerl. If you've downloaded version 5.20r4 or later (which I hope you have), you won't need to worry about it.

Figure 6.15 *Once you click the MacPerl installer icon, and accept the licensing agreement, you can click the Install button to install MacPerl on your computer.*

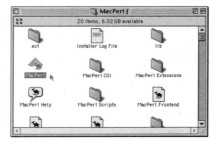

Figure 6.16 *MacPerl and all of its auxiliary files are stored in the MacPerl f folder. The most important element, of course, is MacPerl itself (highlighted here).*

Figure 6.17 *In an Untitled window in MacPerl, create the program that checks the version of CGI.pm.*

Figure 6.18 *When you run the script, the version of CGI.pm is displayed in the MacPerl window.*

Figure 6.19 *You can always download the latest version from Lincoln Stein's Web site.*

Installing CGI.pm

When you install MacPerl, CGI.pm, the standard module for parsing Perl CGI scripts, is automatically installed. However, that doesn't mean you have the latest version. If you'd like to make sure you're on the technological edge, you can install and download the most recent version of CGI.pm manually.

To find out what version of CGI.pm you have:

1. Open MacPerl and choose File > New to begin a new script.

2. On the first line, type **#! perl -MCGI**

3. On the subsequent line, type **print $CGI:: VERSION; (Figure 6.17)**.

4. Choose Script > Run "Untitled" to run the script. The current version of CGI.pm will be displayed **(Figure 6.18)**.

To download the latest version of CGI.pm for Macintosh:

1. Go to *http://stein.cshl.org/WWW/ software/CGI/#installation*.

2. Download and unzip the Sit file containing the CGI.pm module (and auxiliary files) for Macintosh.

3. Place both the CGI.pm file itself and the CGI directory (containing Apache.pm, Carp.pm and six others) in the lib folder inside the MacPerl folder.

✔ Tips

■ For the purposes of learning Perl CGI scripting with this book, any version of CGI.pm that comes with MacPerl 5.004 or later is probably enough.

■ You don't have to make CGI.pm or any of its auxiliary files executable.

Installing Scripts on Mac Servers

Once you've set up your server and installed MacPerl, you're ready to install your scripts.

To install scripts on your Mac server:

1. Open MacPerl.

2. Create your Perl CGI script as described on pages 36–39 **(Figure 6.20)**.

3. Choose File > Save or Save As when you're ready to save your script **(Figure 6.21)**.

4. Name your file and add the .cgi extension **(Figure 6.22)**.

5. Choose a folder within the root Web folder in which to save the script.

6. Then choose CGI Script in the Type pop-up menu under the file name box.

7. Click Save. The file acquires a special icon once it's saved as a CGI script **(Figure 6.23)**.

✔ Tips

■ The shebang line *(see page 35)* isn't strictly required with MacPerl since saving the file as a CGI Script changes its Type and Creator so that MacPerl is automatically invoked to execute the script when the script is called. However, you will need it to check for warnings and to use other switches. And since it is required on Unix and some Windows systems, it's not a bad idea to get into the habit of using it.

■ If you later need to upload the script to a Unix or Windows server, you'll have to open the script with MacPerl and save it as Plain Text.

Figure 6.20 *Write your script in MacPerl. The shebang line isn't strictly required.*

Figure 6.21 *Choose File > Save when you're ready to save and install your script.*

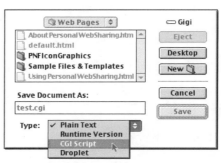

Figure 6.22 *Saving the file as a CGI script is probably the most important step.*

Figure 6.23 *Your CGI scripts will have a special icon that distinguishes them from regular Perl scripts.*

```
1   print "Content-type: text/html\n\n";
2   print "Show me the monkey with my new
        server!";
```

1: MacPerl doesn't require the shebang line.

Even the simplest script requires a Content-type line that tells the server what kind of output to expect. Note that there *must* be a space between the colon and *text/html*.

2: Finally, we'll just output a simple line to make sure that the server's working.

Figure 6.24 *Be sure to use an excruciatingly simple script so that if you get an error, you can be sure the problem is with the server and not your script. You'll get to the complicated stuff soon enough.*

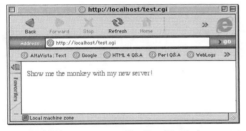

Figure 6.25 *Your server will call on MacPerl to execute the script and then it will display the results in the browser.*

Testing Your Server (Part II)

Now that we've got MacPerl installed, it's a good idea to test your server with an achingly simple Perl script to make sure it can handle Perl scripts in general.

To test how your server handles Perl scripts:

1. Install your server and test it as described on pages 72–76.

2. Install MacPerl *(see page 78)*.

3. Write a very simple Perl script **(Figure 6.24)**, name it *test.cgi*, and install it as described on page 80.

4. Open any Web browser.

5. In the Address box (it's called *Location* in Netscape), type **http://localhost/test.cgi**, where *test.cgi* is the file you created in step 3.

6. You may have to enter your User ID (Owner name) and Password (depending on whether you've restarted your browser since the test on page 77).

7. The browser will display the results of the Perl CGI script **(Figure 6.25)**.

✔ Tips

■ Make sure you test the server with the *simplest possible* Perl script. That way, you can be sure that any problems that arise are due to the server and not the script. You'll have plenty of time to work with more complicated scripts once you're sure your server is functioning properly.

■ MacPerl is very picky about having a space after the colon in the MIME content line. Don't forget it!

Testing Your Server (Part II)

GETTING DATA FROM VISITORS

By far, the easiest and most common way to communicate with your visitors is with a form on your Web page. You decide what you want to ask, create HTML form fields accordingly, and specify the Perl CGI script that will process the answers. Your visitors then fill in their replies and activate the Perl CGI script by clicking the submit button (or active image).

Another way to interact with visitors is by creating a link—with or without embedded data—to a script.

You create forms and links with HTML; no Perl scripting is required. This chapter explains the HTML code you'll need to know, with special emphasis on making the data easy to collect and process. If you are already familiar with using HTML to create forms and links, you can skip this chapter—although you might want to skim through it to catch the scripting-focused tricks that I've added.

This chapter does not include information about creating hidden fields or file upload fields. For information about those topics, consult Chapter 16, *Remembering What Visitors Tell You* and Chapter 20, *Uploading Files*, respectively.

You can also use CGI.pm to create HTML forms. However, it's a bit complex to teach until you have a grasp of Perl itself. For more details, check out CGI.pm's documentation: *http://stein.cshl.org/WWW/software/CGI/*.

Labeling Incoming Data

Perhaps the most crucial part of collecting data from your visitors is making sure the information is properly labeled so you know what you've received. For example, if you receive a piece of data that contains "Maplewood", is that the visitor's preference of materials for the bed they're ordering or is it the name of the town where they want the bed shipped? If the data from a radio button simply says "Yes", what exactly is the visitor agreeing to?

As the designer of the HTML form, you decide on the labels that will accompany incoming data on its journey to your CGI script. In your HTML document, you set the NAME attribute for each form element so that it clearly and distinctly identifies the data or *value* that that particular element collects.

Creating the data itself

There are basically two kinds of form elements: those that allow free-form input (text boxes, password boxes, and larger text areas), and those that the visitor can select but not type in (radio buttons, checkboxes, and menus). For the former, the value is set to the free-form input. For the latter, you, the form designer, will set the VALUE attribute to create the actual data that is sent to the server when the visitor uses one of these fields.

The visitor never sees the VALUE attribute (unless they look at your source code) but when they check a button or checkbox, or select an option in a menu, the corresponding VALUE attribute identifies the visitor's choices to you and to your CGI script. If you don't set the VALUE attribute for radio buttons, checkboxes, or menus, the default value is a vague, pretty useless "on".

```
<FORM ACTION="http://www.cookwood.com/
cgi-bin/perl2e/dataform/display_param.cgi"
METHOD=POST>

Name: <INPUT TYPE="text" NAME="name">
Address: <INPUT TYPE="text" NAME="address"
SIZE=30>
<P>City: <INPUT TYPE="text" NAME="city">
State: <INPUT TYPE="text" NAME="state" SIZE=2
MAXLENGTH=2>
Zipcode: <INPUT TYPE="text" NAME="zip" SIZE=7
MAXLENGTH=5>
Customer Code: <INPUT TYPE="password"
NAME="code" SIZE=8>

<HR><B>Type of wood:</B>
<SELECT NAME="woodtype">
<OPTION VALUE="Mahogany">Mahogany
<OPTION VALUE="Maplewood">Maplewood
<OPTION VALUE="Pine">Pine
<OPTION VALUE="Cherry">Cherry
</SELECT>

<B>Size:</B>
<INPUT TYPE="radio" NAME="size" VALUE="K">
King <INPUT TYPE="radio" NAME="size"
VALUE="Q">Queen <INPUT TYPE="radio"
NAME="size" VALUE="T">Twin <INPUT
TYPE="radio" NAME="size" VALUE="S">Single

<P><B>Extras:</B>
<INPUT TYPE="checkbox" NAME="extras"
VALUE="foot">Footboard
<INPUT TYPE="checkbox" NAME="extras"
VALUE="drawers">Drawers (for underneath)
<INPUT TYPE="checkbox" NAME="extras"
VALUE="casters">Casters
<INPUT TYPE="checkbox" NAME="extras"
VALUE="nosqueak">Squeak proofing

<HR>Please share any suggestions or comments
with us:
<P><TEXTAREA NAME="comments" ROWS=3
COLS=65 WRAP>Comments?</TEXTAREA>
```

Figure 7.1 *Here is part of the HTML code for a typical Web form. Don't worry too much about all the details. Instead, concentrate on the* NAME *and* VALUE *attributes. Notice, for example, how free-form elements have no* VALUE *attribute set, while radio buttons, checkboxes, and the menu have both* NAME *and* VALUE *attributes.*

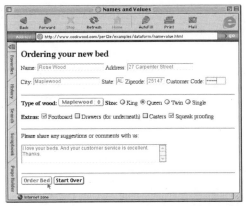

Figure 7.2 *Here is the form on the Web page after the visitor has entered the data. Note that only the high-lighted elements are sent to the server. Everything else, including for example, the radio button labels, are just descriptions so that the visitor knows what to do.*

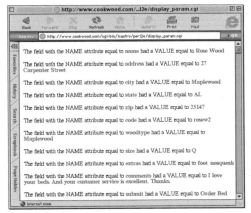

Figure 7.3 *This is the information that arrives at the server and that is processed by the CGI script. Notice that it is the NAME attribute—and not the label that appears in the Web form—that gets sent. Also notice how important it is that the NAME attribute clearly describe the information in the corresponding VALUE— in particular with the identical Maplewood values, but also with non-obvious values like Q.*

HTML labels vs. the NAME attribute

Only the contents of the NAME and VALUE attributes and the text entered by the visitor in free-form fields are sent to the script. Don't confuse either of these with the plain-text labels that you use to identify the different fields on your Web page **(Figure 7.2)**. While the plain-text labels are essential for helping your visitor know where they should type each piece of information, the script doesn't care if they exist at all.

Quotation marks in HTML code

The official HTML 4 specifications do not require the use of quotation marks around attribute values *unless* the values contain something besides letters, digits, hyphens, periods, underscores, or colons. If you're writing XHTML (HTML tags and attributes written with XML syntax), you must quote all attribute values, regardless of their content.

Personally, (despite a good deal of interest in XML and even having written a book about it) I find XHTML's obsession with quotation marks and closing tags to be distracting when one is trying to focus on learning Perl and CGI. Therefore, I have chosen to follow the HTML 4 specifications and not worry exces-sively about quotation marks. We'll have plenty else to think about, I promise.

Creating a Form

A form has three important parts: the FORM tag, which includes the URL of the CGI script that will process the form; the form elements, like fields and menus; and the submit button which sends the data to the CGI script on the server **(Figure 7.4)**.

To create a form:

1. Type **<FORM**.

2. Type **ACTION="script.url"**, where *script.url* is the location on the server of the CGI script that will run when the form is submitted.

3. Type **METHOD=POST>**.

4. Create the form's contents, as described on pages 87–94.

5. Type **</FORM>** to complete the form.

✔ Tips

■ In order for your visitor to send you the data on the form, you'll need either a submit button (if your form contains fields, buttons, and other elements that your visitors will fill in) or an active image. For details about submit buttons, consult *Creating the Submit Button* on page 93. For information on active images, consult *Using an Image To Submit Data* on page 95.

■ You can also use the GET method to process information gathered with a form. However, since the GET method limits the amount of data that you can collect at one time, I recommend using POST.

■ One advantage to using GET is that the query data is part of the URL and thus can be bookmarked and reused. For more details, see page 97.

```
<FORM ACTION="http://www.cookwood.com/
cgi-bin/perl2e/dataform/namevalue.cgi"
METHOD=POST>
```

```
<HR>Please share any suggestions or comments
with us:
<TEXTAREA NAME="comments" ROWS=3
COLS=65 WRAP>Comments?</TEXTAREA>

<HR>
<INPUT TYPE="submit" VALUE="Order Bed">
<INPUT TYPE="reset" VALUE="Start Over">

</FORM>
```

Figure 7.4 *Every form has three parts: the* FORM *tag, the actual form elements where the visitor enters information, and the submit button that sends the collected information to the server (or an active image).*

```
Name: <INPUT TYPE="text" NAME="name">
Address: <INPUT TYPE="text" NAME="address"
SIZE=30>
<P>City: <INPUT TYPE="text" NAME="city">
State: <INPUT TYPE="text" NAME="state" SIZE=2
MAXLENGTH=2>
Zipcode: <INPUT TYPE="text" NAME="zip" SIZE=7
MAXLENGTH=5>
```

Figure 7.5 *While it's essential to set the* NAME *attribute for each text box, you only have to set the* VALUE *attribute when you want to add default values for a text box.*

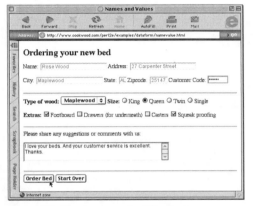

Figure 7.6 *Text boxes can be different sizes to accommodate different types of fields.*

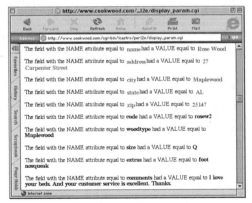

Figure 7.7 *It's important to give descriptive names to your text boxes (with the* NAME *attribute) so that you know what information you're receiving.*

Creating Text Boxes

Text boxes can contain one line of free-form text—that is, anything that the visitor wants to type—and are typically used for names, addresses, and the like.

To create a text box:

1. If desired, type the label that will identify the text box to your visitor (for example, **Name:**).

2. Type **<INPUT TYPE="text"**.

3. Type **NAME="name"**, where *name* is the text that will identify the input data in your script.

4. If desired, type **VALUE="value"**, where *value* is the data that will initially be shown in the field and that will be sent to the server if the visitor doesn't type something else.

5. If desired, define the size of the box on your form by typing **SIZE=n**, replacing *n* with the desired width of the box, measured in characters.

6. If desired, type **MAXLENGTH=n**, where *n* is the maximum number of characters that can be entered in the box.

7. Finish the text box by typing a final **>**.

✔ Tips

■ Even if your visitor skips the field (and you haven't set the default text with the VALUE attribute), the NAME attribute is still sent to the server (with an undefined, empty VALUE).

■ The default SIZE is 20. However, visitors can type up to the limit imposed by the MAXLENGTH attribute. Still, for larger, multi-line entries, it's better to use text areas *(see page 89)*.

Creating Text Boxes

Creating Password Boxes

A password box is similar to a text box, but when the visitor types in it, the letters are hidden by bullets or asterisks (depending on the browser).

To create password boxes:

1. If desired, type the label that will identify the password box to your visitor (for example, **Enter password:**).

2. Type **<INPUT TYPE="password"**.

3. Type **NAME="name"**, where *name* is the text that will identify the input data in your script.

4. If desired, define the size of the box on your form by typing **SIZE=n**, replacing *n* with the desired width of the box, measured in characters.

5. If desired, type **MAXLENGTH=n**, where *n* is the maximum number of characters that can be entered in the box.

6. Finish the text box by typing a final **>**.

✔ Tips

■ Even if nothing is entered in the password box, the NAME is still sent to the server (with an undefined VALUE).

■ You could set default text for VALUE (as in step 4 on page 87), but that kind of defeats the purpose of a password.

■ The only protection the password box offers is from folks peering over your visitor's shoulder as she types in her password. Since the data is not encrypted when the information is sent to the server, moderately experienced crackers can discover the password without much trouble.

Customer Code: <INPUT TYPE="password" NAME="code" SIZE=8>

Figure 7.8 *The* NAME *attribute identifies the password when you analyze the data with your script.*

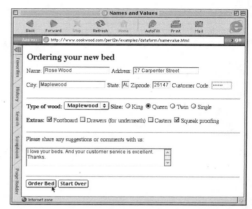

Figure 7.9 *When the visitor enters a password in a form, the password is hidden with bullets.*

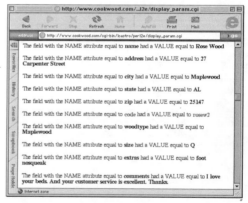

Figure 7.10 *The password data appears as regular text after processing by your script. Password boxes are not high-security! (See last tip.)*

```
<HR>Please share any suggestions or comments
with us:
<P><TEXTAREA NAME="comments" ROWS=3
COLS=65 WRAP>Comments?</TEXTAREA>
```

Figure 7.11 *The* VALUE *attribute is not used with the* TEXTAREA *tag. Default values are set by adding text between the opening and closing tags (as in "Comments?" here).*

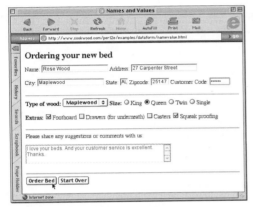

Figure 7.12 *The visitor can override the default text simply by typing over it.*

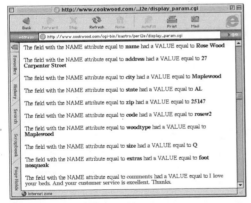

Figure 7.13 *Text areas are great for getting longer comments and suggestions from visitors. They are typically used in guestbooks and bulletin boards.*

Creating Larger Text Areas

In some cases, you want to give the visitor more room to write. Unlike text boxes *(see page 87)*, text areas may be as large as you like, and will expand as needed if the visitor enters more text than can fit in the display area.

To create larger text areas:

1. If desired, type the explanatory text that will identify the text area.

2. Type **<TEXTAREA** (with no space between *TEXT* and *AREA*).

3. Type **NAME="name"**, where *name* is the text that will identify the input data in your script.

4. If desired, type **ROWS=n**, where *n* is the height of the text area in rows. The default value is 4.

5. If desired, type **COLS=n**, where *n* is the width of the text area in characters. The default value is 40.

6. If desired, type **WRAP** so that when the visitor types, the lines are automatically wrapped within the margins.

7. Type **>**.

8. Type the default text, if any, for the text area. You may not add any HTML coding here.

9. Type **</TEXTAREA>** to complete the text area.

✔ Tips

■ There is no use for the VALUE attribute with text areas.

■ Visitors can enter up to 32,700 characters in a text area. Scroll bars will appear when necessary.

Creating Radio Buttons

Remember those old-time car radios with big black plastic buttons? Push one to listen to WFCR; push another for WRNX. You can never push two buttons at once. Radio buttons on forms work the same way (except you can't listen to the radio).

To create a radio button:

1. If desired, type the introductory text for your radio buttons. You might use something like **Select one of the following**.

2. Type **<INPUT TYPE="radio"**.

3. Type **NAME="radioset"**, where *radioset* both identifies the data sent to the script and also links the radio buttons together, ensuring that only one per set can be checked.

4. Type **VALUE="data"**, where *data* is the text that will be sent to the server if the radio button is checked, either by you (in step 5) or by the visitor.

5. If desired, type **CHECKED** to make the radio button active by default when the page is opened. (You can only do this to one radio button in the set.)

6. Type the final **>**.

7. Type the text that identifies the radio button to the visitor. This is often the same as VALUE, but doesn't have to be.

8. Repeat steps 2–7 for each radio button in the set.

✔ Tip

- If you don't set the VALUE attribute, the word "on" is sent to the script. It's not particularly useful since you can't tell which button in the set was pressed.

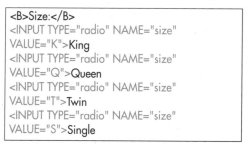

```
<B>Size:</B>
<INPUT TYPE="radio" NAME="size"
VALUE="K">King
<INPUT TYPE="radio" NAME="size"
VALUE="Q">Queen
<INPUT TYPE="radio" NAME="size"
VALUE="T">Twin
<INPUT TYPE="radio" NAME="size"
VALUE="S">Single
```

Figure 7.14 *The* NAME *attribute serves a dual purpose for radio buttons: it links the radio buttons in a given set and it identifies the values when they are sent to the script. The* VALUE *attribute is crucial since the visitor has no way of typing a value.*

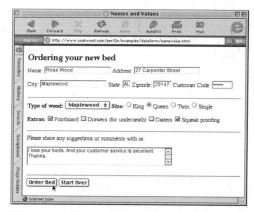

Figure 7.15 *The radio buttons themselves are created with the HTML tags. The labels (King, Queen, etc.) are created with plain text alongside the HTML tags.*

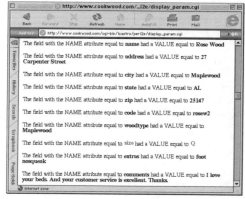

Figure 7.16 *Note that it is the* VALUE *(Q) and not the label (Queen) that gets sent to the script.*

Creating Radio Buttons

```
<P><B>Extras:</B>
<INPUT TYPE="checkbox" NAME="extras"
VALUE="foot">Footboard
<INPUT TYPE="checkbox" NAME="extras"
VALUE="drawers">Drawers (for underneath)
<INPUT TYPE="checkbox" NAME="extras"
VALUE="casters">Casters
```

Figure 7.17 *Notice how the label text (not highlighted) does not need to match the VALUE attribute. That's because the label text identifies the checkboxes to the visitor in the browser while the VALUE identifies the data to the script. (Not all of the checkboxes are shown here.)*

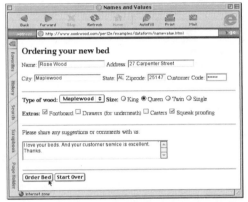

Figure 7.18 *The visitor can check as many boxes as necessary. Each corresponding value will be sent to the script, together with the checkbox set's name.*

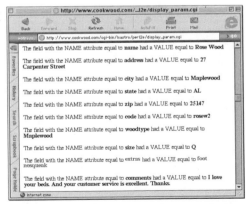

Figure 7.19 *Since the visitor has chosen two checkboxes, both values (but not their labels, of course) are sent to the script.*

Creating Checkboxes

While radio buttons can accept only one answer per set, a visitor can check as many checkboxes in a set as they like. Like radio buttons, checkboxes are linked by the value of the NAME attribute.

To create checkboxes:

1. If desired, type the introductory text (something like **Select one or more of the following**) for your checkboxes.

2. Type **<INPUT TYPE="checkbox"**. (Notice there is no space in the word *checkbox*.)

3. Type **NAME="boxset"**, where *boxset* both identifies the data sent to the script and also links the checkboxes together.

4. Type **VALUE="value"** to define a *value* for each checkbox. The value will be sent to the server if the checkbox is checked (either by the visitor, or by you as described in step 5).

5. Type **CHECKED** to make the checkbox checked by default when the page is opened. You (or the visitor) may check as many checkboxes as desired.

6. Type **>** to complete the checkbox.

7. Type the text that identifies the checkbox to the user. This is often the same as the VALUE, but doesn't have to be.

8. Repeat steps 2–7 for each checkbox in the set.

✔ Tip

- If you don't set the VALUE attribute, the word "on" is sent to the script. It's not particularly useful since you can't tell which box in the set was checked.

Creating Menus

Menus are perfect for offering your visitors a choice from a given set of options.

To create menus:

1. Type the introductory text, if desired.

2. Type **<SELECT**.

3. Type **NAME="name"**, where *name* will identify the data collected from the menu when it is sent to the server.

4. Type **SIZE=n**, where *n* is the number of items that should be displayed at a time.

5. If desired, type **MULTIPLE** to allow your visitor to select more than one menu option (with Ctrl or Command).

6. Type **>**.

7. Type **<OPTION**.

8. Type **SELECTED** if you want the option to be selected by default.

9. Type **VALUE="value"**, where *value* specifies the data that will be sent to the server if the option is selected.

10. Type **>**.

11. Type the option name as you wish it to appear in the menu.

12. Repeat steps 7–11 for each option.

13. Type **</SELECT>**.

✔ Tips

- If you add the SIZE attribute in step 4, the menu appears more like a list, and there is no automatically selected option (unless you use SELECTED).

- If SIZE is bigger than the number of options, visitors can deselect all values by clicking in the empty space.

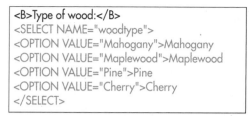

Figure 7.20 *Menus are made up of two HTML tags:* SELECT *and* OPTION. *You set the common* NAME *attribute in the* SELECT *tag and the individual* VALUE *attribute in each of the* OPTION *tags.*

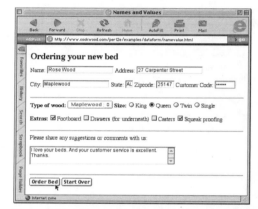

Figure 7.21 *There's no way for a visitor to select nothing in a menu unless you set the* SIZE *attribute. The default selection is either the first option in the menu or the one you've set as* SELECTED *in step 8.*

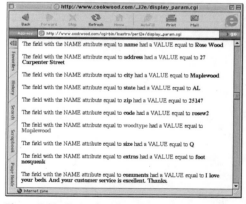

Figure 7.22 *Notice that the* NAME *attribute (woodtype) and not the label (Type of wood:) is what gets sent to the script.*

```
<INPUT TYPE="submit" VALUE="Order Bed">
```

Figure 7.23 *If you leave out the* NAME *attribute, the name-value pair for the submit button will not be passed to the script. Since you usually don't need this information, that's fine.*

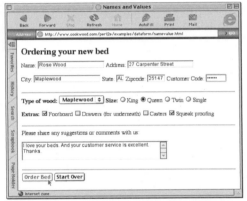

Figure 7.24 *The most important function of the submit button is to activate the script that will collect the data from the* other *fields. You can personalize the button's contents with the* VALUE *attribute. (The phrase* Order Bed *is clearer for your visitors than the default* Submit Query*).*

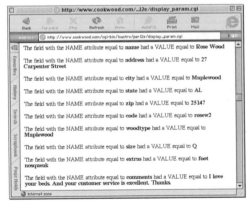

Figure 7.25 *If there is no* NAME *attribute specified for the submit button, not even the submit button's* VALUE *attribute will be gathered by the script.*

Creating the Submit Button

All the information that your visitors enter won't be any good to you unless they send it to the server. You should always create a submit button for your forms so that the visitor can deliver the information to you. (If you use images as active elements in a FORM area, see page 95.)

To create a submit button:

1. Type **<INPUT TYPE="submit"**.

2. If desired, type **NAME="name"**, where *name* is the text that will identify the submit button in your script

3. If desired, type **VALUE="submit message"** where *submit message* is the text that will appear in the button. The default submit message is *Submit Query*.

4. Type the final **>**.

✔ Tips

- The name-value pair for the submit button is only sent to the script if you set the NAME attribute. Therefore, if you omit the NAME attribute, you won't have to deal with the extra, usually superfluous submit data.

- On the other hand, you can create multiple submit buttons (with both the NAME and VALUE attributes) and then write your CGI script to react according to which submit button the visitor presses.

- Although the standard HTML 4 specifications allow for fancier button creation (including fonts and images), many browsers don't recognize the code yet.

Creating the Submit Button

Resetting the Form

If humans could fill out forms perfectly on the first try, there would be no erasers on pencils and no backspace key on your computer keyboard. You can give your visitors a reset button so that they can start over with a fresh form (including all the default values you've set).

To create a reset button:

1. Type **<INPUT TYPE="reset"**.

2. If desired, type **VALUE="reset message"** where *reset message* is the text that appears in the button. The default reset message is *Reset*.

3. Type **>**.

✔ Tips

■ The name-value pair for the reset button is only sent to the script if you set the NAME attribute. Therefore, if you omit the NAME attribute, you won't have to deal with the completely superfluous reset data—which is usually something like "reset, Reset".

■ No information is sent to the server when the visitor clicks the reset button. They have to click the submit button *(see page 93)* to send data.

```
<INPUT TYPE="reset" VALUE="Start Over">
```

Figure 7.26 *You can use any text you wish for the reset button.*

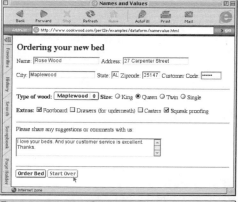

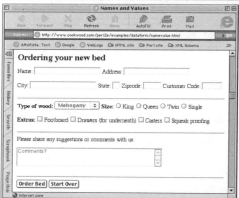

Figure 7.27 *If your visitor clicks the reset button, all the fields are set to their default values (which might be an empty field).*

```
<FORM ACTION="http://www.cookwood.com/
cgi-bin/perl2e/dataform/display_param.cgi"
METHOD=POST>

<BR><INPUT TYPE="radio" NAME="infotype"
VALUE="time">Local time
<INPUT TYPE="radio" NAME="infotype"
VALUE="weather">Local weather
<INPUT TYPE="radio" NAME="infotype"
VALUE="directions">Directions

<INPUT TYPE="radio" NAME="infotype"
VALUE="statistics">City statistics
<P><INPUT TYPE="image" SRC="zonemap.gif"
NAME="coord">
</FORM>
```

Figure 7.28 *If you use an active image, you don't need a submit button.*

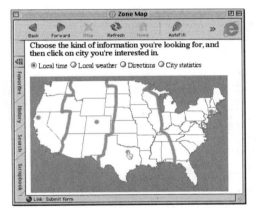

Figure 7.29 *You can have both regular form elements (like the radio buttons) and an image map in the same form. When the visitor clicks the map, all of the data is sent to the script.*

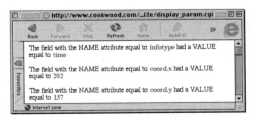

Figure 7.30 *The browser appends a period and an x to the NAME attribute (coord) and uses this name (coord.x) to identify the x coordinate of the location where the visitor clicked. The same happens with the y coordinate. Notice that the information from the radio button is also collected.*

Using an Image to Submit Data

You may use an image—called an active image—as a combination input element and submit button. In addition to submitting the data from the other fields in the form, a click on the image sends the current mouse coordinates to the server in two name-value pairs. The names are generated by adding .x and .y to the value of the NAME attribute. The values correspond to the actual horizontal and vertical locations (in pixels, where 0,0 is the top-left corner) of the cursor.

To use an image to submit data:

1. Create a GIF or JPEG image.

2. Type **<INPUT TYPE="image"**.

3. Type **SRC="image_url"**, where *image_url* is the location of the image on the server.

4. Type **NAME="name"**, where *name* is the base value to which the *x* and *y* coordinates of the mouse will be appended when the visitor clicks on the image.

5. Type the final **>** to finish the active image definition for the form.

✔ Tips

■ Setting the VALUE attribute has no effect. The values are set to the mouse coordinates automatically.

■ *All* the form data is sent when the visitor clicks the active image. Therefore, it's a good idea to explain how to use the active image and to place the image at the end of the form so that the visitor completes the other form elements before clicking the image and sending the data.

Creating a Link to a Script

Some simple—but still useful—scripts require no input at all. For example, you might create a CGI script that outputs the exact time (according to the server). In that case, the visitor doesn't have to input any data, they simply have to ask what time it is. Although you could conceivably create a form with a solitary submit button and no fields, an easier way would be to create a *link* that activates the script.

To create a link to a script:

1. In the HTML document, type **<A HREF= "script.cgi">**, where *script.cgi* is the name of the script that you want to have activated when the visitor clicks the link.

2. Type the label for the link. This is what the visitor will see (usually underlined) on the Web page.

3. Type **</A>**.

✔ Tip

- For more information on the gettime.cgi script used in this example, check the Web site *(see page 22)*. I didn't show it here because I want you to focus on how to activate a script with a link, not on how the script works.

```
<HTML><HEAD>
<TITLE>Time Page</TITLE>
</HEAD>
<BODY>

<H1>What <A HREF="http://www.cookwood.com
/cgi-bin/perl2e/dataform/gettime.cgi">time</A>
is it?</H1>

</BODY></HTML>
```

Figure 7.31 *To make a link activate a CGI script, simply use the CGI script's URL for the* HREF *attribute.*

Figure 7.32 *As with regular links, when the visitor points at the link, the CGI script's URL appears in the status window at the bottom of the browser.*

Figure 7.33 *When the visitor clicks the link, the script is activated, and in this case, displays the correct local time. Notice also that the URL of the script appears in the Address bar.*

```
<HTML><HEAD><TITLE>Time Page</TITLE>
</HEAD><BODY>

<H1>What time is it?</H1>

<P>In <A HREF="http://www.cookwood.com/
cgi-bin/perl2e/dataform/getlocaltime.cgi?zone=
EST&place=Hartford">Hartford, Connecticut</A>?

<P>In <A HREF="http://www.cookwood.com/
cgi-bin/perl2e/dataform/getlocaltime.cgi?zone=
CT&place=Dallas">Dallas, Texas</A>?

<P>In <A HREF="http://www.cookwood.com/
cgi-bin/perl2e/dataform/getlocaltime.cgi?zone=
MT&place=Denver">Denver, Colorado</A>?

<P>In <A HREF="http://www.cookwood.com/
cgi-bin/perl2e/dataform/getlocaltime.cgi?zone=
PT&place=Eureka">Eureka, California</A>?

</BODY></HTML>
```

Figure 7.34 *Each link has two name-value pairs appended to the URL. When the visitor clicks a link, the browser sends the corresponding pair of values to be processed by the script. Note that there are no spaces in any of the URLs.*

Figure 7.35 *Now when a visitor points at a link, not only does the link's URL show up in the status bar at the bottom of the browser, but the data that will be sent to the script also appears.*

Figure 7.36 *When the visitor clicks the link, the data is sent to the script to be processed and the browser displays the result. Notice also that the input appears at the end of the script's URL in the Address bar.*

Using a Link to Input Data to a Script

You can also create links that contain certain pre-input data so that when the visitor clicks the link, that data is sent to the server and processed by the script.

To use a link to input data to a script:

1. Type **<A HREF="script.cgi**, where *script.cgi* is the CGI script that will process the data when the visitor clicks the link.

2. Type **?key=value**, where *key* is the name of the data you're sending and *value* is the actual data itself. There is no space between the script name and the question mark.

3. If desired, type **&key2=value2**, where *key2* is the name of the second piece of data and *value2* is the actual second piece of data. There is no space between the first value (from step 2) and the ampersand (&).

4. Repeat step 3 as desired.

5. Type **">**.

6. Type the label text for the link.

7. Type **</A>**.

✔ Tips

■ If you were sending data from a form, the key would correspond to the contents of the NAME attribute while the value would correspond to the contents of the VALUE attribute.

■ For details on the script used in this example, check the Web site *(see page 22)*. For now, I want you to focus on how to send data to the script, not how the script works.

ENVIRONMENT VARIABLES

One of the keystones of CGI scripting is a collection of data called *environment variables* that are set each time the server runs a CGI script. They contain information about the Web server, its configuration, and about the request that the browser just made. For example, there are environment variables that store a visitor's IP address, what browser they're using, and what server they're using, among others.

The available environment variables may change according to what server you have and what information is sent from the browser.

The environment variables are stored in the special %ENV hash which is set each time a script is run. You do not need to declare the %ENV with my. Don't worry yet about what a hash is or how to get to the information stored in these variables. The important thing is to simply be aware that this information is available. You'll learn how to process and use this data in your scripts on page 102. For more about hashes, Chapter 14, *Working with Hashes*.

Your Visitor's Browser and Platform

One of the more useful environment variables lets you "spy" on your visitors. For example, it's relatively easy to find out which browser and platform your visitor is using.

The HTTP_USER_AGENT environment variable contains the name and version of the visitor's browser. Notice that both Netscape and Internet Explorer identify themselves as "Mozilla", which is actually a code name for Netscape. Explorer then continues on to inform you that it is "compatible", presumably with Mozilla, and that it is really MSIE, which one can assume stands for *M*icrosoft *I*nternet *Explorer*.

The value of HTTP_USER_AGENT also reveals the visitor's computer platform, although each browser uses a different syntax to convey this information. Still, you should be able to match keywords like *Win* or *98*, or *Mac*, to determine your visitor's platform. You could conceivably tailor your output for each browser, ensuring that JavaScript or HTML tags that are compatible with one browser are not used by the other.

```
1  #!/usr/local/bin/perl -wT
1  use strict;
2
3  print "Content-type: text/html\n\n";
4  print "<P>The browser you're using to
   view this page is:
   $ENV{'HTTP_USER_AGENT'}";
```

3: The all important MIME content line.
4: The browser information is stored with the HTTP_USER_AGENT key in the %ENV hash.

Figure 8.1 *For more information on accessing individual values in a hash, see Chapter 14, Working with Hashes.*

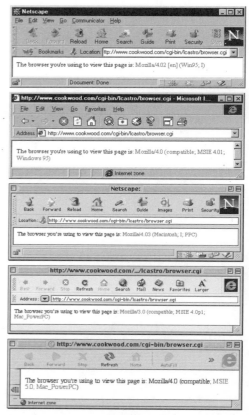

Figure 8.2 *From top to bottom, I've accessed the script shown in Figure 8.1 with Netscape Communicator for Windows, Internet Explorer 4 for Windows, Netscape Communicator 4 for Macintosh, Internet Explorer 4 for Macintosh, and Internet Explorer 5 for Macintosh.*

```
1  #!/usr/local/bin/perl -wT
2  use strict;
3
4  print "Content-type: text/html\n\n";
5  print "<HTML><HEAD><TITLE>Environment
     Variables</TITLE></HEAD><BODY>";
6
7  foreach (keys %ENV) {
8    print "<BR><FONT COLOR=red>$_</FONT>
       is set to <FONT COLOR=blue>
       $ENV{$_}</FONT>";
9  }
10
11 print "</BODY></HTML>";
```

7: This `foreach` loop goes through each of the elements in the special %ENV hash, where the environment variables are stored, and prints each one's name (in red) and value (in blue).

Figure 8.3 *This simple script prints out all of the available environment variables to your browser.*

Figure 8.4 *The environment variables that are currently set will be displayed in the browser.*

Viewing Available Environment Variables

If you would like to see all the environment variables that are available to you, you can create a little script to do just that. Remember, however, that the results depend on what server you use.

To view the environment variables:

1. Copy and install the script shown in Figure 8.3. For more details, consult the appropriate section of Chapters 4, 5, or 6, depending on your server.

2. Open your browser.

3. Type the URL of the script you created in step 1. The environment variables available on your server will appear.

✔ Tip

■ The list of environment variables not only varies from server to server but it depends on how you access the CGI script itself. For example, the CONTENT_LENGTH variable is only set if you're using the POST method to send your script to the server. Or the HTTP_REFERER variable is only set if the script is run by clicking a link or submit button (but not if its URL is typed in the Location box). If you're looking for a particular variable, make sure you've set up and submitted the script in the necessary way.

Storing Data from Environment Variables

You can assign the value of an environment variable to one of your own variables for later processing.

To store data from environment variables:

1. Type **$scalar**, where *scalar* is the name of your variable that will hold the information from the environment variable.

2. Type **=** (the equals sign).

3. Type **$ENV{'env_var'}**, where you type *$ENV* as is (in all uppercase) to access the %ENV hash, and *env_var* is the name (or key) of the desired environment variable within that hash.

4. Type **;** to end the line.

✔ Tips

■ The particular environment variables available to you depend on the server you use. You can see a list of typical environment variables in Figure 8.4 on page 101.

■ The %ENV hash functions like any other hash. For more information on working with hashes, see Chapter 14, *Working with Hashes*.

■ You can get more than one value at a time from the %ENV hash. For more details, consult *Getting Several Values Using Keys* on page 171.

■ Since the environment variable key will always be solely made up of alphanumerics and the underscore, you can omit the single quotes in step 3.

```perl
1   #!/usr/local/bin/perl -wT
1   use strict;
2
3   my $browser = $ENV{'HTTP_USER_AGENT'};
4   my $IP=$ENV{'REMOTE_ADDR'};
5
6   print "Content-type: text/html\n\n";
7   print "<P>You're browsing this page with
        $browser";
8   print "<P>And your IP address is $IP";
```

3: This line declares the $browser variable and stores in it the value of the HTTP_USER_AGENT key (which contains information about what browser and platform the visitor is using).

4: This line declares the $IP variable and then stores in it the value of the REMOTE_ADDR key (which contains the visitor's IP address).

6: The all important MIME content line.

7: We'll print a simple statement with the contents of the $browser variable.

8: And another simple print statement with the $IP variable.

Figure 8.5 *You can use environment variables for simple operations like telling your visitors what you know about them, or you can create more complicated scripts that, for example, count the number of times your site has been visited from each browser.*

Figure 8.6 *While printing this information may wow your visitors, keeping track of it may serve to be a valuable marketing tool. Knowing where your visitors are coming from can help you generate even more traffic; knowing what browsers your visitors use can help you tailor output to their needs.*

GETTING DATA INTO THE SCRIPT

In Chapter 7, *Getting Data from Visitors*, and Chapter 8, *Environment Variables*, I talked about how to get data from your visitor to the server. In this chapter, you'll learn how to pass that data from the server to your Perl script using CGI.pm's `param` function. Once you've entered the data into the Perl script, you can start to process the data and generate the desired output.

Don't worry too much at this point about how the `param` function works. If you like, you can open the CGI.pm module and search for *param* to see how the subroutine is defined. The important bit is to know that it outputs the value of your form data.

For readers of the first edition of this book:

Note that the `param` function does not create a hash of the key-value pairs from the HTML form as my *subparseform.lib* script did. Instead, you use `param` to get either the value(s) of a particular, already known key (using the contents of the HTML tag's NAME attribute) or you use it to get all of the keys (attribute names) from the form.

Processing uploaded files is not covered in this chapter since it is a slightly more complicated procedure. For details about how to let your visitors upload files, Chapter 20, *Uploading Files*.

Getting Single-Valued Form Data

Most, but not all, elements in a form have a single value. It's easy to use CGI.pm to tell you exactly what that value is.

To get single-valued form data:

1. Type **$data =**, where *data* is the scalar variable that will contain the single value from the form.

2. Next type **param(** to call CGI.pm's `param` function.

3. Type **'name'**, where *name* is the content of the HTML form element's NAME attribute. (For more details, consult *Labeling Incoming Data* on page 84.)

4. Type **)** to complete the `param` function.

5. Type **;** to complete the line.

✔ Tips

■ You can use a scalar variable (without quotes) to refer to the name in step 3.

■ CGI.pm considers the NAME attribute to be case sensitive. You must refer to it in step 3 precisely as you created it in the HTML document.

■ You don't have to assign the element's value to a variable. You could print it out directly or perform some other operation on it, as necessary.

■ If your form element—say, a set of checkboxes—has multiple values, you'll have to use the method on page 105.

■ The `param` function can only get the value for one name at a time. If you need to get more than one value, use `param` more than once. (Giving the `param` function multiple arguments has an entire different result. See CGI.pm's documentation for details.)

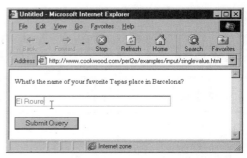

Figure 9.1 *This form has a single element whose* NAME *attribute is set to* tapas.

```
1   #!/usr/local/bin/perl -wT
2   use strict;
3   use CGI ':standard';
4
5   my $value;
6
7   $value = param('tapas');
8
9   print "Content-type: text/html\n\n";
10  print "Your favorite Tapas place in
        Barcelona was $value";
```

3: Start your script in the standard way *(see page 36)*.

7: We use the `param` function to parse the incoming data and to assign the contents of the *tapas* form element to the $data variable.

10: This simple `print` statement outputs the value of the $value variable to the browser.

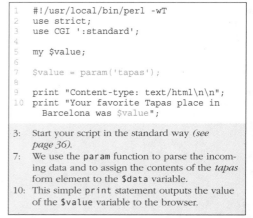

Figure 9.2 *Once you've got the data that a visitor has typed in, you can do practically anything with it. Here I simply print it out.*

Figure 9.3 *The value that the visitor put in the* tapas *element is output.*

Getting Single-Valued Form Data

Figure 9.4 *This form has a group of checkbox elements, all of which have a* NAME *attribute of* dish. *Their values are abbreviated forms of the labels shown.*

```
1   #!/usr/local/bin/perl -wT
2   use strict;
3   use CGI ':standard';
4
5   my @values;
6
7   @values = param('dish');
8
9   print "Content-type: text/html\n\n";
10  print "Your favorite dishes were
       @values";
```

7: We assign the results of the param function to an array variable (@values) when we know that the element in question (*dish*) has more than one value associated with it.

10: This simple print statement outputs the value of the @values variable to the browser.

Figure 9.5 *Since checkbox elements typically have multiple values associated with a single name, we have to assign those values to an array.*

Figure 9.6 *The* dish *element had three values associated with it, all of which are output with this script.*

Getting Multiple-Valued Form Data

If more than one of your HTML form elements has the same NAME attribute—this is most common with checkboxes, but could conceivably happen with any kind of element—it could have multiple values. You will thus have to assign the results of the param function to an array instead of a scalar.

To get multiple-valued form data:

1. In your script, type **@data =**, where *data* is the name of the array variable that will contain the multiple values from the form.

2. Next type **param(** to call CGI.pm's param function.

3. Type **'name'**, where *name* is the content of the HTML form element's NAME attribute. (For more details, consult *Labeling Incoming Data* on page 84.)

4. Type **)** to complete the param function.

5. Type **;** to complete the line.

✔ Tips

■ You may use a scalar variable to refer to the name in step 3. In that case, no quotation marks are necessary.

■ It's perfectly all right to use this method for an element that has a single value. It will simply result in an array that contains a single value.

■ It's not okay to use the single-valued method for multiple-valued form elements. If you try passing the multiple values of a single element to a scalar (e.g., following the instructions on page 104), only the first value will be output. The rest will be ignored.

Getting All the Form Element's Names

If you call CGI.pm's `param` function without specifying which element's data you're interested in, it will supply you with the content of each HTML form element's NAME attribute.

To get all the form elements' NAME attributes:

1. Type **@names =**, where *names* is the array where you will store the contents of each form element's NAME attribute.

2. Type **param()**, with nothing between the parentheses, to call CGI.pm's `param` function and have it parse the incoming data from the form.

3. Type **;** to complete the line.

✔ Tips

■ Note that when you use `param` without arguments, what you get is a list of the names of your HTML form elements, *not their values*. To get their values, you have to apply the `param` function to one of the names *(see pages 104–105)*.

■ You can use `param` without arguments in lots of different expressions. This is just one very simple example since you haven't learned much Perl yet. For another example, see page 107.

■ For more about names and values, consult *Labeling Incoming Data* on page 84.

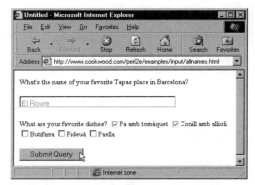

Figure 9.7 *This form has a single text box element called* tapas *and a group of checkboxes named* dish.

```
1  #!/usr/local/bin/perl -wT
2  use strict;
3  use CGI ':standard';
4
5  my @names = param();
6
7  print "Content-type: text/html\n\n";
8  print "This form has elements with the
        following names: @names";

5:  We declare the @names array. Then we use the
    param function without arguments to get a list
    of all the form element's NAME attributes, and
    store the list in the @names array.
8:  This simple print statement outputs the value
    of the @names variable to the browser.
```

Figure 9.8 *Once you've got the data that a visitor has typed in, you can do practically anything with it. Here I simply print it out.*

Figure 9.9 *When you call* param *without arguments, only the names of the elements—but not their values— are output.*

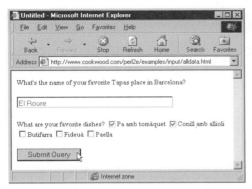

Figure 9.10 *This form is identical to the one shown in Figure 9.7 on page 106. It has one text box element called* tapas *and a group of checkbox elements whose* NAME *attribute is* dish.

```
1  #!/usr/local/bin/perl -wT
2  use strict;
3  use CGI ':standard';
4  print "Content-type: text/html\n\n";
5
6  foreach my $name ( param() ) {
7      my @values = param ($name);
8      print "<p><b>Key:</b> $name
   <b>Value(s):</b> @values";
9  }
```

6: This time I use a `foreach` loop to go through each item in the array of names created by the `param` function with no arguments. Don't worry about the `foreach` loop yet, it's explained in detail on page 130.

7: I then use the `param` function a second time to find out what the corresponding values are for each name in that array.

Figure 9.11 *Getting all the names and all the values requires using the* param *function twice.*

Figure 9.12 *This time we get both the names and the values.*

Getting All the Names and Values

You've learned how to use the `param` function to either get the value(s) from a single form element or to get all the names from all the form elements. You can combine the techniques to get all the names and values from all the form elements.

To get all the names and values from all the form elements:

1. Use the `param` function without arguments to get the contents of the NAME attribute for each element on the form.

2. Use the `param` function on each of those names that result from step 1 to get their corresponding values.

✔ Tips

■ This example goes a bit beyond what you've learned to do in Perl so far. What I want you to understand is the difference between calling `param` with arguments and without, and why it might be useful to use it both ways in the same script.

■ For more information about the `foreach` loop, consult *Repeating a Block for Each Item in an Array* on page 130.

SIMPLE OPERATIONS WITH SCALARS

'elephant' ——————— a string
3 ——————————— a number
$animal ——————— a scalar variable
$animal[2] ————— an individual member
of an array
$animal{'habitat'} —— an individual member
of a hash

Figure 10.1 *Here is a collection of typical scalar elements.*

('elephant', 'tiger') —— a list
@species ——————— an array variable
%tiger_data ————— a hash variable

Figure 10.2 *Here are three examples of things that are not scalars.*

As I discussed in Chapter 2, *Perl Building Blocks (see page 26)*, a scalar is any *individual piece of data*, whether it be a number or a string, a constant or a variable. Scalar variables always start with a dollar sign ($)—the *s* shape is supposed to remind you of the word *scalar*.

Perl has a special default scalar variable, written as $_, which is used by many functions if you don't specify the operand specifically. It can save you lots of time—and typing. I'll discuss which operators and functions use the default variable under the corresponding section.

Note: Each of the example scripts on the pages that follow works in tandem with a form, created with HTML. Unfortunately, there just isn't always enough room to show you the scripts, the HTML code for the form (which reveals the names of the fields), the input that our example visitor types into the fields on the form, *and* the result of the script, given that input. Since the aim of this book is to teach you Perl and CGI, I'll focus on the script code and the result of the script. Where there's room, I'll show you the form and the input and the HTML code behind it. If you're interested, you can find all the forms and Perl scripts online *(see page 22)*.

There are some additional functions that deal with manipulating scalars that contain text that are discussed in Chapter 17, *Formatting, Printing, and HTML*.

Simple Operations with Scalars

Assigning a Value to a Scalar Variable

In Chapter 9, *Getting Data into the Script*, you learned how to store the information that comes from a form into a scalar variable. You can also store constants, other scalars, or the result of an expression in a scalar variable.

To assign a value to a scalar variable:

1. At the beginning of the line, type **$name**, where *name* is the label of the scalar variable.

2. Type **=** (the equals sign is the assignment operator).

3. Type **value**, where *value* is the constant, variable, or expression whose value you want to store.

4. Type **;** to complete the line.

✔ Tips

- You should always declare variables before using them *(see page 34)*. This ensures that they won't override any other variable with the same name, either from your script or from one that you call as a library or module.

- You can declare and assign a value to a variable at the same time, using my `$variable = "value";` **(Figure 10.5)**.

- You're probably more used to seeing the equals sign in a non-active sort of way, as in *5 = 2 + 3*. In Perl, think of the equals sign as something more like *gets* or *is assigned the value of*.

- Strings (but not numbers or variables) should be enclosed in quotation marks. For more details, consult *Quotation Marks* on page 30.

```
1   #!/usr/local/bin/perl -wT
2   use strict;
3   my ($sales_Jan, $sales_Feb, $sales_Mar,
       $sum_1Q, $label_1Q);
4
5   $sales_Jan = 5467;
6   $sales_Feb = 234;
7   $sales_Mar = 8875;
8   $sum_1Q = $sales_Jan + $sales_Feb +
       $sales_Mar;
9   $label_1Q = 'first quarter';
10
11  print "Content-type: text/html\n\n";
12  print "Sales for the $label_1Q were
       $sum_1Q";
```

3: All of the variables are declared *(see page 34)*.
5: Lines 5–7. The variables `$sales_Jan`, `$sales_Feb`, and `$sales_Mar` are each assigned an initial constant value.
8: The right-hand expression evaluates the sum of the three variables. The result of the expression (14576) is assigned to the variable `$sum_1Q`.
9: The string constant (enclosed in quotation marks) is assigned to the `$label_1Q` variable.
11: The all-important MIME content line *(see page 38)*.
12: The variables are interpolated (evaluated) by the double quotation marks and their current values are printed.

Figure 10.3 *You can assign a constant (number or string), another variable (not shown in this example), or the result of an expression to a scalar variable.*

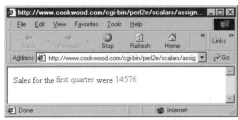

Figure 10.4 *Since the variables are enclosed in double quotation marks, their values (and not their names) are output.*

```
1  #!/usr/local/bin/perl -wT
2  use strict;
3
4  my $counter = 1;
5
6  print "Content-type: text/html\n\n";
7  print "<P>The current value of the
      counter is $counter";
8
9  $counter = $counter + 1;
10 print "<P>The current value of the
      counter is $counter";
11
12 $counter = $counter + 5;
13 print "<P>The current value of the
      counter is $counter";
```

4:   You can declare a variable and assign it a value
     on the same line. Giving a variable an initial
     value is sometimes called *initializing* the
     variable.

7:   We'll output the current value of the $counter
     variable. Notice the <P> tag that will begin each
     print statement in the HTML document on its
     own line.

9:   The right-hand expression adds 1 to the value of
     the variable $counter, which we know is 1
     (line 4) giving a result of 2. This new value is
     then assigned to $counter.

10: We'll output the current value of the $counter
     variable.

12: The right hand expression adds 5 to the value of
     the variable $counter, which this time is 2 (line
     9), giving a result of 7. Again, the result is
     assigned to $counter for future operations.

13: We print the current value of the $counter vari-
     able one last time.

Figure 10.5 *A given variable may have different values over the lifetime of the script.*

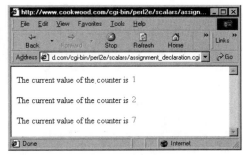

Figure 10.6 *While this is a rather boring script, printing out the current value of a variable can be an effective way of finding the errors in a more complicated script.*

- Make sure you use just one equals sign. There are ways to combine the equals sign with other symbols for different effects *(see pages 119 and 122)*.

- The most common mathematical and string operators are discussed on pages 112–120.

- You can update the value of a variable by using it on both sides of the assignment. For example, $age = $age + 1 adds *1* to the $age variable and then saves the result back in the $age variable itself. This is where it's very important to remember that the equals sign doesn't exactly mean *equals*, it means *gets* or *is assigned the value of* **(Figure 10.5)**.

Assigning a Value to a Scalar Variable

Multiplying, Dividing, Adding, Subtracting

Perl lets you perform basic mathematical operations on scalars with the following symbols: + for addition, - for subtraction, * for multiplication, and / for division. These symbols are called *mathematical operators*. The scalars that you operate on are called *operands*.

To multiply, divide, add, or subtract:

1. Type the first operand. It can be a numerical constant like **12**, a scalar variable like **$distance**, or an entire expression in itself, like **$age + 1**.

2. Type the mathematical operator: *****, **/**, **+**, or **-**.

3. Type the second operand.

✔ Tips

- You can store the result of a mathematical operation in a variable. For example, in `$result = $first * $second`, the product of the values of `$first` and `$second` is stored in `$result`.

- If you use more than one mathematical operator in a given expression, you may need to use parentheses to control the order in which operations are carried out *(see page 113)*.

- If you use a mathematical operator on a string, Perl converts the string to a number (stripping it of any non-numeric symbols, or changing it to zero if there are no numbers at all) and then uses the result in the calculation. The results may not be what you expect. (For more details, consult *Numbers and strings* on page 24.)

```perl
1   #!/usr/local/bin/perl -wT
2   use strict;
3   use CGI ':standard';
4   my ($total, $times, $premium, $average,
      $tax_deduction);
5
6   $total = param('donation');
7   $times = param('times');
8   $premium = param('premium');
9
10  $average = $total/$times;
11  $tax_deduction = $total - $premium;
12
13  print "Content-type: text/html\n\n";
14  print "<P>You donated $total dollars
      last year. Thank you.";
15  print "<P>Since you donated $times
      times, that works out to an average of
      $average dollars per donation.";
16  print "<P>Since your premium was worth
      $premium dollars, you can only take a
      tax deduction of $tax_deduction
      dollars.";
```

10: To get the average donation, we divide the total yearly deductions (`$total`) by the number of contributions (`$times`). The result is saved in `$average`.

11: In line 11, we subtract the premium value (`$premium`) from the total donations (`$total`) and store the result in `$tax_deduction`.

15: This line prints the result of the division.

16: The result of the subtraction is printed here.

Figure 10.7 *Arithmetic operations are particularly useful for Web stores or other sites where you have to calculate numeric data.*

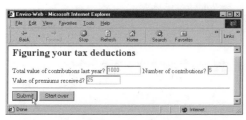

Figure 10.8 *The visitor enters the necessary data and submits the form.*

Figure 10.9 *Saving the results of the calculations in another variable makes it easy to incorporate them into* print *statements (or other operations) later.*

```
1  #!/usr/local/bin/perl -wT
2  use strict;
3
4  my ($div, $parens, $subadd,
     $parens_subadd);
5
6  $div = 40 / 5 + 3;
7  $parens = 40 / (5 + 3);
8  $subadd = 9 - 3 + 5;
9  $parens_subadd = 9 - (3 + 5);
10
11 print "Content-type: text/html\n\n";
12 print "div is $div, parens is $parens,
      subadd is $subadd and parens_subadd is
      $parens_subadd";
```

6: In the right-hand expression, there are two operations, division and addition. Division has precedence, and so we first divide 40 by 5 (getting 8) and then add 3, with a final result of 11, saved in the $div variable.

7: The operators and numbers are the same as in line 6, but here we've added parentheses so that the addition is carried out first. Thus, we first add 5 and 3 and then divide 40 by the result (8), with a final result of 5.

8: In this expression there are two operators of equal precedence. Since they have left associativity, we operate on the two left operands (9 and 3) first. Thus, we subtract 3 from 9, getting 6 and then add 5 for a final result of 11.

9: Again, the numbers and operators are the same as in line 8, with parentheses added to give precedence to the second half of the expression. Thus, we add 3 and 5 and subtract the result (8) from 9, with a final result of 1.

Figure 10.10 *The rules of precedence determine which operations are carried out first in expressions with multiple operators.*

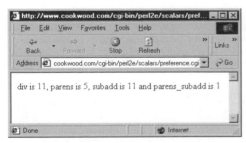

Figure 10.11 *The expected results.*

Using More Than One Operator

What happens if you use several operators in a single expression? Imagine, for example, the expression 2 * 3 + 5. Is the result 11 or 16? For Perl, and indeed most mathematicians, the answer is 11 because the multiplication operator takes *precedence* over the addition operator and is thus completed first.

You can override precedence rules by using parentheses. The expression inside the parentheses is always evaluated before the expressions and operators outside the parentheses. For example, the result of 2 * (3 + 5) is 16 because the parentheses have precedence over multiplication, and thus the numbers within the parentheses are added before the sum is multiplied by 2.

When two operators have equal precedence, Perl then looks at the *associativity* of the operators. Left associativity means the two operands to the left are executed first. Right associativity means the two right operands are executed first. If you check the precedence page on Perl.com (*http://www.perl.com/pub/doc/manual/html/pod/perlop.html*), you'll see that multiplication and division have equal precedence and left associativity. Since left associativity means that with operators of equal precedence the left two operands are executed first, an expression like 12 / 2 * 3 is equivalent, but perhaps more clearly represented by, (12 / 2) * 3, with a result of 18 (and not a result of 2, which is 12 divided by the product of 2 and 3).

What are the basic precedence rules? Exponentiation takes precedence over division, multiplication, taking the remainder of division, and repeating (all of which have equal precedence), which in turn take precedence over addition, subtraction, and concatenation (which have equal precedence).

Raising a Number to an Exponential Power

Multiplying a number by itself a given number of times is known as raising the number to an exponential power. For example, 3 raised to the fourth power (3^4) is equivalent to 3 * 3 * 3 * 3, or 81. Perl uses two asterisks ** as the operator for exponential power.

To raise a number to an exponential power:

1. Type the scalar that you want to raise to an exponential power. You can use a scalar constant, a scalar variable, or even an expression.

2. Type ** (two asterisks).

3. Type the power to which you wish to raise the scalar or expression in step 1.

✔ Tips

■ Don't put a space between the two asterisks.

■ You can assign the result to a scalar variable. For example, if you use `$result = $number ** 5`, with `$number` equal to 3, `$result` will be set to 243 (that is, 3^5).

■ The exponential power operator takes precedence over the simple mathematical operators discussed on page 112. That means that if you use an expression like 2 ** 7 + 1, the answer is *129* (1 added to 2^7) and not *256* (2 to the sum of 7+1). You can override precedence with parentheses. For more on precedence, consult *Using More Than One Operator* on page 113.

```
1   #!/usr/local/bin/perl -wT
2   use strict;
3   use CGI ':standard';
4   my ($number, $power, $result);
5
6   $number = param('number');
7   $power = param('power');
8
9   $result = $number ** $power;
10
11  print "Content-type: text/html\n\n";
12  print "<P>You entered $number with an
        exponent of $power.";
13  print "<P>$number raised to the $power
        power is $result.";
```

9: In the right-hand expression, we raise the value of `$number` to the value of `$power`. The result is stored in `$result`.

12: Lines 12–13. These simple `print` statements remind the visitor what they typed in and print out the result of raising their number to the desired power.

Figure 10.12 *This script spends a bit of time getting the values from the visitor, a millisecond raising the number to a power, and then a bunch more time outputting the data. It's not atypical.*

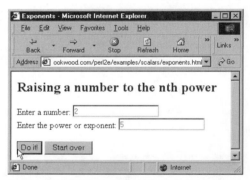

Figure 10.13 *The visitor can enter any number they wish in the form boxes. When they click the Do it (submit) button, the numbers are sent to the server and the script is processed.*

Figure 10.14 *It's a good idea to remind your visitor what information they requested.*

Raising a Number to an Exponential Power

```
1  #!/usr/local/bin/perl -wT
2  use strict;
3  use CGI ':standard';
4  my ($number, $result);
5
6  $number = param('number');
7
8  $result = sqrt ($number);
9
10 print "Content-type: text/html\n\n";
11 print "<P>The square root of $number is
       $result";
```

8: We find the square root of the $number and
    assign it to the $result variable.

Figure 10.15 *You could combine lines 6 and 8 if desired.*

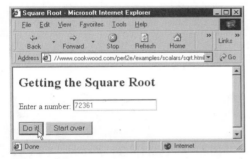

Figure 10.16 *You could do this by hand, but why bother?*

Figure 10.17 *Perl finds the square root and outputs it to the browser.*

Using Mathematical Functions

Perl has several mathematical functions that simplify certain more complex computations. You can get the square root of a number, its absolute value, its integral part, and you can find cosines and sines to your heart's delight.

To use a mathematical function:

1. Type **function (**, where *function* is one of the following:

    sqrt, for taking the square root;

    abs, for getting the absolute value;

    int, for getting just the integer part of a number (i.e., removing the decimal)

    atan2, cos, or sin, for getting the arc tangent, the cosine, or the sine, respectively;

    log or exp, for getting the natural logarithm of a number or *e* raised to a number, respectively.

2. Type the number, the variable that contains the number, or the expression that results in the number for which you'd like to operate the function.

3. Type **)**.

✔ Tips

■ If you don't specify the operand, each of the functions listed will use the default variable: $_. For details on setting the default variable, consult *Loading the Default Variable* on page 131.

■ You can assign the result of the operation to a scalar variable, as in $root = sqrt($number);.

Getting the Remainder of a Division

When you divide 13 by 3, the answer is 4 with a *remainder* of 1. Perl has a built-in function to give you the remainder of a division operation. The operator is called *modulus*.

To get the remainder of a division:

1. Type the first number or scalar variable (the dividend).

2. Type **%** (the percent sign).

3. Type the number (or scalar variable) that you wish to divide into the number in step 1.

✔ Tips

- You can assign the result (that is, the remainder itself) to a scalar variable. For example, if you use $result = $number % 5, with $number equal to 14, $result will be set to 4.

- Perl eliminates the decimal part of a number before taking the modulus. Thus, 34.7 % 5 is calculated as 34 % 5 and results in a remainder, or modulus, of 4.

```
1   #!/usr/local/bin/perl -wT
2   use strict;
3   use CGI ':standard';
4   my ($dividend, $divisor, $result);
5
6   $dividend = param('dividend');
7   $divisor = param('divisor');
8
9   $result = $dividend % $divisor;
10
11  print "Content-type: text/html\n\n";
12  print "<P>You entered $dividend for the
        dividend and $divisor for the
        divisor";
13  print "<P>The remainder of $dividend
        divided by $divisor is $result";
```

9: In the right-hand expression, we want the remainder of $dividend when divided by $divisor. The remainder is stored in $result.

13: This simple print statement reminds the visitor what they typed and gives the remainder of the division.

Figure 10.18 *The* dividend *is the number that you divide the* divisor *into.*

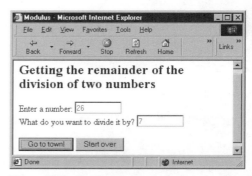

Figure 10.19 *The visitor can enter any numbers they wish in the form boxes. When they click the Go to town! (submit) button, the numbers are sent to the server and the script is processed.*

Figure 10.20 *The script processes the incoming information and then outputs the results.*

```
1   #!/usr/local/bin/perl -wT
2   use strict;
3   use CGI ':standard';
4   my ($first, $married, $fullname);
5
6   $first = param('first_name');
7   $married = param('fiance_last');
8
9   $fullname = $first . ' ' . $married;
10
11  print "Content-type: text/html\n\n";
12  print "Congratulations! Your married
        name would be $fullname.";
```

9: This lines joins the woman's first name ($first)
    with a space (' '), and then with her fiancé's
    last name ($married) and stores the result in
    $fullname.

Figure 10.21 *The period, or concatenation operator, is for connecting strings together.*

Figure 10.22 *The visitor enters both her and her fiancé's names in the appropriate fields. When she clicks Marry Me (the submit button), the information is sent to the server and the script.*

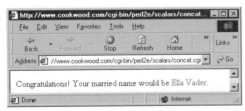

Figure 10.23 *The script takes the woman's first name and concatenates it with a space and the fiancé's last name and then prints out the result. Just one more reason to keep one's own name...*

Connecting Strings Together

Although it might seem logical to use the addition symbol (+) to connect strings together, Perl has a separate operator for connecting or *concatenating* strings: the period.

To connect strings together:

1. Type the first string, in single or double quotation marks *(see page 30)*.

2. Type . (a period).

3. Type the string that you wish to connect to the end of the first string.

4. Repeat steps 2 and 3 as desired.

✔ Tips

■ You can use variables and expressions in both steps 1 and 3, as needed.

■ You can also assign the result to a variable. For example, $string = 'Barry Gold' . 'water' would result in $string containing the value "Barry Goldwater". Notice that the concatenation operator connects the two strings without adding extra spaces.

■ Make sure you use the period (.) for adding strings and the plus sign (+) for adding numbers. For example, 2 + 3 would result in 5, but 2 . 3 results in 23. In a similar way, 'water' + 'melon' results in 0, while 'water' . 'melon' results in *"watermelon"*. Finally, an expression like '3x' + '4y' results in 7 but '3x' . '4y' results in *"3x4y"*. For more information on getting the sum of two numbers, see page 112. For more details on strings versus numbers, consult page 24.

■ Double quotes are a much easier way to concatenate strings *(see page 30)*.

Connecting Strings Together

Repeating a String

Perl has an operator for repeating a string a given number of times. It's not a particularly common function in CGI scripts, but maybe you'll find a use for it.

To repeat a string:

1. Type the string (in the form of a constant or variable) that you want to repeat.

2. Type **x** (a lowercase letter *x*), followed by a space.

3. Type **n**, where *n* is the number of times you want the string to be repeated.

✔ Tips

■ You can use a mathematical expression for step 3. Something like `$repeats * 4` is perfectly legal.

■ You can assign the resulting value (the repeated string) to a variable in order to save it for a later calculation.

■ Don't confuse the repeat operator (x) with the multiplication operator (*) for numbers. For example, because Perl expects the operands next to the repeat operator (x) to be strings, 2 x 3 results in *222* while 2 * 3 (where Perl expects the operands to be numbers) results in the perhaps more expected 6. For more information on numbers and strings, consult *Numbers and strings* on page 24. For more information on multiplying numbers, consult *Multiplying, Dividing, Adding, Subtracting* on page 112.

```
1   #!/usr/local/bin/perl -wT
2   use strict;
3   use CGI ':standard';
4   my ($base, $school, $cheer, $number,
        $repeat, $repeat_number);
5
6   $base = param('base');
7   $school = param('school');
8   $cheer = $base x 2 . $school;
9
10  $number = param('number');
11  $repeat = param('repeat');
12  $repeat_number = $number x $repeat;
13
14  print "Content-type: text/html\n\n";
15  print "<FONT SIZE=+1>The cheer is
        <B>$cheer</B>.";
16  print "<P>And the number, $number,
        repeated $repeat times is
        <B>$repeat_number<B></FONT>";
```

8: The right-hand expression repeats the value of the $base variable twice, concatenates that with $school and stores the result in $cheer. Notice that the repeat operator has precedence over the concatenate operator.

12: If you use the repeat operator on a number, Perl converts the number into a string and then completes the operation.

Figure 10.24 *The repeat operator repeats a string as many times as you can stand.*

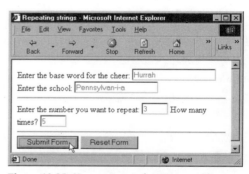

Figure 10.25 *You can't see it, but I've entered a space after Hurrah in the first field.*

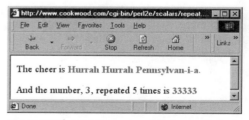

Figure 10.26 *Is this the most contrived example you've ever seen, or what? If you find a good use for the repeat operator in your CGI scripts, I'd like to hear about it.*

```
1   #!/usr/local/bin/perl -wT
2   use strict;
3   use CGI ':standard';
4
5   my $counter = param('counter');
6
7   $counter +=1;
8
9   print "Content-type: text/html\n\n";
10  print "<FONT SIZE=+1>If you add one to
       your number, the result is
       <B>$counter</B>";
11
12  $counter +=5;
13  print "<P>If you add 5 to that, the
       result is <B>$counter</B></FONT>";
```

5: The initial value for $counter is specified by the visitor.

7: The binary operator adds 1 to the value of $counter and then stores the result back into $counter.

12: This line adds 5 to the current value of $counter (which is now 1 plus whatever the visitor had entered), and then stores the result back into $counter.

Figure 10.27 *Notice that the* print *statements in both lines 11 and 14 use the* $counter *variable, since it always contains the latest value.*

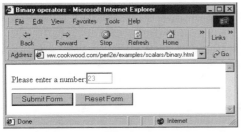

Figure 10.28 *The visitor enters the initial value for the* $counter *variable.*

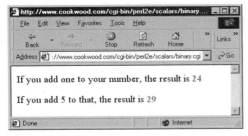

Figure 10.29 *Binary operators save you time and typing.*

Operating and Assigning in One Step

Updating the value of a variable by assigning it the result of an operation on itself is quite common. For that reason, Perl offers a special operator to save you typing called the *binary assignment operator.* It takes the form of the regular operator followed by the equals sign, which makes sense if you think of it as both operating and assigning a value to the variable.

To update a variable with the binary assignment operator:

1. Type **$scalar**, where *scalar* is the name of the variable that both holds the current value and that will hold the result of the operation.

2. Type the operator (*****, **/**, **+**, **-**, **%**, ******, **.**, etc.)

3. Type **=** (the equals sign).

4. Type the second operand.

✔ Tips

■   Using a binary assignment operator is equivalent to carrying out the operation and the assignment individually. In other words, $age = $age + 1 is equivalent to $age +=1. The second variation is simply faster to type.

■   The binary assignment shortcut works for both numbers and strings. In fact, the operators work just as they usually do; this is just a shortcut so you don't have to write out the variable name twice.

Operating and Assigning in One Step

Incrementing (or Decrementing) a Variable

Perl has a shorthand for the common operation of adding 1 to a variable (or subtracting 1 from it). You can use the operator either before or after the variable. In both cases, the variable itself is modified. If the operator precedes the variable, the return value *(see page 29)* of the operation is the incremented value, while if the operator goes after the variable, the return value is the value before it was incremented.

To increment/decrement a variable (and the result):

1. Type **++** (for adding 1) or **--** (for subtracting 1).

2. Type the variable.

To increment/decrement a variable (but not the result):

1. Type the variable.

2. Type **++** (for adding 1) or **--** (for subtracting 1).

✔ Tips

■ Whether you put the autoincrement operator before or after the variable largely depends on whether you're assigning the result to another variable. If you are, you just have to decide if you want the second variable to use the incremented value (use ++ before) or the value before it was incremented (use ++ after).

■ The autoincrement operator (but not autodecrement) works on strings as long as they contain only numbers and letters.

```
1   #!/usr/local/bin/perl -wT
2   use strict;
3   use CGI ':standard';
4   my ($start, $counter, $watch);
5   $start= param('start');
6
7   print "Content-type: text/html\n\n";
8   print "You started with <b>$start</b>";
9
10  $counter = $start;
11  ++$counter;
12  $watch = ++$counter;
13  print "<P>The current value is $watch";
14
15  $counter = $start;
16  $counter++;
17  $watch = $counter++;
18  print "<P>The current value is $watch";
```

9: The autoincrement operator adds 1 to the value of $counter. The result is then assigned back to $counter.

10: The autoincrement operator adds 1 to the value of $counter and then assigns the result back to $counter. *Then*, it assigns the result of the operation to $watch. Note that $counter is equal to $watch.

13: We reassign the initial visitor-entered start value to $counter so that we can compare the two operators on an even footing.

14: The autoincrement operator adds 1 to the value of $counter. The result is then assigned back to $counter. There is no difference here from line 9.

15: The value of $counter is assigned to $watch, and *then* the autoincrement operator adds 1 to the current value of $counter and assigns the result back to $counter. Now $counter and $watch have different values. Compare these results with the results from line 10.

Figure 10.30 *If you're not assigning the result of the entire expression to another variable, the placement of the autoincrement operators doesn't matter (lines 9 and 14). It's when you assign the result to a new variable (*$watch*), as in lines 12 and 17, that the order becomes important.*

Figure 10.31 *Notice how the result changes depending on whether the ++ or -- goes before or after the variable.*

CONDITIONALS AND LOOPS

A simple statement

```
$winnings = $payoff / $ticketholders;
```

Figure 11.1 *Here is a simple statement that divides the scalar* $payoff *by* $ticketholders *and assigns the result to* $winnings *(to see how lottery winnings should be divvied up among friends).*

A condition

```
$payoff != 0
```

Comparison operator
(not equal to)

Figure 11.2 *A condition is either true or false. In this example, the value of the scalar variable* $payoff *is either not equal to 0 (in which case this condition would be true), or it is equal to 0 (in which case this condition would be false).*

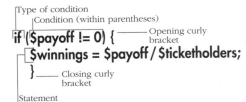

Type of condition
Condition (within parentheses)

```
if ($payoff != 0) {
    $winnings = $payoff / $ticketholders;
}
```

Opening curly bracket

Closing curly bracket

Statement

Figure 11.3 *A conditional statement has three principal parts: the conditional word (*if*) that determines how the condition will be analyzed; the condition itself, which is enclosed in parentheses; and a block, which begins with an opening curly bracket, then contains one or more statements, and ends with a closing curly bracket.*

So far, you've learned how to make definitive statements like "divide this number into that one". In this chapter, you'll learn how to execute statements only under particular circumstances. For example, you may only want to divide those numbers *if* one of them is not equal to 0.

Both conditional statements and loops generally have three parts. First, we have the all important defining word, such as `if` or `while`, that determines how the condition or loop is interpreted. Notice the difference between "Divide this number into that one *if* the payoff is not 0" and "Divide this number into that one *while* the payoff is not zero".

Next, comes the condition itself (even in a loop), which in this example is "the payoff is not zero". When Perl encounters a condition, it has to decide whether it is true or false. In this case, if the value of `$payoff` is, say, 3 million, the expression is evaluated as true. If the value of `$payoff` is 0, the expression is false.

The last element is a *block*—enclosed in curly brackets—of one or more statements that are executed depending on the true or false state of the condition. In this example, the statement "divide the payoff by the ticketholders, and assign the result to winnings" will only be executed if the condition (that the payoff is not zero) is true.

While conditionals and loops are similar, conditionals (like `if` or `unless`) only do something once and maybe don't execute all of their blocks while loops (`while`, `foreach`, etc.) may repeat a process over and over again (depending on the condition).

Comparing Numbers

One typical way to create a condition is by comparing two numbers to see if they are equal, or not equal, or if one is bigger or smaller. The result of a comparison is either true or false.

To compare numbers:

1. Type the first element in the comparison.

2. Type the numeric comparison operator:

Use **>** for greater than, **<** for less than, **>=** for greater than or equal to, **<=** for less than or equal to, **==** for equal to and **!=** for not equal to.

3. Type the second element in the comparison.

✔ Tips

■ There are separate comparison operators for numbers and strings. For more information on comparison operators for strings, consult *Comparing Strings* on page 123.

■ If you use a numeric comparison operator on a string, Perl will convert the string into a number (stripping it of non-numeric symbols and characters and changing it to zero if it has no numbers at all). The results may not be what you expected. For comparing strings, use the string comparison operators *(see page 123)*. For more details on how Perl handles numbers and strings, consult *Numbers and strings* on page 24.

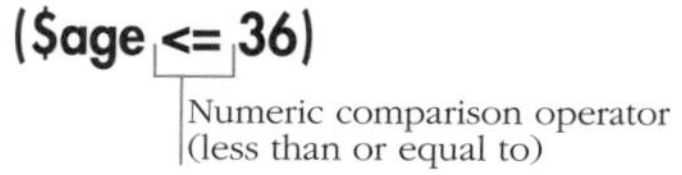

($age <= 36)

Numeric comparison operator (less than or equal to)

Figure 11.4 *In this example, if the value of* $age *is 3 or 25 or anything else less than or equal to 36, the condition will be evaluated as true. If the value of* $age *is higher than 36, the condition is evaluated as false.*

Comparing Numbers

($name eq 'Ralph')

String comparison operator
(equivalent to)

Figure 11.5 *In this example, if the value of* $name *is exactly* Ralph, *the condition is true. Otherwise, it is false.*

Comparing Strings

While it's often useful to compare numbers to see which is bigger and which is smaller, with strings you usually want to know if they are the same or not. The result of a comparison is either true or false.

To compare strings:

1. Type the first string.

2. Type the string comparison operator:

   Use **eq** for equal to, **ne** for not equal to, **gt** for greater than, **lt** for less than, **ge** for greater than or equal to, and **le** for less than or equal to.

3. Type the second string.

✔ Tips

■ Remember that case matters. "Zipper" is not equivalent to "zipper". In fact, it is less than "zipper".

■ To decide whether a string is greater or less than another, Perl looks at the ASCII values of the characters that it contains. So, *Z* (ASCII code = 90) is less than *z* (ASCII code = 122). *Z* is of course greater than *A*, and all letters are greater than the digits 0–9 and many symbols (including the space).

■ Remember that since Perl expects strings with these operators, it will treat numbers as strings as well. For example, 42 gt 147 returns true (even though the number 42 is obviously less than the number 147) because the ASCII value of 4 is greater than the ASCII value of 1.

■ For comparing numbers, see page 122.

■ You can also use regular expressions with conditionals. For more details, see Chapter 15, *Analyzing Data*.

Comparing Strings

Evaluating Conditions without Comparisons

While comparison operators are probably the simplest and most common way to construct a condition, they are not the only way. In fact, you can use any statement as a condition. Perl has a simple set of rules for deciding if a statement is true or false: if the statement is evaluated as 0, the empty string (""), or undef (undefined), it is considered to be false. In all other cases, it is true.

For example, a condition like ($payoff) will return true only if it is not empty, not undefined, and not equal to zero. This is a great way to test if a particular variable has had a value assigned to it, and to execute further statements only if the assignment has already occurred.

Further, a function like print "hello" will return true if it was successful (able to print) and false if not.

✔ Tip

■ Note that if the condition contains an operation, the operation will always be executed. For example, if you use if ($number++), the value of $number will be incremented by 1 regardless of whether the condition evaluates as true or false. (Note that in this particular example, the variable is evaluated *before* it is incremented so that if $number was 0 before this line, the condition returns false and *then* $number is incremented to 1. If the condition was (++$number), then $number would be incremented before being evaluated, and (assuming it was 0 before this line) it would be incremented to 1 and the condition would return true. Whew! For more details on the increment operator, see page 120.)

A condition with no comparison

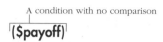

($payoff)

Figure 11.6 *In this example, the condition is true if the value of the variable is not empty, not undefined, and not equal to zero.*

A condition in the form of an expression

($number++)

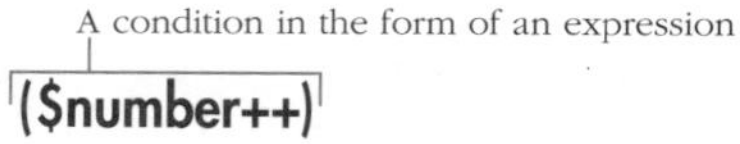

Figure 11.7 *Again, the condition is true if the expression evaluates as anything except 0, empty, or undefined. Note that the expression is executed whether it is true or not. In this case the $number variable is always incremented by 1.*

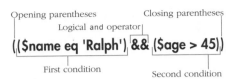

Opening parentheses | Closing parentheses
Logical and operator |
First condition | Second condition

Figure 11.8 *With two comparisons and the logical* and *operator, the entire condition is true if and only if the value of both comparisons is true. In other words, the man in question must be named* Ralph *and* must be *older than 45.*

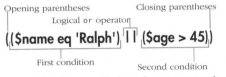

Opening parentheses | Closing parentheses
Logical or operator |
First condition | Second condition

Figure 11.9 *If you use the logical* or *operator, only one of the comparisons needs to return true for the condition to be true. In this case, men older than 45, regardless of their name, or men named* Ralph, *regardless of their age, would match.*

Testing Two or More Comparisons

So far, we've looked at using a single comparison or using none at all. You can also test more than one condition at a time.

To test two comparisons at a time:

1. Type **(** to begin the set of conditions.

2. Type **(condition1)**, where *condition1* is the first condition you want to test.

3. Type **&&** (this is the logical and operator) to test if both conditions are true.

   Or type **||** (two pipe symbols—above the \ on the keyboard— called the logical or operator) to test if at least one (but possibly both) of the conditions is true.

4. Type **(condition2)**, where *condition2* is the second condition.

5. Repeat steps 3–4 as necessary.

6. Type **)** to close the set of conditions.

✔ Tips

- Don't forget the outer set of parentheses that encloses the two conditions and the operator.

- Perl also has the and and or operators which work the same way as && and ||, respectively, and are easier to remember, but have a lower precedence. As long as you use parentheses (which have a higher precedence) to enclose your conditions, you can use either the symbol or word versions of logical or and logical and.

- You can also use *regular expressions*, which we'll discuss in Chapter 15, to make your conditions more flexible.

Testing Two or More Comparisons

Creating a Basic Conditional Statement

You probably heard your first if statement from one of your parents: "*If* you don't eat your spinach, then you can't have dessert." Notice that there is an if, a condition, (you don't eat spinach), and something that will happen if the condition is true (you won't get dessert). *If* statements in Perl aren't much different—except you can always have dessert.

To use if:

1. Type **if (condition) {**, where *condition* is the expression you will test.

2. On the next line, type the statement that should be executed if the condition in step 1 is true. Remember to end each statement with a semicolon.

3. Repeat step 2 as many times as needed.

4. Type **}** (the closing curly bracket).

✔ Tips

- If you only have one short statement that will be executed if the condition is true, you can put the entire if block on one line and omit the semicolon.

- In fact, you can omit the semicolon of the *last* statement in any block. However, most people use it just so that they don't forget it if later they add additional statements.

- If the block contains only one statement, you can flip the order of the elements and omit the parentheses around the condition: `print 'You ate spinach, so you get dessert' if $food eq 'spinach';`.

- White space is unimportant. If you'd rather start the opening curly bracket on its own line (like in C++), that's fine.

```
1   #!/usr/local/bin/perl -wT
2   use strict;
3   use CGI ':standard';
4   my $food;
5
6   $food = param('food');
7
8   if ($food eq 'spinach') {
9     print "Content-type: text/html\n\n";
10    print 'You ate spinach, so you get
        dessert!';
11  }
```

8: If the value of $food, which the visitor inputs through the corresponding Web form, is *spinach*, then the rest of the statements in the if statement (lines 9–10) will be executed. Otherwise, they will be skipped.

9: The all-important MIME content line.

10: As long as the condition in line 8 is true, the program will execute this line, printing the phrase *You ate spinach, so you get dessert!* (Note that if the condition is false, the browser gets no output, and therefore will get an Internal Server Error. We'll correct that on the next page.)

11: You must end an if statement with the final closing curly bracket.

Figure 11.10 *This* if *block contains two statements that will only be executed if the condition evaluates as true.*

Figure 11.11 *If the visitor types* spinach *in the field, the condition is true, both statements in the* if *block are executed, and both the MIME content line and the phrase* You ate spinach, so you get dessert! *are output to the browser.*

```
1   #!/usr/local/bin/perl -wT
2   use strict;
3   use CGI ':standard';
4   my $food;
5
6   $food = param('food');
7
8   print "Content-type: text/html\n\n";
9
10  if ($food eq 'spinach') {
11    print 'You ate spinach, so you get
          dessert!';
12  } else {
13    print 'No spinach, no dessert!';
14  }
```

8: I've taken the MIME content line out of the `if` statement so that it is sent to the browser no matter what the outcome of the `if`.

12: The `else` clause begins after the closing curly bracket of the original `if` statement.

13: As long as `$food` is not *spinach*, the condition in line 10 is false and this line will be executed, printing the line *No spinach, no dessert!*.

14: You must end an `else` clause with a closing curly bracket.

Figure 11.12 *The* `else` *clause lets you add a statement that will be executed only if the condition is false. If the condition is true, the statements in the* `if` *block are executed as usual and the statements in the* `else` *block are skipped.*

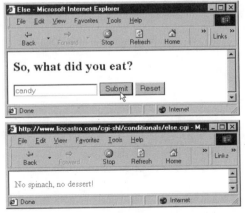

Figure 11.13 *If the visitor types anything other than* spinach *(including nothing at all), the condition is false and the statement(s) in the* `else` *block are executed. In this case, that means the script outputs the sentence* No spinach, no dessert! *to the browser.*

Adding Options for False Conditions

In the example on the preceding page, if the visitor types anything except "spinach", the `print` statements are ignored, resulting in a confused browser and an internal server error. Thankfully, you can add an `else` clause to an `if` block that lets you execute one group of statements if the condition is true and a different group if the condition is false (instead of giving up altogether). The statements in the `else` clause are only executed when the condition is *not* true.

To add options for when the condition is false:

1. Create an `if` statement as described on page 126.

2. After the final curly bracket (from step 4 on page 126), type **else**.

3. Type {.

4. Now press Return, and on the next line, type the statement that should be executed if the condition is false. Remember to end each statement with a semicolon.

5. Type }.

✔ Tips

- Although you could embed other `if` statements within an `else` clause, there is a better way to add multiple conditions (*see page 128*).

- Note that the scope of a variable declared within an `if` block extends to any `else` and `elsif` blocks. (We get to `elsif` on the next page.) For more details about scope, consult *Statements, Blocks, and Scope* on page 32 and *Declaring Private Variables* on page 34.

Adding Multiple, Independent Conditions

An if block with an else clause lets you control two outcomes: what should happen if the condition is true and what should happen if it's false. Perl also lets you add additional conditions that it will test after the if condition evaluates as false and before it resorts to the statements in the else clause.

To add multiple, independent conditions:

1. Create the if statement as described on page 126.

2. Type **elsif**. Notice that there is only one *e* in *elsif*.

3. Type **(condition)**, where *condition* is the expression that should be evaluated as true or false to determine if the following statements should be executed.

4. On the same line, type **{**.

5. Press Return and then type the statements that should be executed if the condition in step 3 is true. Remember to type a semicolon at the end of each statement.

6. Type **}**.

7. Repeat steps 2–6 for each additional condition and statements.

8. Create an else clause as described in steps 2–5 on page 127, whose statement(s) will only be executed if *all* the preceding conditions are false.

✔ Tip

- Each condition is evaluated in order. Once Perl finds a true condition (or the else clause), the corresponding statements are executed and the rest of the block is ignored.

```
10  if ($food eq 'spinach') {
11    print 'You ate spinach, so you get
         dessert!';
12  } elsif ($food eq 'broccoli') {
13    print "Broccoli's OK. Maybe you'll get
         dessert.";
14  } else {
15    print 'No spinach, no dessert!';
16  }
```

9: Lines 1-9 are not shown. They are exactly the same as in Figure 11.12.

10: Supposing the user enters *broccoli* for $food, this first condition will be false and Perl will skip line 11 and look for an elsif or else block.

11: Because the initial condition is false, this line is skipped.

12: The first additional condition follows the if's closing curly bracket. Now, Perl will look to see if $food is *broccoli*. If so, the statements in this block are executed. If not, it jumps to the next elsif, if any, or to the else clause (line 14).

13: If the visitor entered *broccoli*, the elsif condition is true, and this statement is printed. Note that since the phrase contains a single quote, I've enclosed the whole thing in double quotes.

14: The elsif clause has its own closing curly bracket (shown here before the else). Don't forget it.

Figure 11.14 *If the condition in the initial if block is false, each elsif's condition is evaluated in order. If one turns out to be true, its statements are then executed and the rest of the if structure is ignored. If no conditions are true, the else block is executed.*

Figure 11.15 *If the visitor types* broccoli, *the initial if condition is false, and the elsif is evaluated and found to be true. If they type "spinach" the result is the same as in Figure 11.11 on page 126. Anything else gets the result shown in Figure 11.13 on page 127.*

Adding Multiple, Independent Conditions

```
1   #!/usr/local/bin/perl -wT
2   use strict;
3   use CGI ':standard';
4   my $food;
5
6   $food = param('food');
7
8   print "Content-type: text/html\n\n";
9
10  unless ($food eq 'spinach') {
11    print 'No spinach, no dessert!';
12  }
```

10: With an unless block, the condition is evaluated and when it is *false*, the attached statements are executed. If it is true, the attached statements are skipped.

11: As long as the user does not enter a value of *spinach* for $food, this line is executed and the phrase is printed.

12: You must end an unless block with a closing curly bracket.

Figure 11.16 *The* unless *conditional works alone, without* else *or* elsif.

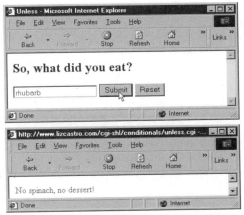

Figure 11.17 *Now the* print *statement will be executed only when the condition is false. In this case, the user entered* rhubarb—*which is certainly not* spinach—*so the phrase is indeed printed.*

Using Unless

Sometimes it's more important (and simpler) to know when a condition is false rather than when it's true. Although you could use an if statement and a convoluted, negative condition, Perl has another conjunction that makes this easy: unless. With unless, the attached statements are only executed if the condition is false.

To execute statements when the condition is false:

1. Type **unless**.

2. Type **(condition)**, where *condition* is the expression that will be evaluated as true or false to determine if the following statements should be executed.

3. Type **{** to begin the block.

4. Type the statements that should be executed if the condition in step 2 is *false*. Remember to type a semicolon at the end of each statement.

5. Type **}** to end the block.

✔ Tip

■ The unless block has neither an else nor an "elsunless". If you need to use multiple, independent conditions, you'll have to construct them using if, elsif, and else.

Repeating a Block for Each Item in an Array

The most common loop in Perl lets you execute a block of statements (that is *loop* through them) for each and every element of an array. It's aptly called `foreach`.

To repeat a block for each item in an array:

1. Type **foreach**.

2. Type **$element**, where *element* is the name of the *index variable* to which each successive item from the array will be assigned.

3. Type **(@array)**, where *array* is the name of the array.

4. Type **{**.

5. Type the statements that should be evaluated for each item in the array specified in step 3.

6. Type **}**.

✔ Tips

- While you could declare the index variable elsewhere, it is almost never used outside of the block and so can be declared right in the foreach statement: `foreach my $element (@array) {`. The `$element` then will have scope for the entire `foreach` loop, but not outside it.

- For more information about arrays, consult Chapter 12, *Working with Arrays*.

```perl
1   #!/usr/local/bin/perl -wT
2   use strict;
3   use CGI ':standard';
4   my ($name, @prey);
5
6   print "Content-type: text/html\n\n";
7
8   $name = param('name');
9   @prey = param('prey');
10
11  foreach my $creature (@prey) {
12    print "<P>$name likes to eat
          $creature.";
13  }
```

9: Make sure to assign the results of the `param` function to an array (`@prey`, in this example) when it's parsing menus and checkboxes that can have more than one option marked. (For more details, consult *Getting Multiple-Valued Form Data* on page 105.)

11: In English, this lines says "take the first element in the `@prey` array, assign it to the `$creature` variable and use it in the following statements. Then take the next element from the `@prey` array and do the same thing. Repeat for each element in the array."

12: This statement prints the value of `$name` and the current value of `$creature`. It will be repeated each time the `foreach` loop gets the next element in the array.

13: The `foreach` loop ends with a curly bracket.

Figure 11.18 *The* `foreach` *loop is essential for working with arrays, as we'll see in Chapter 12.*

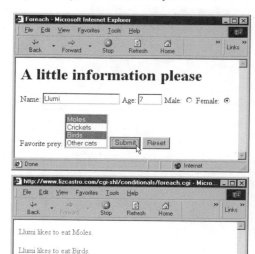

Figure 11.19 *Since the visitor chose* Moles *and* Birds *in the form, these are the elements of the* @prey *array.*

```
1   #!/usr/local/bin/perl -wT
2   use strict;
3   use CGI ':standard';
4   my ($name, @prey);
5
6   print "Content-type: text/html\n\n";
7
8   $name = param('name');
9   @prey = param('prey');
10
11  foreach (@prey) {
12  print "<P>$name likes to eat $_.";
13  }
```

11: In this foreach loop, I don't specify the scalar variable to which each individual element of the array is assigned. Therefore, Perl uses the default variable, $_ for this purpose.

12: This line works the same way as line 12 in Figure 11.18 on page 130. Since I'm letting Perl assign each array member to the $_ variable, that's what I operate on in this line.

Figure 11.20 *This script is equivalent to the one shown in Figure 11.18 on page 130.*

Figure 11.21 *The output is formatted precisely the same way as Figure 11.19 on page 130 (though the input is slightly different—I couldn't resist).*

```
11  print "<P>$name likes to eat<UL>";
12  foreach (@prey) {
13   print "<LI>";
14   print;
15  }
16  print "</UL>";
```

12: Again, I let Perl use the default variable, $_ for each array element.

14: This line is equivalent to print $_;. The print function is one of the functions that automatically operates on $_, given no other operand.

Figure 11.22 *Many functions, like* print *shown above, automatically operate on the default variable ($_) if none other is given.*

Loading the Default Variable

If you don't specify the variable in which you want to store each successive element of the array, Perl automatically loads the default variable, $_, with that data. You can then use $_ in the block to operate on the array's contents. In addition, there are a number of functions that automatically operate on $_ if no other operand is given. This combination of shortcuts can save you lots of time.

To load the default variable with each array element:

1. Type **foreach**.

2. Type **(@array)**, where *array* is the name of the array.

3. Type **{**.

4. Type the statements that should be evaluated for each item in the array specified in step 3. Use $_ when you want to access or operate on the current member of the array.

5. Type **}**.

✔ Tips

■ Using the default variable is purely for convenience. It's easier to let Perl store each member of the array in the $_ variable since you don't have to type its name and since many functions operate on the $_ variable if no other is given (which saves additional typing). For example, print; is the same as print $_;.

■ With either system, if your statements modify the index variable, the array itself will be modified as well. (The index variable is an actual stand-in or alias for the array element, not an independent variable that temporarily stores the array element's value.)

Loading the Default Variable

Repeating a Block While a Condition Is True

So far we've used conditions to decide whether or not to execute one or more statements. Perl also has a number of constructs that let you execute one or more statements *as long as* a condition is true. Typically, one of the enclosed statements changes the values evaluated by the condition, although that's not required.

To repeat a block while a condition is true:

1. Type **while**.

2. Type **(condition)**, where *condition* is the expression that should be evaluated as true or false to determine if the following statements should be executed.

3. Type **{**.

4. Type the statements that should be executed *while* the condition in step 2 is true. Remember to type a semicolon at the end of each statement.

5. If desired, add a statement that modifies the value of the condition.

6. Type **}**.

✔ Tips

■ You could also use --$start as the condition in this example. The first printed value of $start would be one less than the visitor entered (since the value is decremented before it is first printed), but you save a line of code.

■ while loops are most often used to read in data from other files. But we haven't gotten to file operations yet, so we're using a simpler example. For more on while loops and files, see page 253.

```
1   #!/usr/local/bin/perl -wT
2   use strict;
3   use CGI ':standard';
4   my $start;
5
6   $start = param('start');
7   print "Content-type: text/html\n\n";
8   print '<P>Starting countdown...';
9
10  while ($start > 0) {
11      print "$start... ";
12      --$start;
13  }
14  print 'KABOOM!';
```

10: In English, this line says "while $start is greater than 0 (that is, the condition is true), execute the following statements and then evaluate the condition again. If it is true, execute the statements and then evaluate the condition again. If it is false, skip the statements and exit the loop.

11: This statement prints the value of $start followed by three periods and a space.

12: The decrement operator subtracts one from the value of $start. This means that at some point (as long as you start with a non-negative number), the condition in line 10 will become false.

13: The while loop ends with a curly bracket.

Figure 11.23 *Notice that the MIME content line is outside of the* while *loop. Once the Perl script is running, it just creates one page. All the results are output to the same page.*

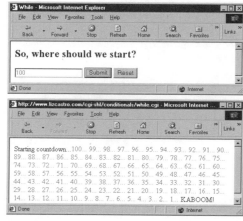

Figure 11.24 *The statements within the* while *loop (printing the value of* $start *and then decrementing it by one), are repeated as long as the condition remains true.*

```
1   #!/usr/local/bin/perl -wT
2   use strict;
3   use CGI ':standard';
4   my $start;
5
6   $start = param('start');
7
8   print "Content-type: text/html\n\n";
9   print '<P>Starting countdown...';
10
11  until ($start <= 0) {
12      print "$start... ";
13      --$start;
14  }
15
16  print 'KABOOM!';
```

11: In English, this line says, "until $start is less
than or equal to 0" (that is, the condition evaluates true), execute the following statements and
evaluate the condition again. If it is not yet true,
execute the statements and evaluate the condition again. Once it is zero or less, skip the
following statements and exit the loop.

12: This statement prints the value of $start fol-
lowed by three periods and a space.

13: The $start value is decremented by one. This
makes it possible for the condition in line 11 to
someday be true (as long as the visitor entered a
starting value greater than 0).

14: The until loop ends with a curly bracket.

Figure 11.25 *Aside from the type of condition used,
the principal difference between this example and the
one in Figure 11.23 is the condition itself.*

Repeating a Block While a Condition Is False

You can also have Perl repeat a set of statements as long as a condition is false, or
perhaps more precisely, *until* it is true.

To repeat a block while a condition is false:

1. Type **until**.

2. Type **(condition)**, where *condition* is the
   expression that should be evaluated as
   true or false to determine if the following
   statements should be executed.

3. Type **{**.

4. Type the statements that should be executed *until* the condition in step 2 is true.
   Remember to type a semicolon at the end
   of each statement.

5. If desired, add a statement that modifies
   the value of the condition.

6. Type **}**.

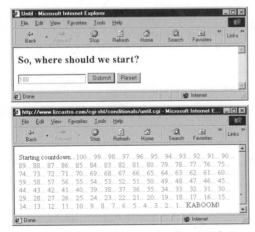

Figure 11.26 *The statements within the* until *loop
(printing the value of* $start *and then decrementing it
by one), are repeated as long as the condition remains
false.*

Executing the Block at Least Once

With a while block *(see page 132)*, if the condition is false from the start, Perl will never get to the statements in the block. If you want Perl to execute the statements at least once, you can use a do block.

To execute the block once before testing the condition:

1. Type **do**.

2. Type **{**.

3. On the next line, type the statements that should be executed at least once, and more times if the condition in step 5 below is true.

4. Type **}**.

5. Type **while** or **until**, depending on whether you want to test if the condition is true or false, respectively.

6. Type **(condition)**, where *condition* is the expression that should be evaluated as true or false to determine if the statements in step 3 should be executed again.

7. Type **;** (semicolon) to end the line.

✔ Tip

■ The do block is not very common in Perl CGI scripts.

```
1   #!/usr/local/bin/perl -wT
2   use strict;
3   use CGI ':standard';
4   my $start;
5
6   $start = param('start');
7
8   print "Content-type: text/html\n\n";
9   print '<P>Starting countdown...';
10
11  do {
12      print "$start... ";
13      --$start;
14  } while ($start > 0);
15
16  print 'KABOOM!';
```

11: In English, this line says, "execute the following statements and then check to see if the value of $start is greater than 0" (that is, the condition is true in line 14). If it is, execute the statements again and check again, continuing in this manner until $start is not greater than 0.

12: This statement prints the value of $start followed by three periods and a space.

13: The $start value is decremented by one.

14: The do block ends with a curly bracket, and is followed by while or until and a condition, and then a semicolon.

Figure 11.27 *With a do block, the statements are always executed at least once, no matter how the condition evaluates.*

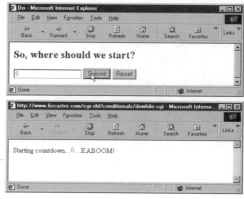

Figure 11.28 *Even if the visitor enters a number that is not greater than 0 (like 0 itself), the statements in the do block are executed at least once. Then the while conditional takes over and the loop is exited.*

```
1    #!/usr/local/bin/perl -wT
2    use strict;
3    use CGI ':standard';
4    my ($start, $i);
5
6    $start = param('start');
7
8    print "Content-type: text/html\n\n";
9    print '<P>Starting countdown...';
10
11   for ($i = $start; $i > 0; --$i) {
12       print "$i... ";
13   }
14
15   print 'KABOOM!';
```

11: In English, this line says, "Set the value of $i (the typical counter variable) to the value of $start. Check to see if $i is greater than 0. If so, execute the statements in the block and then decrement $i and evaluate the condition again. If and when the condition returns false, skip the statements and exit the loop." It's not unusual to declare the $i variable within the loop itself (since it rarely is used outside of the block) as in: for (my $i = ...

12: This statement prints the current value of $i followed by three periods and a space.

13: The for block ends with a curly bracket.

Figure 11.29 *Notice that no statement is required within the block to modify the condition. The third argument of the* for *loop has already taken care of that.*

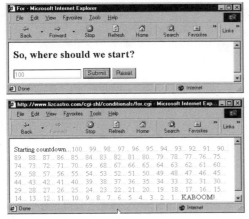

Figure 11.30 *The* for *loop executes the statements for each value of* $i *until the condition is false.*

Repeating a Block a Given Number of Times

The for loop makes it easy to repeat a block a given number of times by following the progress of a counter—a variable whose sole purpose in life is to count how many times the block has been executed. You first must set the initial state of the counter, then decide what condition should cause the statements to stop being executed, and then set the way the counter will be modified.

To repeat a block a given number of times:

1. Type **for**.

2. Type **(**.

3. Type **$i=start**, where *i* is the name of the counter variable and *start* is its initial value (and may be a constant or a variable).

4. Type **;**.

5. Type **condition**, where *condition* is the expression that should be evaluated as true or false to determine if the following statements should be executed. The condition generally takes into account the value of the counter variable.

6. Type **;**.

7. Type **$i++**, or any other expression that increments or decrements the value of the counter variable. (In the example, I use **--$i**.)

8. Type **)**.

9. Type **{**.

10. Type the statements that should be executed as long as the for block is repeated.

11. Type **}**.

Nesting Conditional Statements

Often, the only way to test your incoming data completely is to use more than one kind of conditional. You can nest one inside the other without much extra trouble.

To nest conditional statements:

1. Create the first conditional statement, following the steps on pages 126–130.

2. Within the statement area of the first conditional statement, create the second conditional statement.

✔ Tips

- Probably the trickiest part of nesting conditionals is making sure you have enough closing curly brackets. Make sure you have one closing curly bracket for each opening curly bracket. If you don't, the script won't run.

- One helpful technique is to type the closing curly bracket as soon as you type the opening curly bracket, and then go back and add the inner statements.

- It's typical practice to combine closing brackets all on one line, where applicable. That's OK too, as long as you have the same number of opening brackets as you do closing brackets. White space, as usual, doesn't matter.

```
11  while ($start > 0) {
1   if ($start - int $start) {
1      $start = int $start;
1   }
2          print "$start... ";
3          --$start;
4   }
5   print 'KABOOM!';
```

10: Lines 1–10 are the same as in Figure 11.23.

12: The nested if conditional block is only evaluated if the outside while loop is true. In this example, the condition subtracts the integer portion of $start from $start to see if the visitor entered a decimal.

13: If the visitor has entered a decimal portion of a number (that is, the condition is true), this line strips the decimal portion by setting $start to the integer value of $start.

14: The nested conditional still requires its own closing curly bracket.

15: The rest of the outside while loop continues as before.

Figure 11.31 *A nested conditional block lets you test for additional characteristics or problems in your incoming data.*

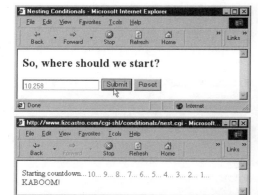

Figure 11.32 *If the visitor enters a decimal number in the form, the script strips the decimal portion so that it can do a normal countdown. (10.258, 9.258, 8.258... just doesn't have the same ring to it.)*

Nesting Conditional Statements

```
1   #!/usr/local/bin/perl -wT
2   use strict;
3   use CGI ':standard';
4
5   my $start = param('start');
6   my $skip = param('skip');
7
8   print "Content-type: text/html\n\n";
9   print '<P>Starting countdown...';
10
11  while ($start > 0) {
12  --$start;
13  if ($start == $skip) {
14      print "(We skip $skip.) ";
15      next;
16  }
17      print "$start... ";
18  }
19  print 'KABOOM!';
```

6: The visitor can specify where to skip out of the loop.

11: The outer loop is the same one we used in Figure 11.23 on page 132. It begins with the $start value given by the visitor, decreases the number by 1, and prints out its value (followed by ...), as long as the number is greater than 0, at which point it prints *Kaboom*.

13: The inner loop checks to see if the number has reached the $skip value entered by the visitor. If so, line 14 is printed, the rest of the outer loop (line 17) is skipped, and we return to line 11 to reevaluate the condition. If the inner block's condition is false, its statements are skipped (as usual) and the rest of the enclosing block is completed.

19: When the outer block is completed, line 19 is printed.

Figure 11.33 *A* next *statement skips the remaining parts of an iteration, but always goes back to reevaluate the loop's condition and continue iterating if the condition is still true.*

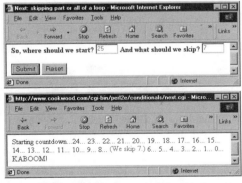

Figure 11.34 *When the inner conditional is true (*$skip *is 7), the rest of the outer loop is skipped and thus does not* print *"7...". The outer loop then continues.*

Skipping a Loop Iteration

By default, all of the statements in a loop are executed each time Perl goes through the loop. Sometimes, however, you may want to skip part or all of a trip through the loop (called an iteration) given a certain condition.

To skip all or part of a loop iteration:

1. Create the loop as usual, following the instructions on pages 130–135.

2. Within the outer loop's block, before the statements you want to skip, create the conditional statement or loop that specifies the circumstances in which the remaining statements in the outer loop should be skipped.

3. In the inner block, type **next;** to jump out of the inner loop, skip the rest of the statements in the outer loop, and then reevaluate the loop condition and go through the loop again if necessary.

4. Type **}** to complete the inner loop.

5. Create the statements in the outer loop that might be skipped.

6. Type **}** to complete the outer loop.

✔ Tips

■ If the inner block has no statements of its own, you can combine steps 2–4 on one line as in next if (condition);.

■ If you have several layers of nested loops, you can label each loop and then use the label in the next statement to determine which one's remaining statements should be skipped. Precede the loop definition with LABEL: to name it (as in LABEL: while ($start>0) {, and then use next LABEL when choosing to skip it.

Jumping out of a Loop Altogether

When you use next to skip part of a loop iteration, as described on page 137, Perl still will go back and reevaluate the condition of the outer loop and continue iterating through it if the condition is still true. If you'd rather end the loop altogether, use last.

To jump out of a loop altogether:

1. Create the outer loop as usual, following the instructions on *(see pages 130–135)*.

2. Within the outer loop's block, create the conditional statement or loop that specifies the circumstances in which Perl should stop running the loop.

3. In the inner block, type **last;** to jump out of the both the inner and outer loops, skipping the rest of the statements in the outer loop, if any.

4. Type **}** to complete the inner loop.

5. Create the statements in the outer loop that might be skipped.

6. Type **}** to complete the outer loop.

✔ Tips

■ If the inner block has no statements of its own, you can combine steps 2–4 on one line as in last if (condition);.

■ If you have several layers of nested loops, you can label each loop and then use the label in the last statement to determine which one's remaining statements should be skipped. Precede the loop definition with LABEL: to name it (as in LABEL: while ($start>0) {, and then use last LABEL when choosing to skip it.

```
1   #!/usr/local/bin/perl -wT
2   use strict;
3   use CGI ':standard';
4
5   my $start = param('start');
6   my $stop = param('stop');
7
8   print "Content-type: text/html\n\n";
9   print '<P>Starting countdown...';
10
11  while ($start > 0) {
12    --$start;
13    if ($start == $stop) {
14      print "(We stop at $stop.)";
15      last;
16  }
17    print "$start... ";
18  }
19  print 'KABOOM!';
```

1: Lines 1–10 are virtually the same as in Figure 11.33 on page 137 except that I've changed the name of the variable in line 6.

11: The outer loop is the same one we used in Figure 11.23 on page 132. It begins with the $start value given by the visitor, decreases the number by 1, and prints out its value (followed by ...), as long as the number is greater than 0, at which point it prints *Kaboom*.

13: The inner loop checks to see if the number has reached the $stop value entered by the visitor. If so, line 14 is printed, and we get out of the loop, skip any remaining statements (like line 17), and go on to line 19. If the inner block's condition is false, its statements are skipped (as usual) and the rest of the enclosing block is completed.*

19: When the outer block is completed, line 19 is printed.

Figure 11.35 *A* last *statement skips out of not only the part of the loop that remains but also any future iterations that may be left.*

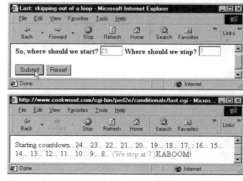

Figure 11.36 *When the inner conditional is true (*$stop *is 7), the rest of the current iteration and all future iterations of the outer loop are skipped and we go right on to KABOOM!.*

WORKING WITH ARRAYS

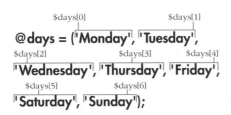

Figure 12.1 *Each element in an array is automatically numbered, starting from 0. You can use the number—together with the array name and some square brackets—to identify, use, and modify individual elements of the array as if they were independent scalar variables.*

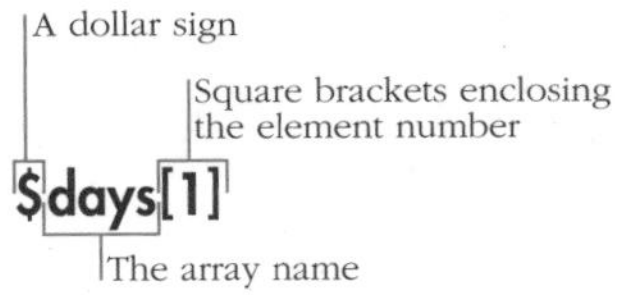

A dollar sign

Square brackets enclosing the element number

$days[1]

The array name

Figure 12.2 *You can refer to a single element from an array by prefacing the array name with the dollar sign and specifying the desired element's index within brackets. This particular expression would be equal to* Tuesday *(not* Monday*), according to the* @array *shown in Figure 12.1.*

While a scalar is an individual piece of data, an array is a *collection* of pieces of data. While scalar variables begin with a dollar sign ($), array variables begin with an at sign (@). The idea is that the *a* in *at* will remind you of the *a* in *array.*

The elements in an array are automatically numbered for easy reference **(Figure 12.1)**. For better or worse, the numbering starts with 0 and not 1. That means that the fifth element is numbered with a *4*—stay alert!

In this chapter you'll learn how to create arrays and to work with them once they're set up.

Note: Each of the example scripts on the pages that follow works in tandem with a form, created with HTML. Unfortunately, there just isn't enough room to show you the scripts, the HTML code for the form (which reveals the names of the fields), the input that our example visitor types into the fields on the form, *and* the result of the script, given that input. Since the aim of this book is to teach you Perl and CGI, I'll show you the script code and the result of the script. You'll usually be able to reconstruct what the HTML code and form looked like. And you can find the HTML—as well as Perl scripts—online at my Web site *(see page 22).*

Assigning a List to an Array Variable

In Chapter 9, *Getting Data into the Script*, you learned how to store multiple-valued data into an array variable. You can also manually input lists of constant data—like the names of the days of the week—when necessary.

To assign a list to an array variable:

1. At the beginning of the line, type **@name**, where *@name* is the label for the array.

2. Type **=** (the equals sign).

3. Type **(element1**, where *element1* is the first item in the list.

4. If desired, type **, nextelement**, where *nextelement* is the next item in the list.

5. Repeat step 4 as desired, remembering to separate each element with a comma (but see first tip).

6. Type **)** to complete the list.

7. Type **;** to finish the line.

✔ Tips

- You must enclose string elements—but *not* variables, numbers, or expressions—in quotes when using strict *(see page 30)*. Make sure you put the separating commas *outside* the quotes! An equivalent but faster technique for single-word data is to precede the parentheses with qw. Then you don't need to use quotes or commas at all *(see page 31)*.

- You can use numbers, strings, scalar variables, expressions, or even arrays as elements to be assigned to the new array. And you may use a combination of each.

```
1    #!/usr/local/bin/perl -wT
2    use strict;
3
4    my @days = qw(Monday Tuesday Wednesday
         Thursday Friday Saturday Sunday);
5
6    print "Content-type: text/html\n\n";
7    print "These are the days of the week:
         @days";
```

5: I have used qw to quote the individual days of the week. That way, I don't have to type commas between each one. Then I assign the entire list to the @days array variable (which I declare with my at the same time.)

Figure 12.3 *Once you've input an array (line 6) you can manipulate it or combine it with visitor input. Here we stick to just printing it out.*

Figure 12.4 *Notice that the members of the array are printed in precisely the same order as they were input, with a space separating each one. We'll get to fancier ways of outputting arrays very shortly, don't worry.*

```
1   #!/usr/local/bin/perl -wT
2   use strict;
3
4   my @time = localtime;
5
6   print "Content-type: text/html\n\n";
7   print "Right now, the elements of the
        time are: @time";
```

4:   This time I assign the list created by the
     `localtime` function to the `@time` array.

Figure 12.5 *The* localtime *function returns a nine-member list of time elements.*

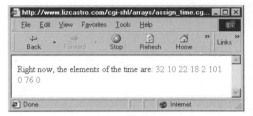

Figure 12.6 *I ran this script shortly after ten in the evening (32 seconds, 10 minutes, 22 hours), on the 18th (day 18) of March (month 2), in 2001 (101), which was a Sunday (day 0), the 76th day of the year. And no, daylight savings time wasn't in effect (0).*

One specific application of assigning lists to array variables is with the `localtime` function. The `localtime` function consults the server and then returns a nine-element list comprised of the current time's seconds, minutes, hours, day of the month, month, year, day of the week, day of the year, and whether it's daylight savings time—in that order. You can assign this list to an array variable.

To assign a list of time and date elements to an array variable:

1. Type **@time**, where *time* is the name of the array that will contain the list generated by the `localtime` function.

2. Type **=**.

3. Type **localtime** to have Perl consult the server for the current, local time.

4. Type **;** to complete the line.

✔ Tips

■ If you're going to need all or most of the time and date pieces, you can assign the `localtime` function directly to more easily identifiable, individual scalar variables. To wit: **($sec,$min,$hour,$mday,$mon, $year,$wday,$yday,$isdst) = localtime;**.

■ If you prefer, you can use `gmtime` instead of `localtime`. In that case, the time will reflect Greenwich Mean Time.

■ The month and weekday elements range from 0 to 11 and 0 to 6, respectively, that is, 2, refers to March, not February. The day of the year also starts at 0. The year is the number of years since 1900.

■ The `localtime` function is not at all crucial for learning about arrays. However, not only does it not have a better, more logical place in this book, it will also help us with several of our array examples.

Assigning a List to an Array Variable

Referring to a Particular Item in an Array

The elements in an array are automatically numbered, starting with 0 (not 1!). You use the numbers, often called an *array index*, to grab and use a particular item in the array.

To get a particular item from an array:

1. Type **$array_name**, where *array_name* is the name of the array that contains the desired element.

2. Type **[n]**, where *n* is the array index of the desired item in the array (the leftmost item is 0, the next item is 1, and so on).

✔ Tips

- Note that when you access an individual member of an array, you use a dollar sign ($) and not an at sign (@). It makes sense when you think of scalars ($) as individual pieces of data and arrays (@) as lists of pieces of data.

- You don't need to declare those individual variables (like $days[0]). When you declare the array with my @days, the individual elements are covered.

- Use a negative value for *n* to get items starting from the end of the list. (The rightmost or last item is numbered -1, the second to last item is -2, and so on.)

- To copy an item from an array to a scalar variable, use $scalar = $array[n].

- You can use a scalar variable for *n*, as in $array[$index];. You can also use expressions, as in $array[$index-1];

- To get more than one item at a time from an array, consult *Referring to Multiple Items from an Array* on page 144.

```
1   #!/usr/local/bin/perl -wT
2   use strict;
3   use CGI ':standard';
4   my (@days, $daynumber, @ordinals);
5
6   $daynumber=param('daynumber');
7
8   @days = qw(Monday Tuesday Wednesday
        Thursday Friday Saturday Sunday);
9   @ordinals = qw(first second third fourth
        fifth sixth seventh);
10
11  print "Content-type: text/html\n\n";
12  print "The $ordinals[0] day of the week,
        in the US at least, is always
        $days[0].";
13  print "<P>You chose $days[$daynumber],
        the $ordinals[$daynumber] day of the
        week.";
```

8: This line assigns the list of days of the week to the array @days. For more on qw, see page 31.
9: Here I assign a list of ordinal numbers to the @ordinals array.
12: In this print statement, I always use the first element of each array: $ordinals[0] and $days[0].
13: In this more interesting example, I'll use the number of the form element that the visitor chooses to determine the item in the array that gets printed, both from the @ordinals and the @days arrays.

Figure 12.7 *Notice that when you access an individual member of the array, you use the dollar sign ($), not the at sign (@).*

Figure 12.8 *In the first sentence, the first item in each array is always used. In the second sentence, the item displayed depends on the choice made by the visitor.*

```
1   #!/usr/local/bin/perl -wT
2   use strict;
3   use CGI ':standard';
4   my (@time,@days,@months,@catdays,
      @catmonths);
5
6   @time = localtime;
7
8   @days = qw(Sunday Monday Tuesday
      Wednesday Thursday Friday Saturday);
9   @months = qw(January February March
      April May June July August September
      October November December);
10
11  @catdays = qw(diumenge dilluns dimarts
      dimecres dijous divendres dissabte);
12  @catmonths = qw(Gener Febrer Mar&#231;
      Abril Maig Juny Juliol Agost Setembre
      Octubre Novembre Desembre);
13
14  print "Content-type: text/html\n\n";
15  print "Today is $days[$time[6]],
      $months[$time[4]] $time[3].";
16  print "<P>In Catalonia, they'd say: Avui
      &eacute\;s $catdays[$time[6]],
      $time[3] de $catmonths[$time[4]].";
```

6: The localtime function gets the date from the system and converts it into nine pieces, which this line assigns to the @time array variable.

8: Lines 8–12 store initial values (days and months in both English and Catalan) in arrays.

15: This line uses the items numbered 6, 4, and 3 in the @time array to get the proper weekday, month, and day of the month, respectively, from the @days and @months arrays.

16: This line uses the same items from the @time array to access the Catalan arrays.

Figure 12.9 *The weekday and month name items in the* @time *array have values from 0–6 and 0–11, respectively. They work perfectly with the array element numbering system but may confuse you if you have trouble thinking of say, 2, as March (and* not *February).*

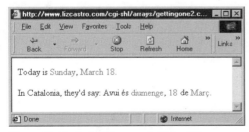

Figure 12.10 *So, in this example,* $time[6] *was equal to 0, and thus* $days[$time[6]] *is the same as* $days[0], *which gives us the first element in the* @days *array, which is* Sunday. *Similarly,* $catdays[$time[6]] *gets* diumenge.

- Copy the first element in an array to a scalar by placing the scalar in parentheses: ($variable) = @array. Copy the first two elements in an array to scalars by placing both scalars in parentheses: ($variable1, $variable2) = @array. And so on. Similarly, you can assign the first two elements to scalars and the remaining elements to another array using ($var1, $var2, @newarray) = @array. Note, however that arrays in the left expression are greedy; they will grab up as many elements of the array as they can. Something like (@newarray, $var1) = @array assigns the entire @array to @newarray and leaves nothing for the $var1 variable, which ends up undefined.

- If you use $variable = @array, the scalar variable is assigned the *length* of the array (i.e., the number of elements it has). Also see *Finding the Length of an Array* on page 152.

- You can use $#array to find out the index number of the last element in the array.

- For a quick way to get the last or first item in an array, consult page 148 and page 149, respectively.

- Getting an item from an array does not necessarily affect the array itself. It depends on what you do with it. If you simply print it out or assign it to a scalar variable, the item and the array remain unchanged. However, if you operate on the item and change its value, the array is also changed. For more details, consult *Adding or Replacing an Item in an Array* on page 145.

Referring to a Particular Item in an Array

Referring to Multiple Items from an Array

You can extract more than one item at a time from an array. This is called taking a *slice*. You can assign the slice to an array or use it in some other expression.

To get multiple items from an array:

1. Type **@array**, where *array* is the name of the array that contains the desired items.

2. Type **[n**, where *n* is the number of the desired item in the array (the leftmost item is 0, the next item is 1, etc.).

3. Type **, m**, where *m* is the number of the next desired item in the array.

4. If desired, repeat step 3 as many times as necessary, remembering to separate each array index with a comma.

5. Type **]**.

✔ Tips

■ If you want to assign the resulting items to another array, use @resulting_items = @array[n, m];. It wouldn't make sense to assign more than one item to a scalar variable; you have to assign a slice to another array.

■ As shown in the example, it's perfectly fine to use an array for *n* and *m*, as in @array[@otherarray]. You can also use scalar variables, as in @array [$index_n, $index_m]; or expressions, as in @array[$index_n, $index_n + 1];.

■ If you know how many pieces are in the slice, you can assign them to individual scalars as in ($var1, $var2) = @array[n,m];.

```
1   #!/usr/local/bin/perl -wT
2   use strict;
3   use CGI ':standard';
4   my (@days, @choice);
5
6   @days = qw(Monday Tuesday Wednesday
        Thursday Friday Saturday Sunday);
7
8   @choice = param('choice');
9
10  print "Content-type: text/html\n\n";
11
12  print "You chose @days[@choice]";
```

6: The @days array is set to the English days of the week.

8: The @choice array contains the choices the visitor has entered in the form.

12: Since the fields' values are numbers, they can be easily used here to access the @days array.

Figure 12.11 *We use the @choice array, set by the visitor, to determine which elements of the @days array should be printed.*

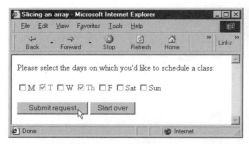

Figure 12.12 *The value of these checkboxes is not their name but rather their number. Monday is 0, Tuesday is 1, and so on, to match the @days array.*

Figure 12.13 *In this example, the script grabs the elements numbered 1 and 3 (corresponding to the values of the T and Th boxes checked) in the @days array and prints them out. (We'll get to prettier ways to print out arrays very shortly. I promise.)*

```
1   #!/usr/local/bin/perl -wT
2   use strict;
3   use CGI ':standard';
4   my (@classes, $newclass, $ID);
5
6   @classes = ('Latin 305', 'Advanced Greek
       Grammar', 'Applied Linguistics',
       'Virgil and the Iliad');
7   $newclass = param('newclass');
8   $ID = param('ID');
9
10  print "Content-type: text/html\n\n";
11  print "<B>You replaced $classes[$ID]
       with $newclass. ";
12
13  $classes[$ID] = $newclass;
14
15  print "Your complete list is
       now:</B><UL>";
16  foreach (@classes) {
17      print "<LI>$_";
18  }
19  print "</UL>";
```

6:   I store the class names in the @classes array.
7:   The name of the new class is received from the visitor and stored in $newclass.
8:   The number of the class to be removed is received and stored in $ID.
11: Before replacing the element in the array, this line takes advantage of the old information to tell the visitor what they're getting rid of.
13: The value of $ID determines which element of the @classes array is substituted with the value of $newclass.
16: The foreach loop goes through each item in the @classes array (assigning each one to the default variable, $_, since I haven't specified one), and then prints each item out, preceded by the LI HTML tag, thereby creating a pretty list.

Figure 12.14 *Identifying an item in an array by its element number is the easiest way to replace it with an updated element.*

Figure 12.15 *Notice that the first time I reference $classes[$ID] (in line 11), the old value is printed. The second time, after the value has been changed in line 13, the new value is printed out (line 17).*

Adding or Replacing an Item in an Array

You can use the fact that array items are numbered to add or replace a particular item in an array.

To add or replace an item in an array:

1. Type **$array**, where *array* is the name of the array that will contain the new item. (Notice that you use a dollar sign and not an at sign.)

2. Type **[n]**, where *n* indicates the position of the new item or the item to be replaced (the leftmost item is 0, the next item is 1, etc.).

3. Type **=** (the equals sign).

4. Type **scalar**, where *scalar* is either a scalar variable or a scalar constant.

5. Type **;** to finish the line.

✔ Tips

■ If you assign a value to a position higher than the next available empty position, the intermediate positions will be undefined. For example, if you added the line $classes[5]='Calculus 241' after line 13, the value of $classes[4] would be undef.

■ For information about replacing several items in an array, see page 150. You can get information about operating on (and thus modifying) all the elements in the array at once on page 153.

Adding or Replacing an Item in an Array

Adding to the End or Beginning of an Array

Perl has two special functions for adding items to the end or beginning of an array.

To add one or more items to the end of an array:

1. Type **push(@array**, where *@array* is the name of the array to which you want to add items.

2. Type **, newelement**, where *newelement* is a scalar constant, a scalar variable, or an array whose elements you wish to add to the end of the array mentioned in step 1.

3. Repeat step 2 as desired for each item you wish to add, using a comma to separate each new item from the previous one.

4. Type **)**.

5. Type **;** to finish the line. The array now contains its original contents followed by the new elements **(Figure 12.16)**.

To add one or more items to the beginning of an array:

1. Type **unshift(@array**, where *@array* is the array to which you want to add items.

2. Type **, newelement**, where *newelement* is a scalar constant, a scalar variable, or an array whose elements you wish to add to the beginning of the array mentioned in step 1.

3. Repeat step 2 as desired for each item you wish to add, using a comma to separate each new item from the previous one.

4. Type **)**.

5. Type **;** to finish the line. The array now contains the new elements followed by its original contents **(Figure 12.19)**.

```
1   #!/usr/local/bin/perl -wT
2   use strict;
3   use CGI ':standard';
4   my (@classes, $newclass);
5
6   @classes = ('Latin 305', 'Advanced Greek
        Grammar');
7   $newclass = param('newclass');
8
9   push(@classes, $newclass);
10
11  print "Content-type: text/html\n\n";
12
13  print "<H2>You added $newclass. Your
        complete list is now:</H2><UL>";
14
15  foreach (@classes) {
16      print "<LI>$_";
17  }
18  print "</UL>";
```

6: For simplicity, I've manually created the array here *(see page 140)*. It would usually come from visitor input.

7: The $newclass variable gets data from the visitor with the param function, as usual.

9: The push function adds the value of $newclass to the end of the @classes array.

Figure 12.16 *You don't need to assign the result of the* push *function to another array. The array specified in the first argument is itself permanently modified.*

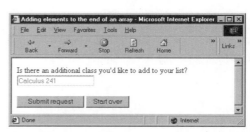

Figure 12.17 *Again, the visitor types the name of the new class and submits the data.*

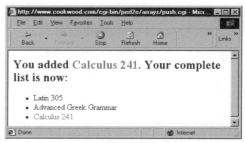

Figure 12.18 *The* push *function adds the new value to the* end *of the array (cf. Figure 12.21).*

```
1  #!/usr/local/bin/perl -wT
2  use strict;
3  use CGI ':standard';
4  my (@classes, $newclass);
5
6  @classes = ('Latin 305', 'Advanced Greek
     Grammar');
7  $newclass = param('newclass');
8
9  unshift(@classes, $newclass);
10
11 print "Content-type: text/html\n\n";
12 print "<H2>You added $newclass. Your
     complete list is now:</H2><UL>";
13
14 foreach (@classes) {
15     print "<LI>$_";
16 }
17 print "</UL>";
```

6: For simplicity, I've manually created the array
    here *(see page 140)*. It would usually come from
    visitor input.
7: The $newclass variable gets data from the visitor.
9: The unshift function adds the value of $new-
    class to the beginning of the @classes array.

Figure 12.19 *You don't need to assign the result of the* unshift *function to another array. The array specified in the first argument is itself permanently modified.*

Figure 12.20 *The visitor adds the new class which will be stored in the* $newclass *variable.*

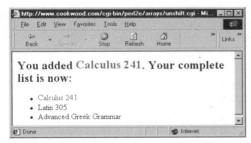

Figure 12.21 *If you use* unshift *to add an element to an array, the new element appears at the beginning of the array (cf. Figure 12.18).*

✔ Tips

■ You don't need to assign the result of the unshift or push functions to another array. The array that they operate on is itself permanently modified.

■ As always, separate each item in the array with a comma. String constants should be quoted *(see pages 30–31)*.

■ Use push or unshift when you want to combine two arrays: push(@array1, @array2);. Note that while @array1 now contains both its former elements and the ones from @array2, @array2 itself remains unchanged.

■ You can also add items to the beginning of an array using assignment: @array = (newelements, @array); or @array = (@array, newelements);, but it's slower.

■ The result of the push and unshift functions is always another array. If you like, you can assign that result to a scalar to get the length of the new array. For more details, consult *Finding the Length of an Array* on page 152.

■ It doesn't make much sense to add a hash to an array because the order of the pairs in a hash is arbitrary, and thus there is no way to control the order of the resulting items.

■ For details on adding elements to specific positions in the array, consult *Adding or Replacing an Item in an Array* on page 145 and consult *Replacing More Than One Item in an Array* on page 150.

Adding to the End or Beginning of an Array

Removing the Last Item from an Array

You can eliminate individual items from the end of an array using the pop function.

To remove the last item in an array:

1. Type **pop(@array)**, where *@array* is the name of the array from which you wish to remove the last item.

2. Type **;** to finish the line.

When you remove an item from an array, by default it disappears into the cyberether. If you're interested in using the removed item for another operation, you'll have to save it to a scalar variable.

To remove an item from the end of an array *and* store it in a scalar variable:

1. Type **$scalar**, where *scalar* is the name of the variable where you will store the element from the array.

2. Type **=**.

3. Type **pop(@array)**, where *@array* is the name of the array from which you wish to remove the last item.

4. Type **;** to finish the line.

✔ Tip

■ Within a subroutine, if you don't specify the array that you want to pop, Perl automatically assumes you mean the @_ array, which is used to pass arguments to the subroutine. For more details, consult *Creating a Subroutine That Takes Input* on page 160.

```
1   #!/usr/local/bin/perl -wT
2   use strict;
3   use CGI ':standard';
4   my (@classes, $removed);
5
6   @classes = ('Latin 305', 'Advanced Greek
       Grammar', 'Applied Linguistics',
       'Virgil and the Iliad');
7
8   print "Content-type: text/html\n\n";
9   print "You started with:<UL>";
10  foreach (@classes) {
11      print "<LI>$_";
12      }
13      print "</UL>";
14
15  $removed = pop(@classes);
16
17  print "<BR>You removed $removed. Your
       complete list is now:<UL>";
18
19  foreach (@classes) {
20      print "<LI>$_";
21  }
22  print "</UL>";
```

6: Again, for simplicity's sake, I've created the base array manually. Hopefully, what the example lacks in usefulness, it makes up in clarity.

15: Two things are going on here. In the right-hand expression, the pop function removes the last element from the @classes array. Then the removed element is stored in the $removed variable.

Figure 12.22 *The only reason I've stored the removed element in the $removed variable is so that I can print it out later. You don't need to store the result of the pop function for the array to be changed.*

Figure 12.23 *Again, I use the $removed variable so I can give visitors more information. Notice that the element no longer forms part of the array.*

Removing the Last Item from an Array

```
1   #!/usr/local/bin/perl -wT
2   use strict;
3   use CGI ':standard';
4   my (@classes, $removed);
5
6   @classes = ('Latin 305', 'Advanced Greek
       Grammar', 'Applied Linguistics',
       'Virgil and the Iliad');
7
8   print "Content-type: text/html\n\n";
9   print "You started with:<UL>";
10  foreach (@classes) {
11      print "<LI>$_";
12      }
13      print "</UL>";
14
15  $removed = shift(@classes);
16
17  print "<br>You removed $removed. Your
       complete list is now:<UL>";
18
19  foreach (@classes) {
20      print "<LI>$_";
21  }
22  print "</UL>";
```

6: Again, for simplicity's sake, I've created the base array manually. Hopefully, what the example lacks in usefulness, it makes up in clarity.

15: Two things are going on here. In the right-hand expression, the shift function removes the first element from the @classes array. Then the removed element is stored in the $removed variable.

Figure 12.24 *The only reason I've stored the removed element in the* $removed *variable is so that I can print it out later. You don't need to store the result of the* shift *function for the array to be changed.*

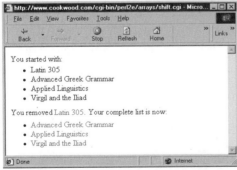

Figure 12.25 *You can print and use the removed element to give extra information to your visitor. Notice that the array no longer contains the removed element.*

Removing the First Item from an Array

You can eliminate one or more individual items from the beginning of an array using the shift function.

To remove the first item from an array:

1. Type **shift (@array)**, where *@array* is the name of the array from which you wish to remove the first item.

2. Type **;** to finish the line. The @array now contains one less item.

When you remove an item from an array, by default it disappears into the cyberether. If you're interested in using the removed item for another operation, you'll have to save it to a scalar variable.

To remove the first item in an array *and* store it in a scalar variable:

1. Type **$scalar**, where *scalar* is the name of the variable where you will store the element from the array.

2. Type **=**.

3. Type **shift (@array)**, where *@array* is the name of the array from which you wish to remove the first item.

4. Type **;** to finish the line. The @array now contains one less item.

✔ Tip

- Within a subroutine, if you don't specify the array that you want to shift, Perl automatically assumes you mean the @_ array, which is used to pass arguments to the subroutine. For more details, consult *Creating a Subroutine That Takes Input* on page 160.

Replacing More Than One Item in an Array

You can replace several items in an array simultaneously by assigning an array with the new items to a slice of the array marking the items that need to be replaced.

To replace more than one item in an array:

1. Type **@array**, where *array* is the name of the array that contains the items to be replaced.

2. Type **[**.

3. Type **n, m**, where *n* and *m* (and any others) are the index numbers of the desired items in the array (the leftmost item is 0, the next item is 1, etc.). The numbers should be separated with commas.

   Or type **@numbers**, where *numbers* is the name of the array that contains the index numbers that identify the desired items in the array referenced in step 1.

4. Type **]**.

5. Type **=**.

6. Type **(scalar_n, scalar_m)**, where *scalar_n* is the new value for the item numbered *n* and *scalar_m* is the new value for the item numbered *m*. Add additional scalar items if you've referenced additional positions in the array in step 3.

   Or, type **@replacement_array**, where *replacement_array* is the name of the array that contains the items you wish to substitute for the ones referenced in step 3.

7. Type **;** to finish the line.

```perl
#!/usr/local/bin/perl -wT
use strict;
use CGI ':standard';
my (@classes, @newclasses, @IDs,
   @added);

@classes = ('Latin 305', 'Advanced Greek
   Grammar', 'Applied Linguistics',
   'Virgil and the Iliad');
@newclasses = param('newclass');
@IDs = param('ID');

print "Content-type: text/html\n\n";
print "<P><B>You replaced: </B>";

foreach (@IDs) {
    print "<LI>$classes[$_]";
}

print "<P><B>with:</B> ";
foreach (@newclasses) {
    if ($_ ne "") {
        print "<LI>$_";
        @added = (@added, $_);
    }
}

@classes[@IDs] = @added;

print "<H2>Your complete list is
   now:</H2><UL>";
foreach (@classes) {
    print "<LI>$_";
}
print "</UL>";
```

7: Lines 7 and 8 receive and store input from the visitor about which classes should be removed and which classes should be their replacements.
13: Lines 13–15 contain a foreach loop that prints out the classes that should be removed. Note that since I don't specify the scalar that will hold each array element, Perl uses the default variable ($_) for that purpose. I can then operate on the $_ variable. It's a nice typing shortcut.
17: Lines 17–23. The foreach loop goes through each element in @newclasses, finds the non-empty ones, and then prints them and adds them to a new @added array.
22: Notice that each block needs its own closing curly bracket (lines 22 and 23).
25: This is the line that actually substitutes the chosen old classes and replaces them with the new ones. Notice I've used the @IDs array, which contains the index numbers, to identify the desired elements in @classes.
28: Now that the @classes array contains the updated list, we can use a foreach loop to print out each element.

Figure 12.26 *The ability to replace particular elements of an array with elements from another array makes arrays versatile and very powerful.*

```
<tr><td align=left><INPUT TYPE=checkbox
NAME=ID VALUE="0">Latin
305</td><td><INPUT TYPE="text"
NAME="newclass" SIZE=30></td></tr>
<tr><td align=left><INPUT TYPE=checkbox
NAME=ID VALUE="1">Advanced Greek
Grammar</td><td><INPUT TYPE="text"
NAME="newclass" SIZE=30></td></tr>
```

Figure 12.27 *An excerpt from the HTML file used to create the form shows the set of checkboxes are named* ID *while each text field is named* newclass. *These names are used to identify the incoming data in lines 8 and 7 respectively of Figure 12.26 on page 150.*

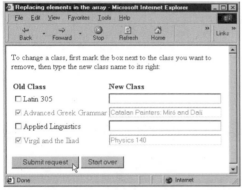

Figure 12.28 *By checking the box next to the old course, the* ID *is set to remove that item (and accept a new one). Typing in the new course creates the replacement element in the* @newclasses *array.*

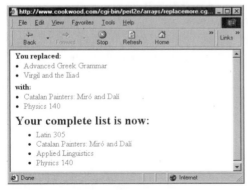

Figure 12.29 *The chosen old classes are replaced with the new ones. Printing out each stage of the script not only gives your visitor information but is also a good debugging tool (see page 284).*

✔ Tips

■ If you already know what elements you want to replace, your example will be a lot simpler than this one (line 25 contains the crucial code). I wanted to give the visitor the ability to *choose* which items to replace.

■ In this example, two items are replaced with an array that contains two items. If the replacement array contains more items than the items marked by the slice, the extra items are ignored. If there are more items to be replaced than there are replacement items, the original items are removed and the unmatched items are left undefined.

■ You can replace a slice of one array with a slice of another. Use @array[m,n] = @otherarray[x,y].

Replacing More Than One Item in an Array

Finding the Length of an Array

Once you or your visitor have entered an array, it's often useful to know how many elements the array contains. There are several ways to get the length of an array.

To store the length of an array in a scalar variable:

1. Type **$scalar**, where *scalar* is the name of the variable that will contain the length of the array.

2. Type **=** (the equals sign).

3. Type **@array**, where *array* is the name of the array whose length you want.

To get the length of an array another way:

1. Type **scalar**. (That's *not* a variable. You really have to type the word "scalar".)

2. Type **(@array)**, where array is the name of the array whose length you're interested in. The result of this expression is the length of the array.

An array name prefaced with $# returns the index number of the last item in the array *(see tip on page 143)*. You can add 1 to this to get the number of elements in the array.

To use the index number to get the length of an array:

Type **$#array + 1**. The result of the expression is the number of elements (or length) of the array.

✔ Tip

■ If you assign the array to another array (e.g., @array = @otherarray), instead of the length, you'll assign the *contents* of the right array to the left one.

```
1    #!/usr/local/bin/perl -wT
2    use strict;
3    use CGI ':standard';
4    my (@classes, $amount);
5
6    @classes = param('class');
7    $amount = @classes;
8
9    print "Content-type: text/html\n\n";
10
11   print "<P><B>You chose $amount classes.
        They are:</B><UL>";
12
13   foreach (@classes) {
14   print "<LI>$_";
15   }
16
17   print "</UL>";
```

7:   This line stores the length of the @classes array in the $amount variable.

11: This print statement uses the $amount variable to display how many classes the visitor has chosen (that is, how many elements are in the @classes array).

Figure 12.30 *The easiest way to get the length of an array is to assign the array to a scalar variable.*

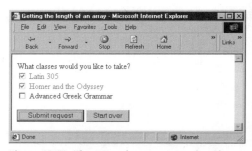

Figure 12.31 *The visitor chooses any number of classes...*

Figure 12.32 *...and by counting the elements in the newly created array, you can determine how many classes they chose.*

```
1   #!/usr/local/bin/perl -wT
2   use strict;
3   use CGI ':standard';
4   my (@classes, $case, $class);
5
6   @classes = ('Latin 305', 'Advanced Greek
       Grammar', 'Applied Linguistics',
       'Virgil and the Iliad');
7
8   $case= param('case');
9
10  print "Content-type: text/html\n\n";
11
12  if ($case eq 'upper') {
13      foreach $class (@classes) {
14          $class = uc($class);
15      }
16  } else {
17      foreach (@classes) {
18          $_ = lc;
19      }
20  }
21  print "<P>Here are your classes, in
       $case case:<UL>";
22
23  foreach (@classes) {
24      print "<LI>$_";
25  }
26
27  print "</UL>";
```

13: Lines 13–15. The foreach loop uses the $class variable to represent each member of the @classes array, as usual.

14: Operating on the $class element permanently changes the item in the @classes array itself.

17: Lines 17–19. Notice that this foreach loop works exactly the same way as the one in lines 13–15, but instead of the $class variable, we use the default variable $_ (which both the foreach loop and the lc (or uc) function will use, if none other is given). I could have written lines 13–15 this way as well, but I wanted it to be crystal clear what was happening.

Figure 12.33 *You can find more information about the* uc *and* lc *functions in Chapter 17.*

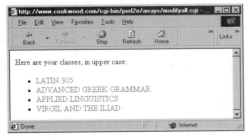

Figure 12.34 *The resulting array is permanently changed.*

Modifying All the Members of an Array

It seems strange but if you operate on the index variable *(see page 130)* when going through an array with a foreach loop, the array itself is permanently changed. You can modify the whole array at once this way.

To modify all the members of an array:

1. Type **foreach**.

2. Type **$item**, where *item* is the name of the index variable that will act as a stand-in for each member of the array.

3. Type **(@array)**, where *array* is the name of the array that you wish to change.

4. Type **{**.

5. On the next line, create an expression that changes the value of the $item variable from step 2. Remember to end the line with a semicolon.

6. On the next line, type **}**.

✔ Tips

■ Beware of functions that seem to change a variable but don't. For example, the *result* of uc($item) is the item's contents in uppercase letters, but the *value* of the $item variable itself remains unchanged. On the other hand, $item++ results in 1 plus the value of $item, *and* the variable $item will now contain the new value. This is why lines 14 and 18 in the example in Figure 12.33 store the value of the uc and lc functions back into $class and $_, respectively. For more details, see page 29.

■ To replace one element of an array, see page 145. To replace several, but not all, of the elements, see page 150.

Modifying All the Members of an Array

Sorting Arrays

You can change an array so that the items it contains are sorted in alphabetical, or ASCII order.

To sort arrays:

1. Type **sort** to sort in ASCII order.

   Or type **sort {$b cmp $a}**, to sort in reverse ASCII order.

   Or type **sort {$a <=> $b}**, to sort numerically in ascending order.

   Or type **sort {$b <=> $a}** to sort numerically in descending order.

2. Type **@array**, where *array* is the name of the array that contains the items that you wish to put in order.

✔ Tips

■ The sort function doesn't affect the array itself. If you want to save the results of the sorting action, you'll have to assign the result to an array (the same one or a different one) with @array = sort @array;.

■ Another way to take advantage of the sort function is to use it in a larger expression, as in print sort @array;. In this case, the array will be printed in ASCII order, but the original positions of the items will be maintained.

■ The ASCII order for numbers is not the same as going from lowest to highest numerically. For example, the numbers 1, 2, 3, 10, 12, 20, 35 are in ascending numerical order. The basic sort function would arrange them according to their ASCII values: 1, 10, 12, 2, 20, 35.

```
1   #!/usr/local/bin/perl -wT
2   use strict;
3   use CGI ':standard';
4
5   my @classes = param('class');
6
7   print "Content-type: text/html\n\n";
8
9   print "<H2>You chose:</H2><UL>";
10
11  @classes = sort @classes;
12
13  foreach (@classes) {
14      print "<LI>$_";
15  }
16
17  print "</UL>";
```

11: This line rearranges the elements of the @classes array in alphabetical (ASCII) order, and then stores the result back into the @classes array.

Figure 12.35 *The* sort *function puts items in ASCII order by default.*

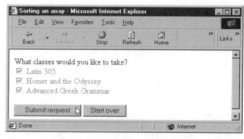

Figure 12.36 *The visitor chooses the classes they want to take. (Note that the contents of the* VALUE *attribute for each of the checkboxes is the actual class name, not a code number, as was the case in Figure 12.27 on page 151.)*

Figure 12.37 *The script confirms the choices in alphabetical order.*

```
1  #!/usr/local/bin/perl -wT
2  use strict;
3  use CGI ':standard';
4
5  my @classes = param('class');
6
7  print "Content-type: text/html\n\n";
8
9  print "<H2>You chose:</H2><UL>";
10
11 @classes = sort @classes;
12 @classes = reverse (@classes);
13
14 foreach (@classes) {
15     print "<LI>$_";
16 }
17
18 print "</UL>";
```

11: This line rearranges the elements of the
    @classes array in ASCII order, and then stores
    the result back in the @classes array.

12: This line reverses the order of the elements in
    the @classes array (now they'll be in descend-
    ing alphabetical order), and stores the result
    back in the @classes array.

Figure 12.38 *Store the result of the* reverse *function
somewhere if you want to use it later in your script.*

Figure 12.39 *Again, the visitor chooses which
classes to take.*

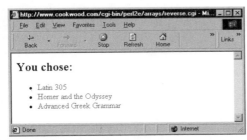

Figure 12.40 *This time the confirmation shows the
classes in reverse alphabetical order (cf Figure 12.37
on page 154).*

Reversing the Order of an Array's Contents

You can completely reverse the order of the
items in an array, putting the last item first,
the second to last item second, and so on.

To reverse the order of the items in an array:

1. Type **reverse**.

2. Type **(@array)**, where *array* is the name
   of the array whose items you want to
   reverse the order of.

✔ Tips

■ The reverse function doesn't affect the
  array itself. If you want to save the results
  of the reversing action, you'll have to
  assign the result to an array (the same
  one or a different one) with @array =
  reverse (@array);.

■ Another way to take advantage of the
  reverse function is to use it in a larger
  expression: print reverse (@array);.
  In this case, the array will be printed in
  reverse order, but the original positions
  of the items will be maintained.

■ You can use the reverse function
  together with sort *(see page 154)* to
  reverse the chosen sort order, as in
  $classes = reverse (sort @classes);.

SUBROUTINES

Subroutine is one of those words that I think sounds so completely technical and uninviting. Just the same, subroutines are extremely useful time-saving devices that you'll want to use throughout your script.

A subroutine is like a mini-program inside your script that completes a certain, specific function that you might have to perform several times. You'll probably want to feed it different parameters (that is, *arguments*) each time you use it. Saving the process in a subroutine lets you perform the entire process as many times as needed without having to type it over each time.

Typical subroutines for CGI Perl scripts do common tasks such as parsing forms and printing out HTML headers and footers.

Note: Because a subroutine is enclosed in a separate block from the rest of your program —and thus has a different scope—private variables declared in a subroutine will not work outside of the subroutine in the rest of the script. It's not a bad thing, but you should be aware of it. For more information about scope, consult *Statements, Blocks, and Scope* on page 32.

Creating a Simple Subroutine

A subroutine is just a block of statements that will be executed when the subroutine is called. For example, you could create a subroutine that prints out the content line that tells your visitor's browser to expect a Web page *(see page 38)*. Then, whenever you want to create Web output, you can call the subroutine to print that line.

To create a subroutine:

1. Type **sub**. The sub function defines the subroutine.

2. Type **name**, where *name* identifies the subroutine for later use.

3. Type **{**.

4. Now press Return, and on the next line, indented, type the statement(s) that should be executed when the subroutine is called. Remember to end each statement with a semicolon.

5. Type **}**.

✔ Tips

■ Although it seems like you should have to place a subroutine *before* the line that uses it, you don't. It doesn't really matter where in your script you put a subroutine, or in which order you put multiple subroutines. The convention is to leave them until the very end, or to store them in a separate file altogether *(see page 164)*.

■ The convention is to use all lowercase letters (and an underscore if desired) for subroutine names.

■ Since the idea of a subroutine is to save you time, you might as well invent names that are short and sweet.

```
1   #!/usr/local/bin/perl -wT
2   use strict;
3
4   sub mime {
5       print "Content-type:
    text/html\n\n";
6   }
```

4: The sub function creates a subroutine called mime and gets ready to define it with the statements listed after the opening curly bracket.

5: This is a simple print statement. When the subroutine is invoked, the program will print "Content-type: text/html" followed by two line breaks, which is precisely the initial information that is required when sending a Web page to a browser.

6: The closing curly bracket completes the definition of the mime subroutine.

Figure 13.1 *By putting a common task like printing out the MIME content line in a subroutine, you save typing time and minimize the possibility of typographical errors. As long as you've created the subroutine properly this time, it will always work correctly in the future. Whereas, if you type this line a zillion times, you're apt to make a mistake at some point.*

```
1   #!/usr/local/bin/perl -wT
2   use strict;
3
4   mime();
5   print "<HTML><HEAD><TITLE>A new
      page</TITLE></HEAD><BODY>\n";
6   print "This page wholly created with CGI
      and Perl!";
7   print "</BODY></HTML>";
8
9   sub mime {
10    print "Content-type: text/html\n\n";
11  }
```

4:   This line calls (executes) the `mime` subroutine. Therefore, the line *Content-type: text/html* will be sent to the browser followed by two new-lines (line 10).

5:   This is a simple `print` statement that prints the header portion of the Web page.

6:   Here is another simple `print` statement that prints out the content of the Web page, in this case a fairly inane sentence: *This page wholly created with CGI and Perl!*.

7:   The final `print` statement outputs the end of the HTML page code.

Figure 13.2 *Typically a subroutine is defined at the end of the script, but its location doesn't really matter.*

Figure 13.3 *By using a subroutine to create the MIME content line, you can be sure that you haven't made any typographical errors.*

Using a Simple Subroutine

Some subroutines are relatively independent and require no additional information before being processed. For example, the subroutine created in Figure 13.1 on page 158 doesn't require any input (officially called *arguments*).

To use a simple subroutine (with no arguments):

1. Type **name()**, where *name* is the label for the subroutine that you defined in step 2 on page 158 and the parentheses are empty.

2. Type **;** to complete the line.

✔ Tips

- Sometimes you'll see programmers call a subroutine with &name. That's fine too.

- CGI.pm has a built-in shortcut for outputting header information. You can find more information in CGI.pm's documentation: *http://stein.csbl.org/WWW/software/CGI/*.

Creating a Subroutine That Takes Input

Usually you'll want to apply the subroutine to some piece of data. For example, imagine that you want to create a subroutine that prints out the first part of an HTML page, but you want to be able to tell it what the title of the page should be. You can pass the title to the subroutine, have the subroutine insert the title, and then print it out with the rest of the HTML page. (Each piece of data passed to the subroutine is called an *argument*.)

Subroutines transfer all the data that is passed to them into the special underscore array, written as @_. You can then use each individual element of this array in your subroutine and perform operations on them as desired.

Remember that the elements of the @_ array are $_[0], $_[1], and so on (but not $_). For more information on accessing individual elements of an array, consult *Referring to a Particular Item in an Array* on page 142.

To create a subroutine that takes input:

1. Create the subroutine *(see page 158).*

2. In the statements, use $_[0] to refer to the first argument passed to the subroutine, $_[1] to refer to the second argument passed to the subroutine, and so on.

✔ Tips

- Both push and shift work on the @_ array in a subroutine if no other array is specified. It's not uncommon to see a line like my $scalar=shift; at the beginning of a subroutine to assign the first argument passed to the subroutine to a scalar variable (and remove it from @_).

- You might also use my ($arg1, $arg2, $arg3) = @_; to pass the contents of @_ to individual (declared) scalar variables.

```perl
1   #!/usr/local/bin/perl -wT
2   use strict;
3   use CGI ':standard';
4   my ($title)=param('title');
5
6   mime();
7   heading($title);
8
9   print 'This is more of that page wholly
        created by CGI and Perl!';
10
11  footer();
12
13  sub heading {
14    print '<HTML><HEAD><TITLE>';
15    print "$_[0]";
16    print '</TITLE></HEAD><BODY>';
17  }
18
19  sub footer {
20    print '</BODY></HTML>';
21  }
22
23  sub mime {
24    print "Content-type: text/html\n\n";
25  }
```

13: The sub function names the subroutine. This one is called heading.
14: This line prints the opening HTML tags.
15: The variable $_[0] will get its value from the argument passed to the subroutine. Therefore, whatever argument is used will be printed here.
16: This line prints the closing TITLE tag, the closing HEAD tag, and then the opening BODY tag—basically everything you need to complete the header.

Figure 13.4 *Using a subroutine to complete common tasks can save you lots of time.*

```
1   #!/usr/local/bin/perl -wT
2   use strict;
3   use CGI ':standard';
4   my ($title)=param('title');
5
6   mime();
7   heading($title);
8
9   print 'This is more of that page wholly
      created by CGI and Perl!';
10
11  footer();
12
13  sub heading {
14    print '<HTML><HEAD><TITLE>';
15    print "$_[0]";
16    print '</TITLE></HEAD><BODY>';
17  }
18
19  sub footer {
20    print '</BODY></HTML>';
21  }
22
23  sub mime {
24    print "Content-type: text/html\n\n";
25  }
```

6: This is the same subroutine that we saw in Figure 13.2.

7: This line calls the `heading` subroutine and passes it the title chosen by the visitor (`$title`).

13: The `heading` subroutine is defined on lines 13–17. For more details, see Figure 13.4.

15: The variable `$_[0]` gets its value from the argument passed to the subroutine (in line 7).

Figure 13.5 *If the subroutine has only one argument as in this example, you access it with* `$_[0]`.

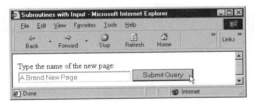

Figure 13.6 *The visitor enters the desired title.*

Figure 13.7 *And then the script uses the visitor's entry as input for the heading subroutine.*

Calling a Subroutine That Takes Input

Once you have set up a subroutine to process the arguments *(see page 160)*, you're ready to pass the actual data to the subroutine.

To call a subroutine that takes input:

1. Type **name**, where *name* identifies the subroutine.

2. Type **(**.

3. Type **argument**, where *argument* is the array or scalar that you want to process with the subroutine.

4. Repeat step 3 for each argument you want to process, separating each one with a comma.

5. Type **)**.

6. Type **;** to complete the line.

✔ Tips

- As usual, the arguments must be enclosed in quotes if they are strings. For more on quoting, see page 30.

- *Argument* is just another word for the data that some function (like a subroutine) processes.

- If you use an array in step 3, its individual elements become the arguments.

- Again, CGI.pm includes a subroutine for creating headers. It's described in CGI.pm's documentation: *http://stein.cshl.org/WWW/software/CGI/*. While the example here works perfectly well, it's really only designed to teach you how to create subroutines that accept input.

Using a Subroutine's Return Value

When you call a subroutine, it generally executes all of the statements that it contains. If you're just printing an HTML header or some other static code, executing a series of statements may be all you're interested in. Like other functions, however, a subroutine not only completes one or more operations, it also has an intrinsic final value, called a *return value*, which you can store for later use *(see page 29)*. The default return value is the value of the last expression evaluated in the block.

To store a subroutine's return value:

1. Type **$scalar** or **@array**, depending on whether the subroutine will have one or more return values.

2. Type **=**.

3. Type **subroutine()** or **subroutine (argument)** to call the subroutine whose return values you want to save.

✔ Tips

■ You can also use a subroutine's value directly in an expression, as if it were a scalar or array. For example, you could use $scalar = subroutine() + 5;.

■ Make sure you know what the return value of the last expression in your subroutine is. For example, if the last statement in your subroutine block is a print statement, since the return value of a print statement is 1, the value of the subroutine will also be 1.

■ For information on setting the return value manually, see page 163.

```
1   #!/usr/local/bin/perl -wT
2   use strict;
3   use CGI ':standard';
4   my ($title, $which);
5
6   $title=param('title');
7
8   mime();
9   heading($title);
10
11  print 'This is more of that page wholly
       created by CGI and Perl!';
12
13  $which = which();
14  print "<P>You're browsing this page with
       $which";
15
16  footer();
17
18  sub which {
19    my $browser = $ENV{'HTTP_USER_AGENT'};
20    if ($browser =~ /MSIE/) {
21      $browser = 'Explorer';
22    } elsif ($browser =~/Mozilla/) {
23      $browser = 'Netscape';
24    } else {
25      $browser = 'something besides
         Netscape and Explorer';
26    }
27  }
```

13: The return value of the which subroutine is stored in the $which variable.

18: The which subroutine uses the HTTP_USER _AGENT environment variable and regular expressions *(see Chapter 15)* to see which browser the visitor is using. Depending on which condition evaluates as true, the last expression evaluated will give the name of the browser being used. The value of the last expression (for example, *'Netscape'*) becomes the return value for the subroutine. Thus, in line 13, the $which variable gets the name of the browser used.

19: I've declared the $browser variable within this subroutine; it's not used elsewhere in the script.

Figure 13.8 *You can effectively use the return value of a subroutine in other expressions.*

Figure 13.9 *The return value of the subroutine is printed, along with the descriptive statement.*

```
1  . #!/usr/local/bin/perl -wT
2    use strict;
3    use CGI ':standard';
4    my ($title, $capped_which);
5
6    $title=param('title');
7
8    mime();
9    heading($title);
10
11   print 'This is more of that page wholly
        created by CGI and Perl!';
12
13   $capped_which = cap(which());
14   print "<P>You're browsing this page with
        $capped_which";
15
16   footer();
17
18   sub cap {
19      my $captext = $_[0];
20      $captext =~ tr/a-z/A-Z/;
21      return $captext;
22   }
```

13: The cap subroutine is performed on the return value of the which subroutine. The return value of the cap subroutine is then saved in the $capped_which variable and output in line 14.

19: The argument of the cap subroutine (namely the return value of the which subroutine) is temporarily stored in $captext. Note that the $captext variable is declared within the subroutine and has no value outside of the subroutine.

20: The value of $captext is capitalized with tr (see page 227) and then stored back in $captext.

21: The new value of $captext is manually set as the return value for this subroutine. Notice that the return value for line 20 is not the capitalized text (that we want), but rather the number of characters substituted by the tr function.

23: The other subroutines are not shown, but they're still there on lines 23 and beyond!

Figure 13.10 *If the last expression evaluated has a return value different from the one you need, you'll have to set the return value manually.*

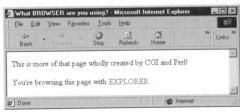

Figure 13.11 *The return value from the* which *subroutine is capitalized by the* cap *subroutine.*

Setting the Return Value Manually

There are many instances in which the last expression evaluated is not the value you're most interested in. Sometimes, for example, you just want to know whether or not the subroutine has executed successfully, or perhaps, which one of its conditional outcomes it has arrived at. You can prescribe a return value manually for the subroutine with the return function.

To set a subroutine's return value manually:

1. Create the subroutine as described on page 158 or page 160.

2. After the last statement in the subroutine, and on its own line, type **return**.

3. Then type **value**, where *value* is the desired return value for the subroutine.

4. Type **;** to end the sentence.

✔ Tips

■ The value you use in step 3 can be a scalar or array variable that you've created or calculated in the subroutine, or it can be a constant.

■ If you have a series of conditional blocks, you may need to create a return statement for each branch of the condition.

■ The return function not only passes a value for the subroutine back to the caller, it also causes the subroutine to exit, skipping all statements that follow.

■ For more details on the difference between the result of a subroutine and its return value, consult *Result vs. return value* on page 29.

Setting the Return Value Manually

Storing Subroutines in an External File

There are some subroutines that you will want to call again and again from almost every CGI script that you write. Instead of tacking such a subroutine onto the end of every script, you can save it in its own file—often called a *library*—and then call it from each script in which it's needed.

To store subroutines in an external file:

1. Create a separate text file as described on page 36. You may omit the shebang line described on page 35.

2. Create the subroutine as described on page 158 or page 160.

3. On the very last line of the file, type **1;**. When you require the subroutine *(see page 165)*, this value will return true, and Perl will know that the external file was accessed successfully.

4. Save the file as usual (in text-only format).

✔ Tips

■ Files that contain subroutines (but no main script) often carry the extension .lib (for *library*) or .pl (for *Perl library*), though it is not essential.

■ You can create one external file that contains several subroutines as shown in this example.

■ External files with subroutines do not need to be executed and therefore need neither the shebang line *(see page 35)* nor extra permissions when run on a Unix server *(see page 56)*.

```
1   sub cap {
2     my $captext = $_[0];
3     $captext =~ tr/a-z/A-Z/;
4     return $captext;
5   }
6
7   sub which {
8     my $browser = $ENV{'HTTP_USER_AGENT'};
9     if ($browser =~ /MSIE/) {
10      $browser = 'Explorer';
11    } elsif ($browser =~/Mozilla/) {
12      $browser = 'Netscape';
13    } else {
14      $browser = 'something besides
              Netscape and Explorer';
15    }
16  }
17
18  sub heading {
19    print '<HTML><HEAD><TITLE>';
20    print "$_[0]";
21    print '</TITLE></HEAD><BODY>';
22  }
23
24  sub footer {
25    print '</BODY></HTML>';
26  }
27
28  sub mime {
29    print "Content-type: text/html\n\n";
30  }
31
32  1;
```

3: Lines 1–30 contain the subroutines we've been using in this chapter. Notice that no shebang line is needed *(see page 35)*.

32: This line ensures that when the external file is called with the require function *(see page 165)*, the function will return true (1), and Perl will know that the external file has been accessed successfully.

Figure 13.12 *Don't forget to add the last line. It looks unimportant, but without it, Perl won't know the file was accessed successfully and won't let you call any of the subroutines that it contains.*

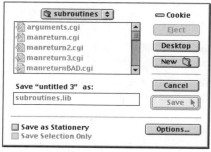

Figure 13.13 *Save the file as text-only. Often, external files with subroutines are given the .lib or .pl extensions, but it's not required.*

```
1   #!/usr/local/bin/perl -wT
2   use strict;
3   use CGI ':standard';
4   my ($title, $capped_which);
5
6   require '/home/user4/lcastro/WWW/cgi-
      bin/perl2e/subroutines/external.lib';
7
8   $title=param('title');
9
10  mime();
11  heading($title);
12
13  print 'This is more of that page wholly
       created by CGI and Perl!';
14
15  $capped_which = cap(which());
16  print "<P>You're browsing this page with
       $capped_which";
17
18  footer();
```

6: The `require` function makes the subroutine library file and the subroutines it contains accessible to this script.

10: Now when we call the `mime` subroutine, for example, Perl will look for it in this script, and if it doesn't find it, it will check the *external.lib* file (where it *will* find it). Then, the subroutine is executed as usual.

Figure 13.14 *This script is virtually identical to the one shown in Figure 13.10 on page 163. However, it's neater, and the subroutines can also be accessed from other scripts.*

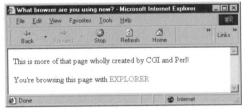

Figure 13.15 *The location of the subroutines is completely invisible to the visitor. This result is exactly the same as when the subroutines were in the main script itself (cf. Figure 13.11 on page 163).*

Calling Subroutines from an External File

Saving subroutines in an external file makes it easy to use them in your other Perl scripts without having to type them out each time. From the Perl script, you have to first make the file that contains the subroutine (often called a *library*) available, and then you call the subroutine as usual.

To call subroutines from an external file:

1. In the main script, type **require 'filename.lib'**, where *filename.lib* is the name and path of the external file that contains the desired subroutine.

2. Type **;** to complete the line.

3. Type **subroutine()** or **subroutine (arguments)** as usual to call the subroutine. For more details, consult *Using a Simple Subroutine* on page 159 or *Calling a Subroutine That Takes Input* on page 161, respectively.

✔ Tips

■ You can also use a scalar variable or an expression as the argument for the `require` function.

■ Once the main script accesses the external file with the `require` function, the subroutines in the external file remain available for the duration of the main script. In other words, you can call the subroutines in the external file as many times as you need but only need to use `require` once.

■ An external subroutine must end with the `1;` line described in step 3 on page 164. Otherwise, the `require` function will fail.

Calling Subroutines from an External File

WORKING WITH HASHES

A *hash* is little more than a special kind of array that contains pairs of associated elements—the *key* and the *value*. In fact, hashes are often called *associative arrays*. While the order of the elements within a pair is crucial (the key, *then* the value), the order of the pairs themselves is not (think of real *country hash*). Unlike array elements, values in a hash are identified by a key (and vice versa), not by an index number. Hash variables begin with a percent sign (%)—perhaps the two circles on either side of the slash suggest a pair of linked values.

Hashes are an extremely important tool. You'll probably use them in almost every Perl CGI script you write.

In this chapter, you'll learn how to assign, add, replace, and delete values in a hash, and to work with a hash's key-value pairs once the hash is set up.

Note: Each of the example scripts on the pages that follow works in tandem with a form, created with HTML. Unfortunately, there just isn't enough room to show you the scripts, the HTML code for the form (which reveals the names of the fields), the input that our example visitor types into the fields on the form, *and* the result of the script, given that input. Since the aim of this book is to teach you Perl and CGI, I'll show you the script code and the result of the script. You'll usually be able to reconstruct what the HTML code and form looked like. And you can find the HTML—as well as Perl scripts—online at my Web site *(see page 22)*.

Assigning a List to a Hash

You can assign a list of key-value pairs to a hash variable for future operations.

To assign a list of key-value pairs to a hash:

1. At the beginning of the line, type **%label**, where *label* is the name of the new hash.

2. Type **=** (the equals sign).

3. Type **(** to begin the list of key-value pairs.

4. Type **key => value** where *key* is the label for the first element and *value* is the corresponding data.

5. To add additional key-value pairs, type a comma and then repeat step 4.

6. Type **)** to complete the list.

7. Type **;** to complete the statement.

✔ Tips

- Keys are case sensitive.

- Keys must be unique and must be strings. If you use the => operator, the key only needs to be quoted if it contains spaces or non-alphanumeric characters.

- You may also separate each key from its value with a comma (**Figure 14.2**). In that case, the key must always be enclosed in quotation marks.

- You can use qw to quote the elements of a list being assigned to a hash. For more details about qw, consult *Quoting without Quotes* on page 31.

- Although you may add the pairs of keys and values in a particular order, Perl does not maintain the pairs in order. You access the values in a hash using its keys (*see page 169*), not the position of its elements.

```
1   #!/usr/local/bin/perl -wT
2   use strict;
3   use CGI ':standard';
4   my (%tiger_data);
5
6   %tiger_data = ('English name' => 'Tiger',
      'Latin name' => 'panthera tigris',
      'current population' => '4500',
      status => 'endangered');
7
8   print "Content-type: text/html\n\n";
9   foreach (keys %tiger_data) {
10    print "<P>The key is <b>$_</b> and the
        value is <b>$tiger_data{$_}</b>";
11    }
```

4: Don't forget to declare your hash variables.

6: Here we assign the list of key-value pairs to the %tiger_data hash variable. You can add extra spaces and tabs to make it look prettier, if you like. Notice that single word keys don't need quotes, as long as you're using the => operator. Keys with spaces should always be quoted.

9: This foreach loop prints out each key and value in the hash. We'll discuss it in more detail on page 175.

Figure 14.1 *The => operator helps you see which values belong to which keys.*

```
6   %tiger_data = ('English name', 'Tiger',
      'Latin name', 'panthera tigris',
      'current population', '4500',
      'status', 'endangered');
```

6: This line 6 is exactly equivalent to line 6 in Figure 14.1. It's just slightly harder to read (which ones are the keys and which are the values?) and slightly harder to type (since the keys must always be quoted).

Figure 14.2 *If you have an existing comma-separated list of key-value pairs, you can assign it to a hash without converting the separator punctuation.*

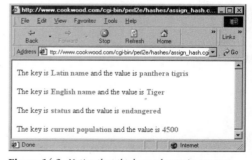

Figure 14.3 *Notice that the key-value pairs are not output in the same order in which they were assigned to the hash.*

```
1   #!/usr/local/bin/perl -wT
2   use strict;
3   use CGI ':standard';
4   my (%tiger_data, $question);
5
6   %tiger_data = ('English name' => 'Tiger',
        'Latin name' => 'panthera tigris',
        'current population' => '4500',
        status => 'endangered');
7
8   $question = param('question');
9
10  print "Content-type: text/html\n\n";
11
12  print "Their <b>$question</b> is
        <b>$tiger_data{$question}</b>";
```

8:   The visitor chooses a question by clicking a
     radio button in the HTML form. The value of that
     button is input into the script and will be the key
     that accesses the proper value in the hash.

12: The phrase $tiger_data{$question} returns
     the value from the %tiger_data hash that corre-
     sponds to the key that is stored in the $question
     variable. Note that $tiger_data{$question} is
     considered declared by line 4.

Figure 14.4 *In an array you pinpoint data by its position. In a hash, you identify what you want by
specifying a label or key.*

Figure 14.5 *The visitor chooses the key by selecting a
radio button (whose* VALUE *attribute contains the key).*

Figure 14.6 *The script uses the key to determine which
value to output. (It's true, by the way, that there are
only about 4500 tigers left in the wild.)*

Getting a Value by Using a Key

Hashes are made up of pairs of elements,
each with the key first and the value second.
You can use the key to access the corresponding value and then use that value in
a larger expression.

To get a value by using a key:

1. Type **$hash**, where *hash* is the name of
   the hash that contains the desired item.
   (Yes, that's a dollar sign—not a percent
   sign—since you're accessing *one* piece of
   data from the hash.)

2. Type **{key}**, where *key* is the label that
   corresponds to the value you want to get
   (or a scalar variable or expression that
   contains that label). And yes, those are
   curly brackets and not parentheses. It
   makes a difference.

✔ Tips

- The key only needs to be enclosed in
  quotes if it contains spaces or non-
  alphanumerics.

- Although hashes begin with a percent
  sign (%), when you want to access an
  individual item, you preface the hash
  name with a dollar sign ($). Remember:
  individual pieces of data are scalars, even
  if they come from hashes.

- Individual pieces of a hash do not,
  however, need to be declared separately
  from the hash variable itself. If you say
  my %tiger_data; the expression
  $tiger_data{key} is also covered.

- Getting a value from a hash doesn't affect
  the hash. The value (and the key) remain
  parts of the hash.

- To assign a value from a hash to a scalar
  variable, use $value = $hash{key};.

Adding or Replacing a Key-Value Pair

You can add new key-value pairs or replace existing ones by assigning the value to the key in the hash.

To add or replace a key-value pair:

1. Type **$hash**.

2. Type **{key}**, where *key* is the label that identifies the value you want to add or replace (or a scalar variable or expression that contains that label).

3. Type **=**.

4. Type **value**, where *value* is the new value that should be associated with the key in step 2.

5. Type **;** to complete the line.

✔ Tips

- Use an existing key to replace a value. Use a new key to create a new key-value pair.

- You can also begin a brand new hash this way. It's not necessary to begin a hash by assigning a list to it as described on page 168.

```
1   #!/usr/local/bin/perl -wT
2   use strict;
3   use CGI ':standard';
4   my (%personal_data);
5
6   %personal_data = ('Your IP Address' =>
    $ENV{'REMOTE_ADDR'}, 'Your Browser
    and Platform' =>
    $ENV{'HTTP_USER_AGENT'});
7
8   $personal_data{'Your name'} =
    param('name');
9
10  print "Content-type: text/html\n\n";
11
12  print "Here's what we know about you";
13  foreach (keys %personal_data) {
14      print "<P>The key is <b>$_</b> and
    the value is
    <b>$personal_data{$_}</b>";
15      }
```

6: We start by assigning a list of information (gleaned from environment variables—see page 99) to the %personal_data hash.

8: We then add a third key-value pair to the hash, by assigning the result of param('name')—that is, what the visitor entered in the *name* field on the HTML form—to the 'Your name' key in the %personal_data hash. Since the hash didn't previously contain a 'Your name' key, a new key-value pair is added to the hash. (Otherwise, the value would replace the current value associated with the 'Your name' key.)

Figure 14.7 *Assigning a value,* param('name')*, to a hash key,* $personal_data{'Your_name'}*, creates the key-value pair in the hash (and even the hash itself if it didn't already exist).*

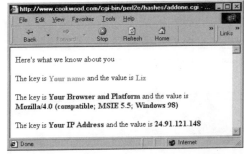

Figure 14.8 *The new key-value pair is output with the rest of the hash. (Again, the order of the pairs is a bit chaotic.)*

```
1   #!/usr/local/bin/perl -wT
2   use strict;
3   use CGI ':standard';
4   my (%tiger_data, @question);
5
6   %tiger_data = ('English name' => 'Tiger',
        'Latin name' => 'panthera tigris',
        'current population' => '4500',
        status => 'endangered');
7
8   @question = param('question');
9
10  print "Content-type: text/html\n\n";
11
12  print "The answers are<UL>";
13  foreach (@tiger_data{@question}) {
14      print "<LI>$_";
15      }
16      print "</UL>";
```

8:   This time, the visitor can ask multiple questions,
     and so we'll have to store those questions in an
     array (@question).

13: We can get all of the answers (that is the values
     from the %tiger_data hash that correspond to
     the keys entered by the visitor) by using
     @tiger_data{@question} and we print them
     out with a now-familiar foreach loop (see
     page 130).

Figure 14.9 *A slice of a hash contains multiple values from that hash and thus must be treated like an array.*

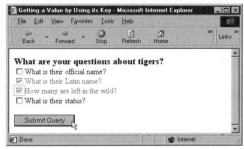

Figure 14.10 *The visitor is now invited to ask multiple questions (with checkboxes instead of radio buttons).*

Figure 14.11 *All of the answers are output.*

Getting Several Values Using Keys

If you need more than one value and you already know the corresponding keys, you can use the keys to access the values. This is called taking a *slice* of the hash.

To get several values using keys:

1. Type **@hash**, where *hash* is the name of the hash that contains the desired items. (You use @ because the result will be several values, not just one.)

2. Type **{key1, key2}**, where *key1* and *key2* (and any others) are the keys that correspond to the desired values from the hash.

   Or type **{@array}**, where *@array* is an array that contains the keys that correspond to the desired values from the hash.

✔ Tips

- Preface the hash name with @—and not % or $—since you're accessing *several* pieces of data.

- To get *all* the values from a hash, consult *Getting All of a Hash's Values* on page 173.

- Getting values from a hash does not alter the hash itself.

- If desired, you can use scalar variables to call the key names in step 2.

- Keys that contain non-alphanumerics or spaces must be delimited with quotation marks.

- You can store the acquired values in another array with @values_array = @hash{key1, key2};.

Getting All of a Hash's Keys

Sometimes it's useful to print or process all of the keys of a hash. Perl has a special function (keys) that makes this easy.

To get all of a hash's keys:

1. Type **keys**.

2. Type **(%hash)**, where *hash* is the name of the hash that contains the desired keys.

✔ Tips

- You can create an array with each of the keys in a hash using @array = keys(%hash);.

- The keys function is typically used in a foreach loop to go through each key-value pair in a hash. For more details, see page 175.

- Once you get the array of keys by using the keys function, you can use the sort function on that array.

- You could (and most programmers would) combine lines 11 and 13 in the example to read foreach (keys %tiger_data) {. I've separated out the lines so you can see more clearly what the keys function does.

```
1   #!/usr/local/bin/perl -wT
2   use strict;
3   use CGI ':standard';
4   my (%tiger_data, @keys);
5
6   %tiger_data = ('English name' => 'Tiger',
        'Latin name' => 'panthera tigris',
        'current population' => '4500',
        status => 'endangered');
7
8   print "Content-type: text/html\n\n";
9   print "The keys are:<UL>";
10
11  @keys= keys (%tiger_data);
12
13  foreach (@keys) {
14      print "<LI>$_";
15      }
16      print "</UL>";
```

11: The result of the keys function is a list (of the hash's keys) which we'll store in an array.
13: We then use a typical foreach loop to output each item of the @keys array.

Figure 14.12 *You'll usually do more interesting things with the keys than simply print them out. Once you have them, you can use them to access the values, for example.*

Figure 14.13 *There is no corresponding HTML form for this script. It simply outputs all the keys in the %tiger_data hash.*

```
1   #!/usr/local/bin/perl -wT
2   use strict;
3   use CGI ':standard';
4   my (%tiger_data, @values);
5
6   %tiger_data = ('English name' => 'Tiger',
        'Latin name' => 'panthera tigris',
        'current population' => '4500',
        status => 'endangered');
7
8   print "Content-type: text/html\n\n";
9   print "The values are:<UL>";
10
11  @values= values (%tiger_data);
12
13  foreach (@values) {
14      print "<LI>$_";
15      }
16      print "</UL>";
```

11: The result of the `values` function is a list (of the hash's values) which we'll store in an array.

13: We then use a typical `foreach` loop to output each item of the `@values` array.

Figure 14.14 *You'll usually do more interesting things with the values than simply print them out.*

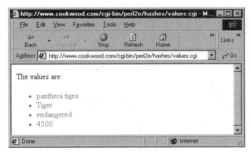

Figure 14.15 *There is no corresponding HTML form for this script. It simply outputs all the values in the* `%tiger_data` *hash.*

Getting All of a Hash's Values

Sometimes it's useful to print or process all of the values of a hash. Perl has a special function (`values`) that makes this easy.

To get all of a hash's values:

1. Type **values**.

2. Type **(%hash)**, where *hash* is the name of the hash that contains the desired values.

✔ Tips

■ You can create an array with each of the values in a hash using `@array = values(%hash);`.

■ You could (and most programmers would) combine lines 11 and 13 in the example to read `foreach (values %tiger_data) {`. Note that you don't need the extra parentheses around the hash name. I've separated out the lines so you can see more clearly what the `values` function does.

■ It's much more common to get the keys of a hash (with the `keys` function described on page 172) then to get the values of a hash (as described above).

Getting Each Key and Value in a Hash

There are two principal ways to access a hash's keys and values at the same time.

Perl's each function goes through each key and value in a hash sequentially. Each time you use the each function, it returns the next pair of items.

To get the first key and value:

Type **each (%hash)**, where *hash* is the name of the hash that contains the desired keys and values.

To get the *next* key and value:

Use **each (%hash)** again later in your script.

✔ Tips

■ Each time you use each (%hash), you get the next key-value pair in the hash. You can use a loop statement (like while or foreach) to go through each pair in the hash without having to type the each function successive times.

■ When you get to the end of the hash, the each function returns an empty list.

```
1   #!/usr/local/bin/perl -wT
2   use strict;
3   use CGI ':standard';
4   my (%tiger_data, $key, $value);
5
6   %tiger_data = ('English name' => 'Tiger',
        'Latin name' => 'panthera tigris',
        'current population' => '4500',
        status => 'endangered');
7
8   print "Content-type: text/html\n\n";
9   while (($key, $value) =
        each (%tiger_data) ) {
10      print "<P>Their <b>$key</b> is
        <b>$value</b>";
11  }
```

9: The condition assigns the first key-value pair from %tiger_data to the scalar variables $key and $value. If the assignment is successful, the condition evaluates as true and the statements in the while block are executed. Using each means that the next time the condition is evaluated, the *subsequent* key-value pair will be assigned to the scalar variables. This will continue until there are no more pairs, at which time the each function returns an empty list which makes the condition false, and the block is exited.
10: When the condition is true, the $key and $value are printed.

Figure 14.16 *The* each *function gets each key-value pair in the hash, one after the next.*

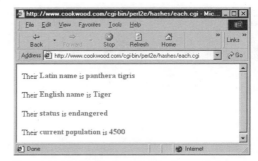

Figure 14.17 *Combining the* while *loop with the* each *function is an easy and quick way to go through and operate on (or print out, as shown here), each key-value pair in a hash.*

```
1   #!/usr/local/bin/perl -wT
2   use strict;
3   use CGI ':standard';
4   my (%tiger_data, $key, $value);
5
6   %tiger_data = ('English name' => 'Tiger',
      'Latin name' => 'panthera tigris',
      'current population' => '4500',
      status => 'endangered');
7
8   print "Content-type: text/html\n\n";
9   foreach $key (keys %tiger_data) {
10    print "<P>Their <b>$key</b> is
      <b>$tiger_data{$key}</b>";
11  }
```

9:   The `foreach` loop always operates on a list and
     this example is no exception. In this case, the
     list is created when you use the `keys` function
     on `%tiger_data`.

10: The `$key` variable is used to access the key in
     each key-value pair in the `%tiger_data` hash,
     and then it is used in `$tiger_data{$key}` to
     access the corresponding value.

Figure 14.18 *Again, you may want to do something
more interesting than print out the keys and the values
in a list. You can use whatever statements you like in
the* foreach *loop.*

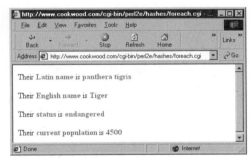

Figure 14.19 *The result is identical to using the*
while *loop and* each *function (see Figure 14.17 on
page 174).*

You can also use the `keys` function *(see
page 172)* combined with a `foreach` loop
(see page 130) to go through each key-value
pair in a hash.

To use the keys function to get key-value pairs:

1. Type **foreach**.

2. Type **$key**, where *key* is the name of the
   scalar that will hold each individual key
   as you go through the loop. (It doesn't
   have to be called "key". You could even
   leave it out entirely and use the default
   variable--see page 131 for details.)

3. Type **(keys %hash)**, where *hash* is the
   name of the hash that contains the
   desired key-value pairs. The word "keys"
   is the name of the function and must be
   typed as is.

4. Type **{**.

5. Type the statements that should be executed each time the script gets the next
   key-value pair from the hash. You can
   use **$hash{$key}** to access each value
   from the hash.

6. Type **}**.

✔ Tips

■ For tips on controlling the order in which
  you access a hash's keys and values, consult *Getting the Pairs in a Specified
  Order* on page 176.

■ For more information on the `keys` function, consult *Getting All of a Hash's
  Keys* on page 172.

■ For details on printing out a hash with an
  HTML table, consult *Outputting Data in
  a Table* on page 236.

Getting the Pairs in a Specified Order

It's tempting to look at a list assigned to a hash and think that the hash's pairs will be output in the same order in which they were assigned. But it won't work. A hash's pairs have no order. Instead, you can control the output order by organizing or sorting the keys.

To get a hash's pairs in order:

Type **sort (keys (%hash))**, where *hash* is the name of the hash whose pairs you want to work with in a particular order.

✔ Tip

■ You can sort the keys in many different ways. For more details on the sort function, consult *Sorting Arrays* on page 154.

```
1   #!/usr/local/bin/perl -wT
2   use strict;
3   use CGI ':standard';
4   my (%tiger_data, $key, $value);
5
6   %tiger_data = ('English name' => 'Tiger',
       'Latin name' => 'panthera tigris',
       'current population' => '4500',
       status => 'endangered');
7
8   print "Content-type: text/html\n\n";
9   foreach $key (sort (keys %tiger_data)) {
10    print "<P>Their <b>$key</b> is
        <b>$tiger_data{$key}</b>";
11  }
```

9: We add the sort function to this line so that it will sort the keys before accessing each key-value pair in the hash.

Figure 14.20 *The* sort *function by itself orders the keys in ASCII order.*

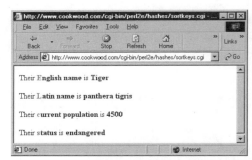

Figure 14.21 *Sorting the keys in ASCII order is not exactly the same as sorting them alphabetically. Notice how all the capital letters come first, followed by all of the lowercase letters.*

Getting the Pairs in a Specified Order

```
1   #!/usr/local/bin/perl -wT
2   use strict;
3   use CGI ':standard';
4   my (%tiger_data, $key, @sortarray);
5
6   %tiger_data = ('English name' => 'Tiger',
       'Latin name' => 'panthera tigris',
       'current population' => '4500',
       status => 'endangered');
7
8   print "Content-type: text/html\n\n";
9   @sortarray = ('status', 'English name',
       'Latin name', 'current population');
10
11  foreach $key (@sortarray) {
12      print "<P>Their <b>$key</b> is
       <b>$tiger_data{$key}</b>";
13      }
```

9: We create an array with the keys in the desired order.

11: When it's time to access the hash, we call the keys from the array created in line 9 and use those keys to get the values from the hash in the desired order.

Figure 14.22 *This method only works if you know what the keys are ahead of time.*

Figure 14.23 *Using a predefined array to determine the output of a hash lets you access the hash in any order you need.*

Another way to output the hash pairs in a particular order—if you know what all of the keys are ahead of time—is to create an array that lists the keys in order. Then you can output the hash using the ordered array.

To set the order manually:

1. Create an array that contains the hash's keys in the desired order.

2. Use the array to determine how the hash's pairs are output.

✔ Tip

- This method only works if you know what all of the keys are. Otherwise, you clearly can't set their order.

Removing Key-Value Pairs

Sometimes you'll want to get rid of a key-value pair altogether—perhaps because the data is obsolete as in the case of a hash with user names and passwords.

To remove a key-value pair:

1. Type **delete**.

2. Type **$hash**, where *hash* is the name of the hash that contains the key-value pair that you want to eliminate.

3. Type **{key}**, where *key* is the key that identifies the value (and thus the entire pair) that you want to eliminate.

4. Type **;** to finish the line. The referenced key-value pair is permanently removed from the hash.

✔ Tips

■ Keys need to be quoted if they contain non-alphanumerics or spaces: delete $hash{'first name'};.

■ You can assign the result of the delete function to a scalar variable: $value = delete $hash{key};. The result is the value that corresponds to the key used.

```
1   #!/usr/local/bin/perl -wT
2   use strict;
3   use CGI ':standard';
4   my (%tiger_data, $question, $removed);
5
6   %tiger_data = ('English name' =>
    'Tiger', 'Latin name' => 'panthera
    tigris', 'current population' =>
    '4500', status => 'endangered');
7   $question = param('question');
8
9   print "Content-type: text/html\n\n";
10
11  $removed = delete
    $tiger_data{$question};
12
13  print "You removed the pair: $question,
    $removed";
14
15  print "<P>The following pairs
    remain:<UL>";
16  foreach (keys %tiger_data) {
17      print "<LI>$_, $tiger_data{$_}";
18      }
19      print "</UL>";
```

11: The delete function removes the key-value pair whose key matches the visitor's input (and assigns it to the $removed variable).

Figure 14.24 *You don't have to assign the removed value to anything. You can simply send it into the cyberether, if you prefer.*

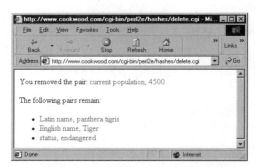

Figure 14.25 *This script reveals the key-value pair that has been removed and then prints out the pairs that remain in the hash.*

Removing Key-Value Pairs

```
1   #!/usr/local/bin/perl -wT
2   use strict;
3   use CGI ':standard';
4   my (%tiger_data, $question);
5
6   %tiger_data = ('English name' => 'Tiger',
        'Latin name' => 'panthera tigris',
        'current population' => '4500',
        status => 'endangered');
7
8   $question = param('question');
9
10  print "Content-type: text/html\n\n";
11
12  if (exists $tiger_data{$question} ) {
13    print "<P>Yes, I have the answer to
          that question. <P>Their $question is
          $tiger_data{$question}.";
14  } else {
15    print "<P>Sorry, I don't know the
          answer to that question.";
16  }
```

12: The condition tests to see if there is a key equal to the visitor's input. If so, the question can be answered.

13: If the condition is true, this `print` statement outputs the explanatory message that contains the question, `$question`, and the answer, `$tiger_data{$question}`.

15: If there is no key in the hash that matches the visitor's input, the "Sorry" message is printed.

Figure 14.26 *The example prints a message depending on the results of the* exists *function.*

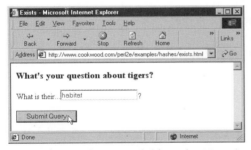

Figure 14.27 *In this open-ended form, the visitor can ask any question they like.*

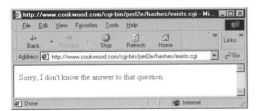

Figure 14.28 *The visitor is informed if the question does not match any of the keys in the hash.*

Checking to See If a Key Exists

If you don't want to list all the keys in a hash to see if the one you're after appears, you can simply check to see if your key is part of the hash.

To check to see if a key is part of the hash:

1. Type **exists**.

2. Type **$hash**, where *hash* is the name of the hash that may or may not contain the key in question.

3. Type **{key}**, where *key* is the key that you are looking for in the hash.

✔ Tips

■ If the key does exist in the hash, the `exists` function returns a value of 1 (true). If the key does not exist, the value returned is 0 (false). You can use the `exists` function effectively in `if` blocks. For more information on constructing an `if` block, consult *Creating a Basic Conditional Statement* on page 126.

■ The `exists` function returns true as long as *the key* exists in the hash—even if the corresponding value is undefined or empty.

Analyzing Data

Once you receive a chunk of incoming information from a Web visitor, you'll want to see what it contains. Perl has several ways of looking inside incoming data and then acting accordingly. Three of the most important are the match and substitution operators and the `split` function.

The match operator just checks to see if a variable *contains* the specified data *(see page 182)*. Then you can set up a conditional to do one thing if the data's there, and another if it's not.

The substitution operator not only looks to see if a variable contains the specified data but, once it finds such data, lets you change it into something else *(see page 183)*.

The `split` function lets you search for an expression in a string of values in order to divide that string into its individual components *(see page 185)*.

What can you look for? Perl is a powerful language for analyzing Web data because you can not only look for straightforward values such as "Smith" and "Hartford, CT" but also generalized patterns that will match a wider range of possibilities. For example, `/^\d{5}-\d{4}$/` would match *any* nine-digit U.S. postal code, as long as it was made up of five digits, a dash, and four more digits.

If that string of funny looking characters gives you pause, relax. This chapter not only explains how to set up those three operators, but also how to construct (and understand) the patterns at their core.

Finding Something

Finding something with Perl's match operator is a lot like using the Find command in your word processor: you want to know if the given text is present but you don't plan to change that text.

To find something:

1. Type **$scalar** where *scalar* is the variable that contains the string that you want to search.

2. Type **=~ m/**. (The equals sign and tilde together are called the *binding operator.* The *m* stands for match.)

3. Type the pattern that describes what you're looking for *(see pages 186–202)*.

4. Type **/**.

5. If desired, type **i** to *i*gnore whether the letters are upper- or lowercase.

✔ Tips

■ The match operator returns true as long as the variable *contains* the pattern. Unless you specify otherwise, it doesn't matter if it *also* contains non-matching data.

■ If your pattern itself contains a lot of forward slashes, you can use some other delimiter so as not to confuse the slashes in your pattern with the slashes in the matching operator. For example, you could use m#pattern#.

■ As long as you use slashes to delimit the pattern, you can omit the *m*. So, `$scalar =~ /pattern/;` is the same as `$scalar =~ m/pattern/;`.

■ Match a pattern contained in the default variable, `$_`, by omitting the scalar variable and the binding operator: `/pattern/;` is equivalent to `$_ =~ /pattern/;`.

```
1   #!/usr/local/bin/perl -wT
2   use strict;
3
4   print "Content-type: text/html\n\n";
5
6   my $browser = $ENV{'HTTP_USER_AGENT'};
7
8   if ($browser =~ m/MSIE/) {
9      print "<P>You're using IE";
10  } elsif ($browser =~ m/Mozilla/) {
11     print "<P>You're using Netscape";
12  } else {
13     print "<P>You're using something
           else";
14  }
```

1:   Lines 1–2. The `use CGI.pm` line is not required since we're not using any visitor-entered input.

6:   The visitor's browser information is automatically saved in the `HTTP_USER_AGENT` environment variable *(see page 100)*.

8:   This line asks if the scalar variable `$browser` contains the sequence of letters *MSIE* (which is the identifying code for Explorer).

10: If the first condition fails (that is, the visitor isn't using Internet Explorer), the second condition checks if `$browser` contains *Mozilla*. If it does, we know the visitor is using Netscape.

Figure 15.1 *In this example, I've used the simplest of search patterns: words. Don't get hung up on the search patterns yet, focus on the syntax of the match operator. We'll get to constructing search patterns on page 186.*

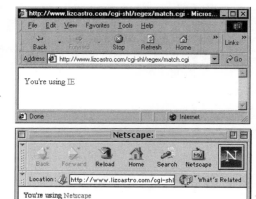

Figure 15.2 *You'll probably want to do more with the information about your visitor's browser than just parrot it back to them.*

```
1   #!/usr/local/bin/perl -wT
2   use strict;
3   use CGI ':standard';
4
5   print "Content-type: text/html\n\n";
6   my $comments = param('comments');
7
8   if ($comments =~ s/<IMG[^>]*>//gi) {
9     print "<P>Sorry, images are not
        permitted. Please limit your
        comments to text.";
10  }
11  if ($comments) {
12    print "<P>Your text comments were
        <P><B>$comments</B>";
13  } else {
14    print "You didn't have any text
        comments.";
15  }
```

8: The condition checks to see if the submitted comments ($comments) contain any IMG tags (ignoring case). If it does find any, it removes them (by substituting nothing—the contents of the two final slashes) and returns true (and thus goes on to print the error message in line 9). The final g ensures that all substitutions (and not just the first one) are made.

11 If there's anything left in the $comments variable after the substitution, this condition returns true, and the comments are printed. Otherwise, line 14 is output.

Figure 15.3 *Don't analyze that ugly looking search pattern in line 8 yet. We'll get to them on page 186. For now, I want you to learn how to set up the substitution operator.*

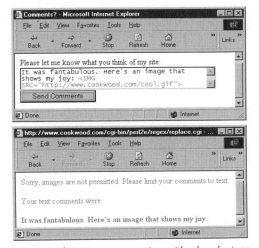

Figure 15.4 *Images can sometimes either bog down or offend. This little script gets rid of all images that your visitor might try to enclose.*

Finding and Replacing

As in a word processor, you can either just find, or you can find and replace. That is, you can *change* the matched strings that you find.

To find and replace:

1. Type **$scalar** where *scalar* is the name of the variable that contains the original text and that will be used to store the changed text.

2. Type **=~ s/**.

3. Type the pattern that describes the text you're looking for *(see pages 187–201).*

4. Type **/**.

5. Type the text with which you want to replace the text found in step 3.

6. Type **/**.

7. If desired, type **i** to *i*gnore the case of the letters that you're searching.

8. If desired, type **g** to replace *all* occurrences of the text described in step 3 (that is, *g*lobally). Otherwise, only the first match will be replaced.

✔ Tips

■ That little *s* in step 2 stands for *substitution*. It's not optional.

■ If you omit the scalar and the binding operator (=~), the substitution operator searches and replaces in the default variable, $_. In other words, s/pattern/ replacement/; is the same thing as $_ =~ s/pattern/replacement/;.

Finding and Replacing

Seeing and Using What Was Found

When using the match and substitution operators, it's not always obvious, especially with more general search patterns, what exactly was matched. Also, if the pattern appears more than once in the search string, you might want to know which occurrence triggered the match.

After a match, Perl sets the values of three special variables. $& will contain the data that the pattern matched. $` (the key above the tilde in the top left corner of the keyboard) will contain any text that preceded the matched text, and $' (a straight single quote) will contain any text that came after the matched text in the searched string.

You can use these variables in your scripts and even in the replacement section of the substitution operator.

✔ Tips

- Once you use one of these variables, Perl makes sure to set it for every search you perform, and may considerably slow down your program in the process. Therefore, only use them when absolutely necessary. Once you have used them, you needn't be frugal; using them once has the same impact as using them a hundred times.

- If you've used parentheses in your pattern, Perl also remembers what the contents of each set of parentheses matched and stores this data for later use. For more details, consult *More on Using What You Already Matched* on page 202.

- If nothing matches, $&, $` and $' will all be empty.

```perl
1   #!/usr/local/bin/perl -wT
2   use strict;
3
4   print "Content-type: text/html\n\n";
5   my $browser = $ENV{'HTTP_USER_AGENT'};
6
7   if ($browser =~ /MSIE/) {
8   print "You're using IE";
9   } elsif ($browser =~ /Mozilla/) {
10  print "You're using Netscape";
11  } else {
12  print "You're using something else";
13  }
14
15  print '<HR>';
16  print qq(<P>The environment variable was
        "<b>$browser</b>");
17  print qq(<P>The unmatched text to the
        left was "<b>$`</b>");
18  print qq(<P>The matched text was
        "<b>$&</b>");
19  print qq(<P>The unmatched text to the
        right was "<b>$'</b>");
```

17: The $` variable contains the portion of the $browser variable that didn't match that was to the left of the matching section.

18: The $& variable contains exactly what matched, if anything.

19: The $' variable contains the portion of the $browser variable that didn't match that was to the right of the matching section.

Figure 15.5 *You won't normally want to print each variable out—unless you're showing someone how the variables work.*

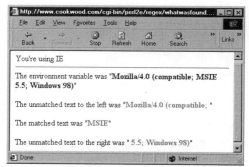

Figure 15.6 *In this example, we were looking for MSIE in the environment variable, which is printed out just below the horizontal rule. The $& variable shows that MSIE was indeed found. $` displays the text from the beginning of the search string to the matched part. The $' variable shows the piece of the search string that didn't match starting from the matching part and going until the end of the string.*

```
1   #!/usr/local/bin/perl -wT
2   use strict;
3   use CGI ':standard';
4   my ($data, @data, $choice);
5
6   $choice= param('choice');
7   $data = 'Tiger,panthera tigris,4500,
        endangered:Florida Panther,Puma
        concolor coryi,50,endangered:Giant
        River Otter,Pteronura brasiliensis,
        1000,endangered';
8
9   @data = split (/:/ , $data);
10
11  print "Content-type: text/html\n\n";
12  print "<TABLE BORDER=1><TR align=left>
        <TH>Name</TH><TH>Latin Name</TH>
        <TH>Current Population</TH><TH>Status
        </TH></TR>";
13
14  foreach (@data) {
15    my ($name, $latin_name, $pop, $status);
16    ($name, $latin_name, $pop, $status) =
        split (/,/);
17      if ($name =~ /$choice/i) {
18      print "<TR><TD>$name</TD>
          <TD>$latin_name</TD><TD>$pop</TD
          ><TD>$status</TD></TR>";
19      }
20  }
21  print "</TABLE>";
```

7: In a real case, this data might come from an external file or database (but we don't get to that until Chapter 19). Note that commas separate fields and colons separate records.

9: First, we split the data into three records and store those records in the `@data` array.

16: Here, we split each record into fields, using the comma as a divisor. We assign the fields directly to four scalar variables. Notice that the `split` function operates on the `$_` variable here (each successive element of the `@data` array).

17: If the visitor-entered choice matches the contents of `$name`, the corresponding data is output in a pretty table (which would be impossible if it were just one long line of data).

Figure 15.7 *I use* `split` *twice in this script: once to divide the stream of data into records, and then again to divide each record into individual fields.*

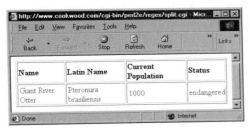

Figure 15.8 *The data is divided into pieces which are then fit into a nice-looking table.*

Splitting a Value into Pieces

Splitting a scalar variable into pieces is particularly useful when parsing information from an external file, like a log file or database.

To split a scalar into pieces:

1. Type **@new** where *new* is the name of the array variable that will contain the split pieces.

2. Type **=**.

3. Type **split (**.

4. Type **/pattern/** where *pattern* is the regular expression that describes the element that divides the pieces. For information about creating regular expressions, see pages 186–202.

5. Type **, $old**, where *old* is the name of the scalar variable that contains the string you want to split. Don't forget the comma.

    Or type nothing to split the contents of the default variable, **$_**.

6. Type the closing parenthesis **)**.

7. Type a semicolon **;** to finish the line.

✔ Tips

■ If you don't specify the element that divides the pieces, Perl automatically uses the regular expression **/\s+/** and thus, will divide the string into word shaped pieces. (See page 192 for more on \s and page 197 for more on +.)

■ Combining the previous tip and the second half of step 5, you can see that `@list = split(/\s+/, $_);` is the same as `@list = split;`.

■ You can assign the results of the split scalar directly to a list as in `($name, $address, $age) = split (/,/ ,$data);`.

Splitting a Value into Pieces

Constructing Search Patterns

Suppose you need a new Web page coder for your design firm. You could put an ad in the classifieds that asks for "Web designer" and you'd probably get quite a few responses. However, instead of wading through piles of resumes, it might be smarter to be more specific with your response so that the folks who apply more closely reflect your needs. On your second try, you might require knowledge of HTML, Perl, and JavaScript, and three years experience doing Web page coding. This time, you'd get fewer responses but they'd (hopefully) be closer to what you need.

When you analyze incoming data from a Web site, you need to take a similar tack. You use *patterns* to analyze data and make sure that it's what you're looking for. Instead of asking for four years experience, you might require that the data begin with an opening parentheses, be followed by three digits, then have a closing parentheses, a space, three more digits, a dash, and finally four more digits. If the data matched that description, you could be pretty sure that it's a U.S. telephone number.

Those patterns are obliquely called *regular expressions*, which is sometimes abbreviated into the nicely shorter, but even more obtuse *regex*. For example, one pattern that matches a telephone number like *(280) 421-9876* is: `/^((\(\d{3}\))? *\d{3}(-| )\d{4},? *)+$/`. Pretty scary looking, huh? The trick is to look at each element individually and not get overwhelmed by the multitude of symbols. The rest of this chapter will teach you how to read and construct your own regular expressions or search patterns—including this one for U.S. phone numbers.

Jeffrey E. F. Friedl has written an excellent if somewhat advanced book on regular expressions, titled *Mastering Regular Expressions*.

Tips for Constructing Search Patterns

A lengthy string of funny looking characters and symbols can be a bit daunting. And the truth is that creating a search pattern that matches what you want it to while filtering out the dreck can be tricky indeed. Here are some tips.

Those forward slashes

Although the forward slashes are part of the match or substitution operators, and not part of the pattern itself, I use them to visually delimit the search patterns in this book.

Combine general and specific components

Perl lets you be as specific or as general as you need. The pattern `/noose/` will match only those characters in that order, while `/.*/` will match *any* quantity of *any* character (including nothing). Often, the most powerful and useful patterns come from combining specific and general components. For example, `/.*oose/` would match "noose", "goose", and even "caboose", among many others.

Spaces

You may want to add spaces between all those chunks of expressions. But don't. Just put one piece right up alongside the next one and have faith that Perl will know what goes where. Spaces are counted like any other character.

Special symbols

When deciphering other folks' regular expressions, keep in mind that the symbols `[, ], (, ), *, +, ., ^, $, -, |, \, and ?` all have special meanings (which are explained throughout this chapter).

Tips for Constructing Search Patterns

Matching a Single Character

To match any particular character, whether it be a letter or number, or some special symbol, you simply state that particular character. To match *any* single character (except a newline), you use the period (.).

To match a particular character:

Type the character you want to match.

To match any character:

Type a . (period).

✔ Tips

- Some symbols—like period (.) described above—have a special meaning when used within a pattern. To look for the symbol itself (and not use its special meaning), precede it with a backslash. So, to search for a period, you'd have to use / \ . /. It's easy to see how patterns can quickly look so incomprehensible.

- To match optional or multiple occurrences of single characters, consult *Choosing How Many to Match* on page 195.

- The wildcard symbol (.) is particularly useful when combined with quantifiers to match a whole string of unspecified characters *next to* the determining constant text that you're searching for. For more on quantifiers, consult *Choosing How Many to Match* on page 195.

```
1   #!/usr/local/bin/perl -wT
2   use strict;
3   use CGI ':standard';
4
5   print "Content-type: text/html\n\n";
6
7   my $phrase = param('phrase');
8
9   if ($phrase =~ /e/) {
10  print "<P>Sorry, that sentence did in
        fact have an e. I told you: it's harder
        than it seems.";
11  } else {
12  print "<P>Congratulations, that
        sentence had no e. Quite a feat!";
13  }
```

9: Here's the simplest of regular expressions, a single character. This line checks to see if there are any letter e's in the variable $phrase. If so, line 10 is executed. If not, Perl skips to lines 11–12.

Figure 15.9 *In this example the regular expression is used by the match operator.*

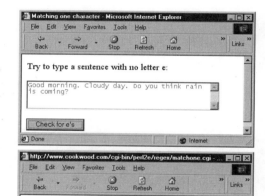

Figure 15.10 *This simple script looks through the entered phrase to see if it contains any letter e.*

```
1   #!/usr/local/bin/perl -wT
2   use strict;
3   use CGI ':standard';
4
5   print "Content-type: text/html\n\n";
6
7   my $phrase = param('phrase');
8
9   $phrase =~ s/damn/hoot/;
10
11  print "<P>Your more proper sentence is
    <P><B>$phrase";
```

9: The regular expression /damn/ tries to find the letters *d, a, m, n,* in that order, with no intervening characters or spaces. (This line then substitutes the first occurrence of those letters with the letters *h, o, o, t.* For more details about substituting, see page 183.)

Figure 15.11 *Although* damn *may look like a word (OK, and it is a word), for understanding regular expressions, you're better off looking at it as a sequence of characters.*

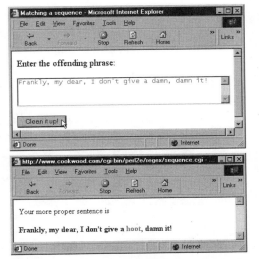

Figure 15.12 *Notice that only the first occurrence of the* damn *sequence is replaced. To replace both occurrences, you'd have to append a* g *to the end of line 10 in Figure 15.11 (see page 183).*

Matching a String of Characters

Often, you'll want to match a whole series of characters, in order. This series of characters might be a word or even a whole sentence, but doesn't have to be.

To match a string of characters, in order:

Type the string of characters in the order in which they should appear in the search string.

✔ Tips

■ The series of characters must appear one after the other in the search string in the same order and without extra intervening characters or spaces to qualify as a match. Therefore, /lemon/ won't find a match in *purple monkey*, even though *purple monkey* contains the five letters searched for in the proper order (since there's an extra space). And /candle grip/ doesn't match *perl and cgi*, even though the letters are the same because they're not in the same order.

■ You can use the period (.) as a wildcard for any character *(see page 188)* in combination with any other characters. For example, /p.p/ matches *pap* and *pep*, as well as *p5p, p%p,* and *p p,* among many others.

■ The pattern may appear surrounded by other letters (that is, part of another word, for instance) and still qualify as a match. For example, /water/ matches both *watermelon* and *Goldwater,* as well as just *water.* For details on limiting searches to free-standing words, consult *Limiting the Location* on page 193.

Matching a Character from a Group

You can also specify a group or *class* of characters that you want to search for in the search string. If any one character in the group is in the search string, the match will be successful.

To match a character from a group:

1. To begin the class definition, type [.

2. Type the characters in the class.

3. Type].

✔ Tips

- Only one of the group's characters has to be present in the search string for the match to be successful.

- The order of individual characters doesn't matter (in contrast with sequences as described on page 189). So [perl] and [lerp] are equivalent groups.

- You can specify a range of characters with the hyphen. For example, [a-z] is an abbreviated way of saying "any lowercase letter from *a* to *z*"; [0-3] would match 0, 1, 2, or 3.

- You can specify more than one range at a time. No spaces are necessary between ranges. Therefore, [a-zA-Z] would match any letter in the English alphabet, lower- or uppercase.

- You can add the hyphen to the class by preceding it with a backslash. So, [a\-z] would match the letter *a*, the hyphen, and the letter *z* (but not the letters *b*, *c*, and so on). Or add the hyphen by listing it first within the brackets: [-a-z] matches the hyphen and the letters *a* to *z*.

```
1   #!/usr/local/bin/perl -wT
2   use strict;
3   use CGI ':standard';
4   my ($number, %catalan, %spanish,
       %french);
5   print "Content-type: text/html\n\n";
6
7   $number = param('number');
8   %catalan = (1 => "un", 2 => "dos", 3 =>
       "tres", 4 => "quatre", 5 => "cinc");
9   %spanish = (1 => "uno", 2 => "dos", 3 =>
       "tres", 4 => "cuatro", 5 => "cinco");
10  %french = (1 => "un", 2 => "deux", 3 =>
       "trois", 4 => "quatre", 5 => "cinq");
11
12  if ($number =~/^[1-5]$/) {
13    print "<P>You chose the number
       $number. That number translated into
       Catalan is <B>$catalan{$number}</B>.
       In French, it's <B>$french{$number}
       </B>. In Spanish, it's
       <B>$spanish{$number}<B>.";
14  } else {
15    print "<P>Sorry, you didn't choose a
       number between 1 and 5. Try again.";
16  }
```

12: The regular expression searches for any number in the range of 1 to 5. The caret and the dollar sign are explained on page 193.)

Figure 15.13 *Regular expressions are ideal for checking to see that incoming data satisfies the necessary criteria. (Here the input must be a number from 1 to 5 since those are all the translations that we have.)*

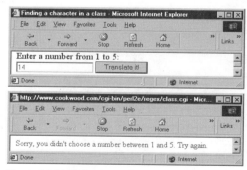

Figure 15.14 *If the visitor does not enter the data properly, they get an explanatory message (instead of throwing the server into a tizzy).*

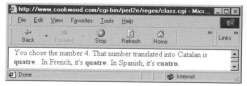

Figure 15.15 *As long as the visitor enters a supported number, the main part of the script is executed.*

```
1   #!/usr/local/bin/perl -wT
2   use strict;
3   use CGI ':standard';
4   my $zip;
5
6   print "Content-type: text/html\n\n";
7
8   $zip = param('zip');
9
10  if ($zip =~/[^0-9\-]/) {
11    print "US zipcodes should only contain
        the numbers or the dash. Try
        again.";
12  } else {
13    print "You entered $zip for your US
        zipcode";
14  }
```

10: The regular expression tries to find anything that is *not* a number or a hyphen. If it does find such an offending character, an error message is printed (line 11). Note that the second hyphen is backslashed to remove its special *range* meaning.

Figure 15.16 *To make sure the incoming data contains no extraneous characters, that is, anything that's not a digit or a hyphen, use a negated class.*

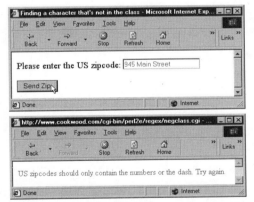

Figure 15.17 *Never assume that your visitors will follow your instructions. Instead, use regular expressions to check all incoming data. Then, if you have to reject data, make sure you explain to your visitor what the problem is.*

Matching a Character That's Not in the Group

Sometimes you'll want to match a character that is not part of a specified group or class. You can search for those characters that don't belong to the group by preceding the class with a caret (^).

To match a character that's not in the group:

1. Begin the class definition with [.

2. Type ^ (that's Shift+6 on most keyboards).

3. Type the members of the class.

4. Type].

✔ Tips

■ For more information on constructing classes, consult *Matching a Character from a Group* on page 190.

■ If the caret (^) appears anywhere except as the first character in the class, it will be considered one of the members of the class. Therefore, [^a-z] would match any character that is *not* a lowercase letter, but [A-Z^a-z] would match any letter—including lowercase ones—or the caret.

■ Negated classes are tricky. While [^a-z] matches any character that's not a lowercase letter, it would still match *a1*, despite the presence of the *a*. Why? Because it is satisfied by matching the 1—which is not a lowercase letter. (Note that the example in Figure 15.16 keeps letters out but doesn't guard against *extra digits*. We'll get there shortly.)

■ When you use the negative caret, you're requiring that the search find you *something* that's not in the class. Finding nothing is not enough.

Matching a Character That's Not in the Group

Using Class Shorthands

Although you can spell out your own classes as described on pages 190–191, Perl also understands a set of abbreviations for specifying common classes.

To use a class shorthand:

Type **\d** to match any digit. The longhand equivalent is [0-9].

Or type **\D** to match any character that is *not* a digit. The longhand equivalent is [^0-9].

Or type **\w** to match any upper or lowercase letter, digit or the underscore. The longhand equivalent is [a-zA-Z0-9_].

Or type **\W** to match any character that is *not* an upper or lowercase letter, a digit, or the underscore. The longhand equivalent is [^a-zA-Z0-9_].

Or type **\s** to match any space, tab, newline, return, or formfeed. The longhand equivalent is [\t\n\r\f].

Or type **\S** to match any character that is *not* a space, tab, newline, return, or formfeed. The longhand equivalent is [^ \t\n\r\f].

✔ Tips

■ Each of these abbreviations matches a *single* character. If you want to match more than one character of the given class, you'd have to specify that explicitly *(see page 195)*.

■ Notice that \w is the class of characters that are valid in Perl variable names.

```
1   #!/usr/local/bin/perl -wT
2   use strict;
3   use CGI ':standard';
4   my $phone;
5
6   print "Content-type: text/html\n\n";
7   $phone = param('phone');
8
9   if ($phone =~ /\(\d\d\d\) \d\d\d-
        \d\d\d\d/) {
10    print "You entered a phone number of
        $phone";
11  } else {
12    print "Please enter the phone number
        in the form <P>(123) 456-7899<P>";
13  }
```

9:   The regular expression tries to find data that matches the pattern.

Figure 15.18 *Using* \d *(the class shorthand) instead of* [0-9] *saves a lot of typing.*

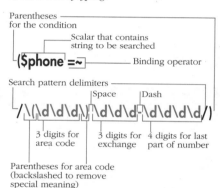

Figure 15.19 *Regular expressions can start to look pretty complicated. Here's a full description of line 9 from Figure 15.18.*

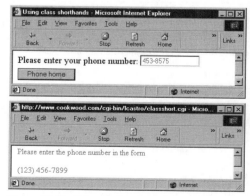

Figure 15.20 *If the number entered does not fit the desired pattern, the visitor gets an error and more information.*

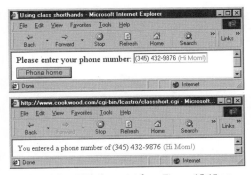

Figure 15.21 *With the script from Figure 15.18 on page 192, visitors can add extra data (as long as they also add a correctly formatted telephone number).*

```
1   #!/usr/local/bin/perl -wT
2   use strict;
3   use CGI ':standard';
4   my $phone;
5
6   print "Content-type: text/html\n\n";
7   $phone = param('phone');
8
9   if ($phone =~ /^\(\d\d\d\) \d\d\d-
    \d\d\d\d$/) {
10    print "You entered a phone number of
        $phone";
11  } else {
12    print "Please enter the phone number
        in the form <P>(123) 456-7899<P>";
13  }
```

9:   The caret (^) and the dollar sign ($) ensure that the telephone number will only match if it is the only thing entered (that is, it's at the beginning and at the end of the entered string).

Figure 15.22 *Limiting the possible location of a match ensures that the visitor can only enter a properly formatted telephone number with no extra goodies.*

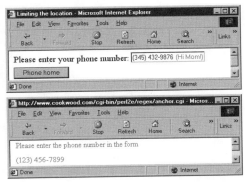

Figure 15.23 *Now when the visitor tries to be cute (or malicious), they are rebuffed.*

Limiting the Location

If you're looking for *wine*, you don't want to find *swine*. If you're looking for a three-digit number, you probably don't want to find it *within* a four-digit number. By limiting, or *anchoring*, the location of the found string to the beginning and/or end of a line, or to the beginning or end of a word, you can better control the results.

To require an element to appear at the beginning of the search string:

1. Type **^** as the very first character in the regular expression.

2. Type the element.

To require an element to appear at the very end of the search string:

1. Type the element.

2. Type **$**.

To require an element to appear at the beginning of a word:

1. Type **\b**.

2. Type the element.

To require an element to appear at the end of a word:

1. Type the element.

2. Type **\b**.

To require an element *not* to appear at the beginning of a word:

1. Type **\B**.

2. Type the element.

continued on the next page

Limiting the Location

To require an element *not* to appear at the end of a word:

1. Type the element.

2. Type **\B**.

✔ Tips

- So, to search for a string that contains a single element, you could use /^element$/.

- And to search for a free-standing word, you could use /\bword\b/. Such a regular expression would match *word* but not *sword*, nor *wordy*.

Choosing How Many to Match

By default, Perl will search for only one of each element that you add to a regular expression. That is, /a/ will match any search string that contains at least one *a*; /baby/ will match any search string that contains at least one instance of the string *baby*; and /[a-z]/ will match any search string that contains at least one lowercase letter. However, if you wanted to search for strings with, say, 3 *a*'s or two instances of *baby*, or individual words (combinations of the letters from *a* to *z*), you'd need to find more than one of the specified element. Perl has a number of *quantifiers* that let you do just that.

Perhaps the most important thing to remember about a quantifier is that it applies only to the individual element directly preceding it—even if that's just a single character. This is hard to remember when you're used to seeing words, like say, *fish,* as a single unit. But if you add the quantifier after the *h*, as in /fish*/, it applies only to the *h*, not to the entire *fish*.

You can make a quantifier affect more than one character by using parentheses. The parentheses group characters or strings as if they were one element. Therefore, in /(fish)*/ the * quantifier affects the entire *fish*, not just the *h*.

A class is considered an independent unit. You don't need to add parentheses around it for the quantifier to apply to the whole class. So, /[a-z]*/ matches the same as /([a-z])*/, and is much prettier to boot. (Although the parentheses have yet another purpose which you won't achieve if you leave them out. For more details, consult *More on Using What You Already Matched* on page 202.)

Suppose part of the string you're looking for contains an element that might or might not be present. To have your string match whether that element *is there or not*, you use the ? quantifier.

To include optional elements:

1. Type the element that can either be present or not.

2. Type **?**.

✔ Tips

■ The ? quantifier will only match one of the elements. If there is a string of similar elements in a row, only the first will be matched by the element quantified with ?.

■ The ? quantifier only affects the element immediately preceding the ?. To have the ? affect an entire string of characters, enclose that string in parentheses.

```
1   #!/usr/local/bin/perl -wT
2   use strict;
3   use CGI ':standard';
4   my $phone;
5
6   print "Content-type: text/html\n\n";
7   $phone = param('phone');
8
9   if ($phone =~ /^(\(\d\d\d\))? ?\d\d\d-
       \d\d\d\d$/) {
10    print "You entered the phone number
         <B>$phone</B>";
11  } else {
12    print "Please enter the phone number
         in the form <P>(123) 456-7899<P>(The
         area code is optional.)";
13  }
```

9: There are two optional elements in this regular expression. The first question mark applies to the area code and surrounding parentheses. The second applies to the space between the area code and the number.

Figure 15.24 *The question mark applies to the element immediately preceding it. Enclose elements in parentheses where necessary (as here).*

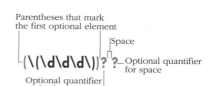

Figure 15.25 *Adding quantifiers (and necessary parentheses) make regular expressions even more bizarre looking. Taking them apart makes them easier to understand.*

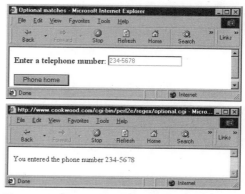

Figure 15.26 *Now the script accepts numbers with an area code as well as those without it.*

Choosing How Many to Match

```
1   #!/usr/local/bin/perl -wT
2   use strict;
3   use CGI ':standard';
4   my $phone;
5
6   print "Content-type: text/html\n\n";
7   $phone = param('phone');
8
9   if ($phone =~ /^((\(\d\d\d\))? ? \d\d\d-
    \d\d\d\d,? ?)+$/) {
10      print "You entered the phone
        number(s) <B>$phone</B>";
11  } else {
12      print "Please enter the phone
        number(s) in the form <P>(123) 456-
        7899<P>(The area code is optional.)";
13  }
```

9: I've enclosed the expression from Figure 15.24 on page 196 in parentheses and added a plus sign to allow visitors to enter one or more telephone numbers. Notice that I've also added an optional comma and optional space after the telephone number.

Figure 15.27 *Parentheses are crucial in determining what a quantifier applies to. Without the parentheses, the quantifier applies only to the single character immediately preceding it.*

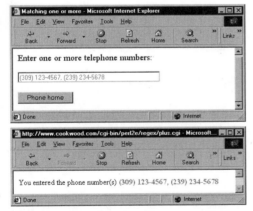

Figure 15.28 *Now the script will accept more than one telephone number, but will still require that at least one number be entered and that each number be properly formatted.*

Let's make our example fit even more situations. Say we want to let visitors enter more than one telephone number but we still want to make them enter *at least one*. The solution is to surround the previous regular expression with parentheses and add the plus (+) quantifier. The plus quantifier requires that at least one, but possibly more, of the element be present.

To match one or more elements:

1. Type the element that you want there to be at least one of (up to an unlimited number) in the search string.

2. Type **+**.

✔ Tips

- I've also added an optional comma and space after the telephone number in case the visitor feels compelled to separate the phone numbers in some way.

- The match will fail if there is not at least one of the elements in the search string.

- It doesn't matter how many of the elements are in the search string (as long as there is at least one).

Choosing How Many to Match

There's still something that might trip up our visitors in our phone example. If they put an extra space between the area code and the phone number, they'll get an error message. In order to accept data with extra characters (like spaces in this example) as long as it fulfills the rest of the formatting requirements, you use the asterisk (*) quantifier. The asterisk lets you match elements if they're present, but not worry too much if they're not. I describe such elements as *multiple optional*.

To include multiple optional elements:

1. Type the element that you want to search for in the search string.

2. Type *****. The match is successful whether the element is present or not.

✔ Tip

■ At first glance, a quantifier that matches whether something is there or not might seem pretty useless. Nothing could be farther from the truth. It offers you the flexibility to accept minor variations in an otherwise rigid pattern.

```perl
1   #!/usr/local/bin/perl -wT
2   use strict;
3   use CGI ':standard';
4   my $phone;
5
6   print "Content-type: text/html\n\n";
7   $phone = param('phone');
8
9   if ($phone =~ /^((\ (\d\d\d))? *\d\d\d-
    \d\d\d\d,? *)+$/) {
10  print "You entered the phone number(s)
    <B>$phone</B>";
11  } else {
12  print "Please enter the phone number(s)
    in the form <P>(123) 456-7899<P>(The
    area code is optional.)";
13  }
```

9:   The first asterisk allows an unlimited number of spaces (or none) after the area code. The second asterisk allows an unlimited number of spaces (or none) after each telephone number.

Figure 15.29 *Asterisks make the most sense when they're part of a larger regular expression.*

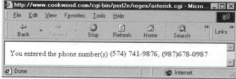

Figure 15.30 *Here the visitor has gone crazy, adding lots of extra spaces between the first area code and its number and again after the comma. Then she left off the space after the second area code. This script accepts all of that, as long as the rest of the pattern matches properly. Note that the spaces are lost in the displayed result since HTML doesn't recognize extra spaces.*

```
1   #!/usr/local/bin/perl -wT
2   use strict;
3   use CGI ':standard';
4   my $phone;
5
6   print "Content-type: text/html\n\n";
7   $phone = param('phone');
8
9   if ($phone =~ /^((\(\d{3}\))? *\d{3}-
      \d{4},? *)+$/) {
10  print "You entered the phone number(s)
      <B>$phone</B>";
11  } else {
12  print "Please enter the phone number(s)
      in the form <P>(123) 456-7899<P>(The
      area code is optional.)";
13  }
```

9: The number within curly brackets indicates exactly how many of the preceding element (in this case the \d) are required for a match.

Figure 15.31 *The regular expression in line 9 above is equivalent to the one in Figure 15.29 on page 198. But it's shorter, easier to type, more legible, and nicer looking.*

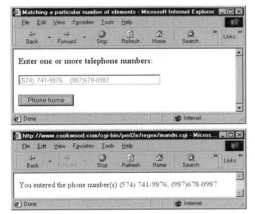

Figure 15.32 *The script works exactly as before. But it's neater.*

There's one shortcut we can add to our phone number regex. Instead of repeating \d over and over again, you can use a number to denote how many should be required for a match.

To match at least *m* and at most *n* elements:

1. Type the elements to match.

2. Type **{m,n}** where *m* is the minimum number of instances necessary for the element to appear in the search string and *n* is the maximum.

✔ Tips

- If you leave off the second number completely (as in the example), both *m* and *n* are set by the first number. So, {3} requires exactly three repetitions of the element to match successfully. No more, no less.

- If you leave off the second number, but keep the comma, the *n* is set to infinity. Therefore, {3,} requires at least three instances of the element to be successful but will also be successful with four or five or however many more.

- If you like, you can think of the ? as {0,1}, the + as {1,}, the * as {0,} and anything without a quantifier as having {1} by default.

- It's not particularly obvious at first, but \d{3} is successful at matching *1234*. Why? Because it can match exactly three digits *(123)* at the beginning of the string. Remember not to think about word or numbers as units. Perl doesn't either. To match only three-digit numbers, you need to anchor the expression *(see page 193).*

Choosing How Many to Match

Curbing a Quantifier's Greediness

A quantifier's greediness has nothing to do with manners. Instead, it means that a quantifier will match as much of the string as it can, as long as that doesn't mean that the entire regular expression will fail. This is especially important in less specific expressions where it's easier for a quantifier to grab more than its due.

For example, suppose you want to cull either the area code or the telephone exchange (the first three digits of the number) out of the phone number. You might think something like /.*(\d{3}).*/ would do just fine. You've got an unlimited number of characters, then 3 digits and then some more characters. The problem is that first .* is *greedy*. It not only takes up to the first three numbers, but it keeps going until it risks failing to match—which in this case is just before the last three numbers in the string. Since the last .* can match something or nothing, the first .* leaves it nothing with little compunction.

One way to get around greediness is to enclose an unlimited quantifier in specific elements that must match. For example, the * quantifier in /\(\d*\)/ is greedy but since the expression has to match a closing parentheses, the quantifier is limited to the area code—as long as there are no additional closing parentheses in the search string.

You can make quantifiers non-greedy by adding a ? to them (*?, +?, ??). Non-greedy quantifiers will match as little of the search string as possible while still attempting to match the entire regular expression.

```
1   #!/usr/local/bin/perl -wT
2   use strict;
3   use CGI ':standard';
4   my $phone;
5
6   print "Content-type: text/html\n\n";
7   $phone = param('phone');
8
9   if ($phone =~ /^((\(\(\d{3}\))? *\d{3}
    (-| )\d{4},? *)+$/) {
10      print "You entered the phone
    number(s) <B>$phone</B>";
11  } else {
12      print "Please enter the phone
    number(s) in the form <P>(123) 456-
    7899<P>(The area code is optional.)";
13  }
```

9: The highlighted section allows the visitor to sep-
    arate the three digit exchange from the last four
    digits of the number with *either* a dash *or* a
    space.

Figure 15.33 *You must enclose the dash, vertical bar,
and space within parentheses. Otherwise, the alternation would look for either the first half of the entire
expression (the area code and exchange) or the second
half (the last four digits of the phone number), which
wouldn't make much sense.*

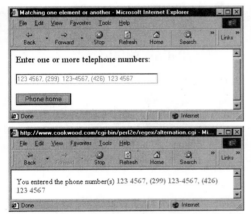

Figure 15.34 *Now the visitor can type the telephone
number with a dash or with a space. While it's important to check incoming data for proper formatting, the
more flexibility you can allow, the happier your visitors
will be.*

Matching One Element or Another

One final tool in Perl's regex arsenal is alternation, a fancy word that means "or". It is
often useful to be able to match one of two
patterns, or one of two elements within a
larger pattern. Alternation makes this possible.

To match one element or another:

1. Type the first element that you want to
search for.

2. Type | (the vertical bar—above the \ on
most keyboards).

3. Type the next element to search for.

4. Repeat steps 2–3, as desired.

✔ Tips

■ In contrast with the quantifiers that affect
only the single preceding element,
alternation affects as much of the
regular expression as it can. Therefore,
/ice tea|coffee/ matches *ice tea* or
coffee. (Note that there are no spaces
between the a and the | and the c.
Use parentheses to limit alternation:
/ice (tea|coffee)/ matches either *ice
tea* or *ice coffee*.

■ For a simple choice between individual
characters, you could use a character
class. For example, /[nr]ice tea/
would match either *nice tea* or *rice tea*.
Alternation lets you choose between two
or more complete regular expressions.

■ Elements in an alternation are matched
in the order in which they appear. So,
/ice tea|coffee/ will match the *ice tea*
in "Would you like ice tea or some hot
coffee?" and then simply stop, never
checking to see if the second choice is
present.

Matching One Element or Another

More on Using What You Already Matched

You've already seen how parentheses can extend the power of quantifiers *(see page 195)* and limit the reach of alternation *(see page 201)*, but parentheses serve one more useful function. Perl will automatically remember what was matched by the contents of each set of parentheses. This information is stored in special numbered variables, where the number reflects the order of the parentheses starting from the left.

To mark what you want to remember:

1. Enclose in parentheses the part of your search pattern that you want to reference.

2. In your mind (or on scratch paper), number the opening parentheses from left to right, starting with 1. Note the number of the parentheses whose match you're interested in.

To use the matched data later in the same pattern:

After the referenced parentheses in the search pattern, type **\n**, where *n* corresponds to the number of the parentheses (that you noted in step 2 above).

To use the matched data either in the replacement text itself or in an independent statement:

In the replacement text of a substitution expression *(see page 183)* or in an independent statement after a matching expression, type **$n**, where *n* corresponds to the number of the parentheses (that you noted in step 2 above).

```
1   #!/usr/local/bin/perl -wT
2   use strict;
3   use CGI ':standard';
4   my $address;
5
6   print "Content-type: text/html\n\n";
7   $address = param('address');
8
9   if ($address =~ /(\d{5}(-\d{4})?)/) {
10  print "I found a zip code of $1. Is that
       correct?";
11  } else {
12  print "No zip code was found.";
13  }
```

9:   The regular expression in this conditional checks for five-digit numbers, optionally followed by a dash and four more digits. The first set of parentheses encloses the entire nine-digit zip code. The second set of parentheses encloses just the optional section.

10: The variable $1 is set to whatever was matched by the first set of parentheses.

Figure 15.35 *Even though the second set of parentheses is mostly for applying the optional ? quantifier to the dash and four digits, it also serves to save that information into the $2 variable (which is not used in this script).*

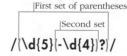

Figure 15.36 *The parentheses are numbered from left to right according to the position of the left parenthesis. In this example, the first set of parentheses encloses the entire regular expression while the second set encloses just the optional dash and four digits.*

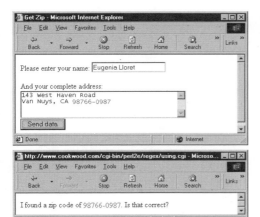

Figure 15.37 *The data that was matched by the first parenthesized section of the regular expression is saved in the $1 variable and then printed out.*

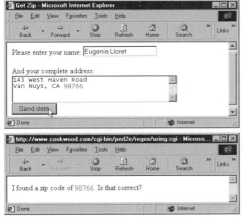

Figure 15.38 *If the visitor only types a five digit number (with no optional dash and extra four digits), that will be the data that is matched by the parenthesized section of the regular expression and saved in the $1 variable.*

To store what was matched in one or more variables:

1. Type **($scalar1, $scalar2)**, where *$scalar1* and *$scalar2* (and any others) are the variables in which you want to store the matched pieces of the search string.

2. Type **=**.

3. Type **$base**, where *base* is the name of the variable that contains the string to be searched.

4. Type **=~**.

5. Type **/pattern/**, where *pattern* is the regular expression that describes what you're looking for. Be sure to enclose in parentheses the parts of the pattern that you want to store.

6. Type **;** to finish the line.

✔ Tips

■ If you have more scalar variables in step 1 than parenthesized elements in step 5, the rightmost scalar variables will be undefined. If you have more parenthesized elements than scalar variables, the rightmost elements will not be stored.

■ You could just as easily store the parenthesized elements in an array (or a hash, if that makes sense). Type @array for step 1 where *array* is the name of the array.

■ If you append a g to the end of the match operator as in m/pattern/g, all of the matches throughout the search string will be saved to the specified variables (and not just the first match that Perl comes across).

■ In this example, a five-digit house number would give unexpected results.

More on Using What You Already Matched

REMEMBERING WHAT VISITORS TELL YOU

Each time your visitor activates a CGI script by pressing a submit button, by default, the browser treats that person as a new, separate individual, even if it's the same exact person that submitted a CGI script a second earlier.

Nevertheless, it's often useful to remember information about a visitor from one page to the next. For example, if you ask a visitor to fill out his name, address, and phone number, and then direct him to another page where he can order your handcrafted maple furniture, you don't want to bother him again later for the same personal information. Or, if you allow your visitors to set particular preferences for viewing your pages—like background color, language, or anything else—being able to remember the visitor's settings each time she visits your site will make your visitor feel special and well taken care of.

There are two simple ways of remembering things about your visitors: cookies and hidden fields. This chapter will explain the basic concepts behind each one and tell you how to put them to use.

About Hidden Fields

HTML forms allow for a special kind of field that doesn't appear in the browser, and yet is part of the form. These hidden fields seem counterproductive at first glance: if your visitors can't see them, how will they fill them in? The answer is they won't. Instead, you will use hidden fields to store information gathered from an earlier form so that it can be combined with the present form's data.

Imagine, for example, that on the first page, you ask for a visitor's name, address, and telephone number. You then want to send them to your catalog page where they can choose which piece of furniture they wish to order. Instead of asking them for their personal data a second time, you can use a CGI script to collect the data from the first form and then generate the hidden fields that will contain this data in the second form. Then, when you go to process the data from the second form, all of the fields, including both the items ordered and the personal data, will be analyzed.

Don't get carried away by the word *hidden*. While hidden fields are not shown by the browser, they still form part of the HTML code that makes up the page (so the CGI script can get at them), and thus are not at all invisible if someone should look at the source code for your page *(see Figure 16.4 on page 209)*.

```
<FORM METHOD=POST
ACTION="whatever.cgi">

<INPUT TYPE="hidden" NAME="quantity"
VALUE="7">

<INPUT TYPE="submit" VALUE="Submit Data">
```

Figure 16.1 *An excerpt from the HTML file used to create the form shows the syntax for hidden elements. It doesn't make much sense to write such code yourself and thus I'm reluctant to create such an example. On the following page you'll see how to use a CGI script to generate this HTML code.*

Adding Hidden Fields to a Form

Although you hardly ever add hidden fields to an HTML document yourself, you'll have to know how to do it so you can make your Perl script create them.

To add hidden fields to a form:

1. Within the form on your HTML page, type **<INPUT TYPE="hidden"**.

2. Type **NAME="name"**, where *name* is a short description of the information to be stored.

3. Type **VALUE="value"**, where *value* is the information itself that is to be stored.

4. Type **>**.

✔ Tips

■   It doesn't matter where the hidden fields appear in your form since they won't appear in the browser anyway. As long as they are within the opening and closing FORM tags, you're OK.

■   HTML 4 does not require quotation marks around attribute values if those values are comprised solely of a combination of letters, digits, and the hyphen, period, underscore, and colon. Since quotation marks have a special meaning in a Perl script and will thus need to be backslashed to get rid of that special meaning, sometimes it's simpler to leave them out altogether where possible. Still, if you prefer to use them—for example, to write conforming XHTML code, be sure to read up on the qq function *(see page 31)* and here documents *(see page 234)*. They make life with quotes much simpler.

■   CGI.pm contains pre-defined subroutines for creating hidden fields. You can find more details in CGI.pm's documentation.

Storing Collected Data in a Hidden Field

Hidden fields are best generated by the same CGI script that processes the initial form—that is, the one that contains the data to be stored. Then you'll create a second script to process the final form—the one that contains both the new data and the stored data.

To store collected data in a hidden field:

1. In your Perl script, generate the HTML code for the page that should appear when the initial form has been submitted. This page may contain some kind of confirmation that the first bit of information has been received and processed, together with a new form to collect the new data. For more information on printing HTML tags, consult *Formatting Output with HTML* on page 232.

2. Store all the field names from the original HTML form in an array by typing **@keys = param()**, where *keys* identifies the set of field names. For more details on using the param function without parameters, see consult *Getting All the Form Element's Names* on page 106.

3. Then type **foreach $key (@keys) {**, where *$key* is the name of the variable that will temporarily store each member of the @keys array, and *@keys* matches the array name you used in step 2.

4. Type **$value= param($key);** to find what value the visitor has entered in each field and store it in the *$value* variable.

5. Type **print qq(<INPUT TYPE="hidden" NAME="$key" VALUE="$value">\n);**, where *$key* matches the variable for the foreach loop defined in step 3 and *$value* matches the variable created in step 4.

Figure 16.2 *Here is the form that gathers the information that we want to store in the hidden fields.*

```
1   #!/usr/local/bin/perl -wT
2   use strict;
3   use CGI ':standard';
4   my ($name, @keys);
5
6   $name= param('name');
7
8   print "Content-type:text/html\n\n";
9   print "<HTML><HEAD><TITLE>Using Hidden
        Fields</TITLE></HEAD><BODY>\n";
10  print "Thanks, $name, for entering your
        personal data. Now choose which items
        you'd like to purchase.\n";
11
12  print qq(<FORM METHOD=POST
        ACTION="hidden2.cgi">\n);
13  print qq(Item <INPUT TYPE="text"
        NAME="item">\n);
14
15  @keys = param();
16
17  foreach my $key (@keys) {
18  my $value= param($key);
19  print qq(<INPUT TYPE="hidden"
        NAME="$key" VALUE="$value">\n);
20  }
21
22  print qq(<INPUT TYPE="submit"
        VALUE="Send order">\n);
23  print "</FORM></BODY></HTML>\n";
```

6: The param function parses the incoming name field and assigns it to the $name variable.

8: Lines 8–13 generate the beginning of the HTML page, including the form and its *new* field. Notice how I've used the qq function to avoid having to backslash double quotes. This makes it easy to ensure that multi-word attribute values are properly quoted in the generated HTML code.

15: In Line 15, we store all of the field names from the original HTML page into the @keys array by calling the param function without parameters.

17: Lines 17–20 go through each field name, find its corresponding value with param and create a hidden field with that name and value.

22: Lines 22–23 complete the form and the HTML page itself. Again, I use qq to simplify the inclusion of double quotes (*see page 31*).

Figure 16.3 *This script has two jobs. First, it parses the data from the form (shown in Figure 16.2 above) and second, it generates a new form into which it stores the collected data in hidden fields.*

Figure 16.4 *Here is the generated form (in which the visitor has entered new data). Notice that the hidden fields are invisible in the browser (top) but are clearly present in the source code.*

```
1   #!/usr/local/bin/perl -wT
2   use strict;
3   use CGI ':standard';
4
5   my ($name, $state, $item);
6   $name=param('name');
7   $state=param('state');
8   $item=param('item');
9
10  print "Content-type:text/html\n\n";
11  print '<HTML><HEAD><TITLE>Using Hidden
        Fields</TITLE></HEAD><BODY>';
12
13  print "The item ordered by $name from
        $state is";
14  print "<P>$item";
15  print "<P>Thanks. It's on its way.";
16  print '</BODY></HTML>';
```

6:   Lines 6–8 store the values, both from the visible and from the hidden fields, in the `$name`, `$state`, and `$item` variables.

13: Line 13 prints the data from the hidden fields.

14: Line 14 prints the new data.

Figure 16.5 *The CGI script called by the generated form is different from the one that actually generated the form. To keep things simple, this script just parses the incoming data and prints it out. You'll probably want to do more than that. (Thankfully, you won't have space constraints.)*

Figure 16.6 *The data from the new field* (item) *is analyzed and processed together with the data from the hidden fields* (name *and* state). *All of the data is displayed in this final result.*

6. Type **}** to complete the `foreach` loop that creates the hidden fields for each key-value pair that was collected from the initial form.

✔ Tips

- Processing the hidden fields is just like processing any form data—use CGI.pm.

- I've used the simplest possible example so that you can understand the underlying technique. Once you get the idea, you can embellish in lots of ways—including reading in the HTML tags from a template *(see page 253)*, creating more complicated scripts that complete more serious processing of the information gathered, and whatever else you can think up. Just remember the basic premise: the script that processes the data to be stored should generate the hidden fields in the next form.

- CGI.pm has a lot of fancy features for creating and keeping track of hidden fields, but I think they're a bit more complicated than we need to get into at this point. Plus, I think it's important to see exactly what's happening, as shown in this example. You can find out more about CGI.pm at *http://stein.cshl.org/WWW/software/CGI/*.

- Hidden fields are useful but transitory. Once your visitor leaves your site or even jumps to a page that's outside the realm of the interconnected scripts that store and generate the hidden fields, the connection between that visitor and the information you're currently collecting is lost.

- The qq function is great for outputting strings that contain both double quotes and variables that need to be interpolated (as with hidden fields). For more details, see *Quoting without Quotes* on page 31.

Storing Collected Data in a Hidden Field

About Cookies

If you want to respond to each visitor personally, it would be ideal if they would simply identify themselves in some way each time they visit the pages on your site. Of course, it's unlikely that folks will take the time to do that. Instead, Netscape Communications created a way to *mark* visitors when they come to your site and then look at that mark when they return. The mark is called a *cookie* ("for no compelling reason," according to Netscape's documentation, although the image of Hansel and Gretel marking the way home with bits of cookie would be a good excuse).

For example, imagine that a visitor comes to your site and tells you, via a form, that they would prefer to read the information from your site in French. You could send a cookie to their browser that says language=French. The browser will save the cookie (until it expires) and offer it to you in an environment variable the next time the visitor comes to your site. You can then read the cookie, find out that this particular visitor prefers French, and even though you know nothing more about them, you can provide the content in that language to a satisfied, and now duly impressed, visitor.

Cookies are pretty safe (although crackers are terribly resourceful) since they are text files and not executable and thus cannot harbor nasty viruses. Nevertheless, visitors sometimes don't like them because they don't want to be tracked. Most browsers allow the visitor to reject all or some of the cookies that get sent their way *(see page 220)*. You'll want to keep that in mind.

Figure 16.7 *If you open the* cookies.txt *file in your Netscape directory on your Windows machine, you'll see something like this. The first column gives the domain, the third column shows the path, the fourth column denotes whether the cookie must travel on secure connections, the fifth gives the expiration date, and the sixth and seventh give the name and value of the information stored in the cookie.*

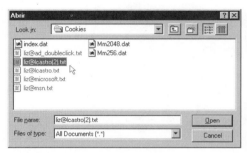

Figure 16.8 *Internet Explorer for Windows stores each cookie in its own individual file in the Cookies folder, inside the Windows folder.*

Figure 16.9 *When you open a cookie stored with Internet Explorer for Windows, you'll see the name and value on the first and second lines, respectively, followed by the domain name.*

Figure 16.10 *When you open Netscape for Macintosh's MagicCookie file (that is stored in the Netscape folder, in the Preferences folder, in the System Folder), you'll see something like this. The first column is for the domain, the third for the path, the fourth for security, the fifth for the expiration date, and the sixth and seventh for the name and value of the information stored in the cookie.*

Figure 16.11 *To view the cookies that Internet Explorer for Mac saves, open that browser and choose Edit > Preferences.*

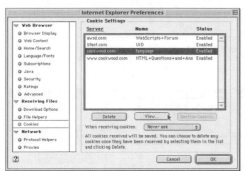

Figure 16.12 *Still in Explorer for Mac, click Cookies in the left-hand column (under Receiving Files) and then, in the list at right, choose the cookie you want to view and click the View button.*

Figure 16.13 *Explorer labels each bit of information stored in the cookie.*

Looking at Your Browser's Cookies

Perhaps the best way to understand cookies is to take a look at them. If you've been traveling around the Web, and allow other sites to send you cookies *(see page 220)*, your browser will have saved a text file that contains those cookies. You can open the cookie file in any text editor.

To look at (and edit) your browser's cookies:

1. Open your text editor.

2. If you use Netscape for Windows, there will be a file called *cookies.txt* in the directory that contains Netscape **(Figure 16.7)**.

   For Explorer for Windows, look in the Cookies folder in your Windows folder. Explorer creates individual files for each cookie **(Figures 16.8 and 16.9)**.

   For Netscape for Macintosh, open the MagicCookie file inside the Netscape folder in the Preferences folder inside your System Folder **(Figure 16.10)**.

   For Explorer for Macintosh, choose Edit > Preferences **(Figure 16.11)**. Then click Cookies in the left-hand column (under Receiving Files). Then, select the desired cookie and click View **(Figure 16.12)**. Explorer displays the stored data **(Figure 16.13)**.

3. Delete unwanted cookies stored by Netscape by selecting the entire cookie and pressing Delete. In the case of Explorer for Windows, delete the whole unwanted cookie file. In Explorer for Mac, select the cookie and press the Delete button in the Internet Explorer Preferences box.

Looking at Your Browser's Cookies

Sending a Cookie

To save information on your visitor's browser you'll have to do two things. You'll first collect some information to save and give it a name, and then you'll create and send that information to the visitor's browser.

To send a cookie:

1. Collect the data that you want to send to the visitor and decide on the name that will identify that data.

2. In your Perl script, before printing anything to the browser—that is, before the MIME content line *(see page 38)*—type **print "Set-Cookie:**.

3. Type **name**, where *name* is either a variable or a constant that identifies the data to be stored in the cookie. Don't type a space between steps 2 and 3.

4. Type **=** to separate the name and value with an equals sign.

5. Type **value**, where *value* is either a variable or a constant that represents the actual data that you want to store.

6. Type **\n"** to add a newline at the end of the Set-Cookie header.

7. Type **;** to complete the sentence.

✔ Tips

- The data can come from processing a form, opening an external file, analyzing an earlier cookie, or it may just be a constant. It's up to you.

- The name and the value cannot contain semicolons, commas, or white space. If you need to include such characters you must first convert them to their hexadecimal equivalents.

```
1   #!/usr/local/bin/perl -wT
2   use strict;
3   use CGI ':standard';
4   my $language = param('language');
5
6   print "Set-Cookie:language=
    $language\n";
7
8   print "Content-type: text/html\n\n";
9   print '<HTML><HEAD><TITLE>Thanks for
    choosing!</TITLE></HEAD><BODY>';
10  print "You chose $language. Next time
    you visit, I'll greet you
    accordingly.";
```

4: Line 4 analyzes and stores the incoming data, as usual.

6: This line sends a cookie called *language* to the server. The cookie's value corresponds to whatever the visitor typed in the language field on the form—which is stored in the $language variable. Notice the single newline (\n) at the end of the print statement. It's important that this line appear before the Content-type header in line 8.

8: Lines 8–10 give feedback to the visitor as usual. Remember that the browser doesn't like having nothing to do.

Figure 16.14 *You have to print the Set-Cookie header (line 6) before printing the MIME content line for the HTML page with the feedback (line 8).*

Figure 16.15 *The visitor doesn't see anything different about the form. They simply make their selection and submit the form as usual.*

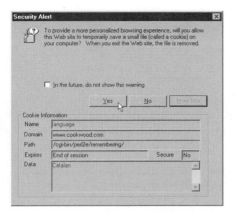

Figure 16.16 *Depending on the preferences that the visitor has set for the browser (see page 220), an alert may appear advising the visitor that a cookie is about to be sent and allowing them to refuse it. The alert will contain the name and value of the information contained in the cookie as well as the expiration date (see page 214), domain (see page 215), and path (see page 216). (IE5 for Windows makes you click the More Info button to get to this data.)*

Figure 16.17 *There is no outward evidence for the visitor (except the alert shown in Figure 16.16, which only appears in certain circumstances) that a cookie has been sent. It's up to you to tell your visitors what's going on.*

■ You can send several cookies with the same script. Simply repeat steps 1–7 as necessary.

■ Cookies can include additional data. For more details, see pages 214–217.

■ *You* decide exactly what information you want to store. You can save a visitor's name (which you'll have to ask them for), or note if they've visited you before, and if so, how many times. It's up to you. You can store any information at your disposal in a cookie, including data you cull from environment variables *(see page 99)*.

■ You don't have to store juicy data in the cookie itself—you can store an identification code for the visitor and then use that code to access data stored in another file. If you create codes for your visitors that link them to sensitive information, you'll want to encrypt them in some way so that sneaky visitors cannot change their own cookies *(see page 211)* in an attempt to get to other folks' data.

■ Devise an alternate system (or error message) for visitors who don't accept cookies. Pages that don't work for no apparent reason are annoying.

■ You can send up to 20 cookies, with a maximum size of 4Kb—which is approximately 4000 characters, a sizable amount—per cookie. Each visitor can store up to 300 cookies from all the sites they've visited.

■ CGI.pm offers a more complete but also more complicated system of sending cookies. For example, you can send a cookie that contains an entire array or a hash, and it escapes the white space and other disallowed characters for you. Consult CGI.pm's documentation for details.

Sending a Cookie

Setting a Cookie's Expiration Date

By default, cookies are temporarily stored in the browser's RAM and disappear when the visitor quits out of the browser. If you want to be able to access the information at a later date, you have to add an expiration date to the cookie. The expiration date simply determines how long the cookie will remain in the cookie file—assuming the visitor doesn't manually erase it first *(see page 211)*.

To set a cookie's expiration date:

1. Follow steps 1–5 on page 212 to begin the `Set-Cookie` header.

2. Type `;` to separate the name-value pair from the expiration date.

3. Type **expires=Wdy, DD-Mon-YYYY HH:MM:SS GMT**, where *Wdy* is the (optional) three-letter abbreviation for the day of the week, *DD* is the two-digit number of the day of the month, *Mon* is the three-letter abbreviation for the name of the month, *YYYY* is the four-digit representation of the year, *HH* is the two-digit number for the hour, in 24-hour format and corresponding to Greenwich Mean Time, *MM* is the two-digit number for the minutes, and *SS* is the two-digit number for the seconds. Type *GMT* as is—it means *Greenwich Mean Time*.

4. Complete the Set-Cookie line by following steps 6–7 on page 212.

✔ Tip

■ 24-hour format (often referred to as *military time*) means that 12am is 00, 1am is 01, and so on, and that 1pm is represented as *13*, 2pm is *14*, and so on up to *23* for 11pm.

```
1   #!/usr/local/bin/perl -wT
2   use strict;
3   use CGI ':standard';
4   my $language = param('language');
5
6   print "Set-Cookie:language=$language;
        expires=3-May-2002 00:00:00 GMT\n";
7
8   print "Content-type: text/html\n\n";
9   print "<HTML><HEAD><TITLE>Thanks for
        choosing!</TITLE></HEAD><BODY>";
10  print "You chose $language. Next time
        you visit, I'll greet you
        accordingly.";
```

6: This line now contains an expiration date for the cookie. Notice the format for the date and the semicolon that separates it from the cookie's data.

Figure 16.18 *Setting an expiration date for a cookie is the only way you can get rid of it. (The visitor can manually edit their cookie file, but few know how—see page 211.)*

Figure 16.19 *The cookie will be sent when the visitor activates the form.*

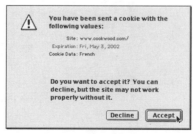

Figure 16.20 *Depending on the preferences set for the browser, an alert may appear with information—including the expiration date—about the cookie.*

Figure 16.21 *You must always give your visitor some output.*

```
1   #!/usr/local/bin/perl -wT
2   use strict;
3   use CGI ':standard';
4   my $language = param('language');
5
6   print "Set-Cookie:language=$language;
       expires=3-May-2002 00:00:00 GMT;
       domain=help.cookwood.com\n";
7
8   print "Content-type: text/html\n\n";
9   print "<HTML><HEAD><TITLE>Thanks for
       choosing!</TITLE></HEAD><BODY>";
10  print "You chose $language. Next time
       you visit, I'll greet you
       accordingly.";
```

6: This line now contains a limited domain for the
    cookie. Don't forget to separate it from the rest
    of the `Set-Cookie` line with a semicolon.

Figure 16.22 *Only requests for cookies that come from the* help.cookwood.com *domain will be honored.*

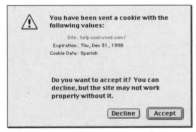

Figure 16.23 *Depending on the preferences the visitor has set for the browser, an alert may appear with information—including the domain—about the cookie.*

Limiting a Cookie to a Domain

While a visitor's browser may store up to 300 cookies from a variety of different Web sites, the browser will only let *you* read cookies that came from *your* full domain. In order to determine which cookies came from you, the browser looks at the domain attribute— which is set by default to the same domain that sent the cookie. If your domain is divided into smaller subdomains (*home.domain.com*, *help.domain.com*, etc.), you can set the cookie's domain to any of the more limited domains so that only those domains have access to their cookies.

To limit a cookie to a domain:

1. Follow steps 1–5 on page 212 to begin the `Set-Cookie` header.

2. If desired, set the expiration date as explained on page 214.

3. Type ; to separate the rest of the `Set-Cookie` header from the domain.

4. Type **domain=www.domain.com**, where *www.domain.com* is the name of the domain that will be able to read the cookie once it is has been sent.

5. Complete the Set-Cookie line by following steps 6–7 on page 212.

✔ Tips

■ The domain you use must have at least two periods if it belongs to one of the seven special top-level domains (*com, edu, net, org, gov, mil,* or *int*), or three periods if it ends some other way.

■ You can only set cookies for the domain you're sending the cookie from.

■ To allow cookies to be sent back to any part of a given domain, use `.domain.com` (with an initial period).

Limiting a Cookie to a Domain

Limiting a Cookie to a Part of Your Server

If you don't have to save CGI scripts in the cgi-bin directory, and thus are setting cookies from different locations, you may want to limit a part of your server's access to cookies. You can do this by specifying the path (or a part of the path) from which a cookie can be read.

To limit a cookie to a particular area of your server:

1. Follow steps 1–5 on page 212 to begin the `Set-Cookie` header.

2. If desired, set the expiration date and domain (*see pages 214–215*).

3. Type `;` to separate the rest of the `Set-Cookie` header from the domain.

4. Type **path=/directory**, where *directory* is the path that will be authorized to read the cookie once it is has been sent.

5. Complete the Set-Cookie line by following steps 6–7 on page 212.

✔ Tips

■ The domain (*see page 215*) is checked before the path. If the domain doesn't match, the path is not even looked at.

■ As you might expect, / is the most general path possible, and thus refers to the largest area on the server.

■ If you don't specify a path, it is automatically set as the same path as the file that sent the cookie.

■ If all your scripts are in the cgi-bin directory then it doesn't make much sense to alter the path.

```
1   #!/usr/local/bin/perl -wT
2   use strict;
3   use CGI ':standard';
4   my $language = param('language');
5
6   print "Set-Cookie:language=$language;
    expires=3-May-2002 00:00:00 GMT;
    domain=www.cookwood.com;path=/help\n"
    ;
7
8   print "Content-type: text/html\n\n";
9   print "<HTML><HEAD><TITLE>Thanks for
    choosing!</TITLE></HEAD><BODY>";
10  print "You chose $language. Next time
    you visit, I'll greet you
    accordingly.";
```

6:   This line now sets a limited path for the cookie. Don't forget to separate it from the rest of the `Set-Cookie` line with a semicolon.

Figure 16.24 *Now, only requests for cookies that come from the paths that match /help (including /helpers and /help/files on the* help.cookwood.com *domain will be honored.*

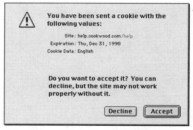

Figure 16.25 *Depending on the preferences the visitor has set for the browser, an alert may appear with information—including the path—about the cookie.*

```
1   #!/usr/local/bin/perl -wT
2   use strict;
3   use CGI ':standard';
4   my $language = param('language');
5
6   print "Set-Cookie:language=$language;
      expires=3-May-2002 00:00:00 GMT;
      domain=www.cookwood.com;
      path=/help;secure\n";
7
8   print "Content-type: text/html\n\n";
9   print "<HTML><HEAD><TITLE>Thanks for
      choosing!</TITLE></HEAD><BODY>";
10  print "You chose $language. Next time
      you visit, I'll greet you
      accordingly.";
```

6:   This line now limits the cookie to secure con-
     nections. Don't forget to separate it from the rest
     of the Set-Cookie line with a semi-colon.

Figure 16.26 *Only requests for cookies that come from secure servers will be honored.*

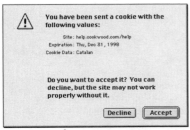

Figure 16.27 *IE does not provide information about the secureness of a cookie.*

Limiting Cookies to Secure Connections

If you are saving particularly sensitive information—or an identification code that leads to sensitive information—via a cookie, you might want to limit sending the cookie to secure connections. This means that the cookie will only be sent to secure servers.

To limit cookies to secure connections:

1. Follow steps 1–5 on page 212 to begin the Set-Cookie header.

2. If desired, set the additional attributes as explained on pages 214–216.

3. Type **;** to separate the rest of the Set-Cookie header from the domain.

4. Type **secure**.

5. Complete the Set-Cookie line by following steps 6–7 on page 212.

✔ Tip

■   Don't use secure unless you're really on a secure server (https). Otherwise, you won't get the cookies back.

Limiting Cookies to Secure Connections

Reading and Using a Cookie

OK, you've stored a bit of information on your visitor's computer. Now how do you read it and use it? In fact, the server sends you all the information in all of the cookies available to you (given the domain and the path) each time you send a script to the server. That information is stored in the HTTP_COOKIE environment variable. You can use CGI.pm to analyze that variable to see what it contains.

To read and use a cookie:

1. Type **$cookie_value =**, where *$cookie_value* is the variable where you will store the information gleaned from the cookie.

2. Type **cookie** to begin CGI.pm's cookie function.

3. Type **('cookie_name')**, where *cookie_name* is the name you gave the cookie when you sent it, back in step 3 on page 212.

4. Type **;** to complete the line.

5. Create the part of the script that uses the information read from the cookie.

6. If desired, create an error message that prints if no cookies are set in the HTTP_COOKIE variable.

```
1  #!/usr/local/bin/perl -wT
2  use strict;
3  use CGI ':standard';
4  my ($language, %greeting);
5
6  print "Content-type: text/html\n\n";
7  $language = cookie('language');
8  %greeting = (Catalan => 'Bon dia.
   <P>Benvingut a la nostra p&agrave;gina
   Web.', Spanish => 'Buenos d&iacute;as.
   <P>Bienvenidos a nuestra p&aacute;gina
   Web.', French => 'Bon jour.
   Bienvenue!', English => 'Hello.
   <P>Welcome to our Web page.');
9
10 if ($language) {
11   print '<HTML><HEAD><TITLE>Greeting
     </TITLE></HEAD><BODY>';
12   print "<CENTER><H1>
     $greeting{$language}</H1></CENTER>";
13   print '</BODY></HTML>';
14
15 } else {
16   print "Couldn't find any cookies.
     Perhaps you've got your browser set
     to refuse all cookies?";
17 }
```

7: Line 7 uses CGI.pm's cookie function to get the information from the cookie called "language" and then stores it in the $language variable.
10: The if clause checks to see if there is any cookie information.
12: If there is cookie information, it is used to access the desired data from the %greeting hash (line 8).
15: Lines 15–17. If the if condition is false (that is, no cookie information was found and thus $language is empty or undefined), then the else clause prints out an error message.

Figure 16.28 *Since you can store up to 20 individual cookies on the visitor's browser, you'll have to specify the cookie you want to use by name (line 7).*

Figure 16.29 *So, the visitor fills out the form and activates the script that sends the cookie.*

Figure 16.30 *You confirm that you've received the information.*

Figure 16.31 *In this example, I used the cookie to save information about the visitor's preferred language. Then I used that information to actually print out a greeting in that language—Catalan in this case—the next time they visit.*

Figure 16.32 *If no cookie information is available, the visitor will see this error.*

✔ Tips

- For more information on using environment variables, consult Chapter 8, *Environment Variables.*

- Although you may have set the expiration date, domain, and other cookie information, only the name and value are available in the `HTTP_COOKIE` environment variable.

- Although I don't explain it in this book, since I find it a bit more complicated than a beginner needs, you can use CGI.pm to store an entire array or hash in a cookie. In that case, when you go to retrieve the cookie, you'd have to store that data in an appropriate variable: for example, `@cookie_info` for arrays, and `%cookie_info` for hashes. You can find more information about CGI.pm's `cookie` function in CGI.pm's online documentation.

Reading and Using a Cookie

How (and Why) Visitors Refuse Cookies

Some folks are not interested in anyone keeping tabs on them. They may have unfounded worries of you copying personal data from their computers or infecting them with a virus. (Neither is possible—you can only store non-executable files with data they have given you, along with environment variables.) And they may know that some sites compile information about which pages folks visit and then use it for marketing purposes. Therefore, some visitors may either refuse all or some of the cookies that are sent their way.

To control cookies:

1. In Explorer for Windows, choose Tools > Internet Options, click the Security tab, and then the Custom Level button **(Figure 16.33)**.

   For Explorer for Mac and Netscape (on both Mac and Windows), choose Edit > Preferences in your browser. Then, for Explorer, click Cookies under Receiving Files in the left list **(Figure 16.34)**. Or for Netscape, click Advanced under Category in the left list **(Figure 16.35)**.

2. Choose whether to accept all cookies, whether you want the browser to ask you about each cookie, or if you want to refuse all cookies.

3. Click OK to save the preferences.

✔ Tip

■ Tell your visitors what you're doing to put them at ease. Remind them that you can't access, save, or share their personal data unless they give it to you first. Stating your privacy policy is a good way to assure your visitors.

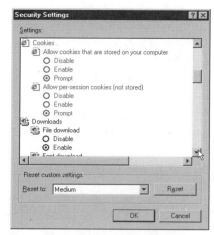

Figure 16.33 *With Internet Explorer for Windows, you choose Tools > Internet Options and then click the Security tab, and finally the Custom Level button. The cookie controls are below the set of ActiveX preferences but before the Downloading preferences.*

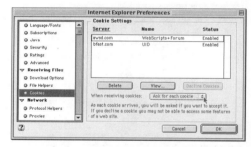

Figure 16.34 *In Explorer for Mac, click Cookies at left and then choose the desired option from the pop-up menu.*

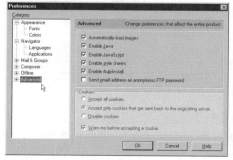

Figure 16.35 *In Netscape for Windows or Mac (they're virtually identical in this respect), choose Edit > Preferences, click the Advanced tab at the left, and then choose the cookie option at right.*

FORMATTING, PRINTING, AND HTML

Even outside of the CGI world, Perl is renowned for its strengths in manipulating text. You can use Perl to format your text in special ways before it ever makes it to the browser. I discuss some of Perl's more useful formatting functions in the first part of this chapter.

Of course, once you're ready to output information with a browser, you'll want to do some formatting with HTML. There are a number of shortcuts and tricks that will help you do just that, and I'll explain these starting on page 232.

Formatting Output with Perl

Perl has a couple of important functions for formatting data. The first, printf, lets you format output as you print. The second, sprintf, uses exactly the same parameters, but instead of printing out the result, saves the resulting string in another variable that you can then process as necessary. Both functions apply one or more format patterns (created by you) to the specified scalars.

To format output with Perl:

1. Type **printf (** to simply print out the formatted data.

    Or type **$formatted = sprintf (**, where *$formatted* is the name of the scalar variable in which you wish to store the newly formatted data (which will be a string).

2. Type **model,,** where *model* contains text and/or format patterns that you wish to apply to your data. We'll discuss format patterns on pages 223–225.

3. Type **data**, where *data* is one or more comma-separated scalars containing the data you want to format.

4. Type **)**.

5. Type **;** to complete the print statement.

✔ Tips

■   Multiple format patterns should be separated by the same characters that you want to have appear between the multiple pieces of data. Think of each format pattern as both a placeholder and model for its corresponding piece of data. Any text that is not part of a format pattern will be output as is.

■   The sprintf function returns a string, not a number.

```
1   #!/usr/local/bin/perl -wT
2   use strict;
3   use CGI ':standard';
4
5   print "Content-type:text/html\n\n";
6
7   my $price = param('price');
8   my $tax = param('tax')/100;
9
10  my $salestax = $price * $tax;
11
12  my $formattax = sprintf ('$%.2f',
        $salestax);
13
14  print "You'll have to pay $formattax in
        sales tax, unformatted it would look
        like $salestax";
```

7: In the real world, I'd use a regular expression to make sure the visitor had typed numbers (and no extraneous symbols or text) in the price and tax fields.

12: This line formats the contents of the $salestax variable and stores the results in the $formattax variable (which we print in line 14).

Figure 17.1 *The* sprintf *function makes it easy to format your data properly.*

Figure 17.2 *The visitor enters the price and the tax.*

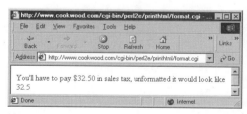

Figure 17.3 *The sales tax is calculated and then printed out, first in dollars and cents and then without formatting (for comparison).*

The percent sign begins the pattern

Zeros will be used for padding, if necessary.

The output will have at least 2 characters.

%02d ── The *d* indicates that the output will be an *integer*, or whole number. It also ends the pattern.

Since there is no hyphen after the %, the result will be aligned to the right.

Figure 17.4 *Here's a typical pattern for integers that you might want to use for dates and times. A number like 3 would be output as 03, (two characters are required in the output, a zero is used as the padding). A number like 423 would be output as 423 (it has at least 2 characters already and needs no padding).*

```
1   #!/usr/local/bin/perl -wT
2   use strict;
3
4   my ($sec,$min,$hour)=localtime;
5
6   print "Content-type: text/html\n\n";
7   printf 'According to my server, right
        now the time is %02d:%02d:%02d',
        $hour, $min, $sec;
```

4: We assign the first three values from the `localtime` function to individual scalars *(see page 141)*. The other six values are silently ignored, which is fine, since we don't need them here.

7: The `printf` function contains some extra text at the beginning which will be printed as is, and also includes three format patterns, which will be used for the three variables that follow the string ($hour, $min, and $sec).

Figure 17.5 *If you're going to print the formatted numbers right away, you might as well use* `printf` *rather than* `sprintf`.

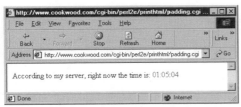

Figure 17.6 *The time is properly formatted. Imagine how strange it would look if it was displayed without the padding (as 1:5:4).*

Creating a Format Pattern for Integers

While you may be satisfied with outputting an integer as is, there are specific situations—like with dates and times—in which it is useful to add padding or change the alignment.

To create a format pattern for integers:

1. Type the **%** (percent sign) to begin the pattern.

2. Type **-** (a hyphen) if you want the integer aligned to the left, or nothing to have it aligned to the right.

3. Type **0** (a zero) to pad extra zeros to the left of the integer, or nothing to fill extra spaces with, well, spaces.

4. Type **m**, where *m* is the minimum number of characters that the output should contain.

5. Type **d**, which stands for *d*ecimal (base 10) number. (It *doesn't* mean the number has a decimal point).

✔ Tips

■ Extra padding (zeros or spaces, depending on what you've typed in step 3) will only occur if there are fewer digits in the original number than the quantity specified with *m* in step 4.

■ Padding, if any, will be added to the right if the number is left aligned or to the left if it's right aligned. Padding to the right is always spaces, and not zeros, for obvious reasons.

■ You may specify characters that should be output as is before, after, and between patterns.

Creating a Format Pattern for Integers

Creating a Format Pattern for Non-Integers

With numbers that have a fractional part, like 25.54 or 7.3, the pattern is slightly different.

To create a format pattern for non-integer numbers:

1. Type the **%** (percent sign) to begin the pattern.

2. Type **0** (a zero) to pad extra zeros to the left of the integer, or nothing to fill extra spaces with, well, spaces.

3. If desired, type **m**, where *m* is the minimum number of characters that the output should contain.

4. If desired, type **.n**, where *n* is the number of digits that should appear to the right of the decimal point. The default for *n*, if you skip this step, is 6.

5. Type **f**, which stands for *f*loating point number.

✔ Tips

■ You can add a + or a space between step 1 and step 2 to have a + or a space appear before positive numbers.

■ If there are more digits in the fractional part of the number than the number specified by *n*, the extra digits are omitted. If *n* is larger than the number of fractional digits in the input, zeros are added as necessary.

■ Extra padding (zeros or spaces, depending on what you've typed in step 2) will only occur if there are fewer digits in the original number than the quantity specified with *m* in step 3.

■ You may type characters before and after the pattern that should be output as is.

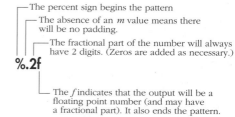

Figure 17.7 *Here's a typical pattern for formatting dollars and cents. The output will always have two digits in the fractional part of the number (to the right of the decimal point).*

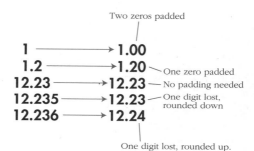

Figure 17.8 *Here are some example outputs using the format shown in Figure 17.7.*

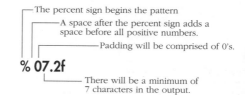

Figure 17.9 *In this example, we want the output to contain exactly seven characters. Two of these will be digits to the right of the decimal point, one will be the decimal point itself, and one will be a leading space if it's a positive number (or a hyphen if it's a negative number). That leaves three digits for the whole part of the number. If the input has less than three digits for the whole portion, it will be padded with zeros as necessary. If the input has more than three digits to the left of the decimal point, the 7 in the pattern has no effect.*

Creating a Format Pattern for Non-Integers

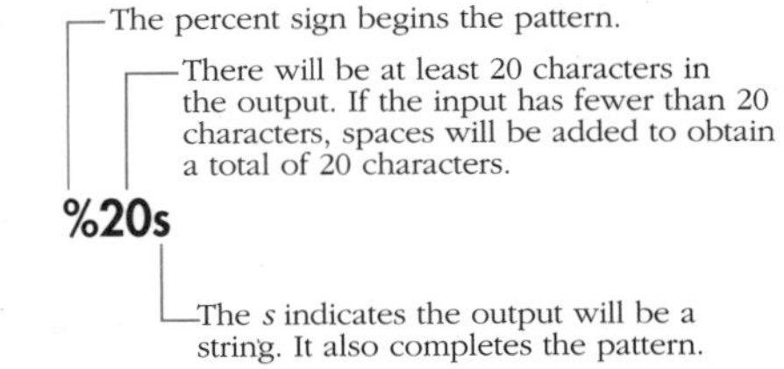

The percent sign begins the pattern.

There will be at least 20 characters in the output. If the input has fewer than 20 characters, spaces will be added to obtain a total of 20 characters.

%20s

The *s* indicates the output will be a string. It also completes the pattern.

Figure 17.10 *When only the* m *value is given, it determines the minimum number of characters in the result. In this example, there will be at least 20 characters in the result.*

There will be at most 20 characters in the output. If the input has more than 20 characters, it will be truncated.

%.20s

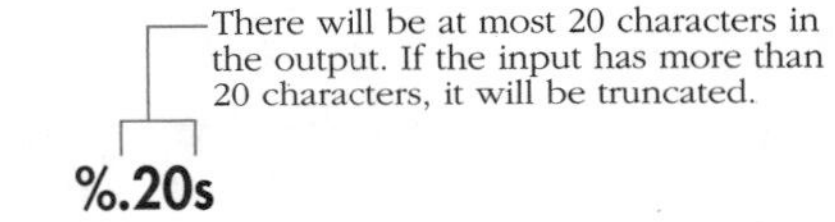

Figure 17.11 *If just the* n *value is given, it determines the maximum number of characters in the result. Input values with more than* n *characters are truncated as necessary.*

This is the *m* value.
And this is the *n* value.

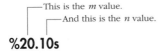

%20.10s

Figure 17.12 *If both the* m *and* n *values are given, the string will first be truncated to the value of* n *characters and then spaces are added to reach* m *characters.*

Creating a Pattern for Strings

While you'll probably not use it as much, you can also create a pattern for outputting strings.

To create a pattern for a string:

1. Type **%** (the percent sign) to begin the pattern.

2. Type **-** (a hyphen) if you want the string aligned to the left, or nothing to have it aligned to the right.

3. Type **m**, where *m* is the minimum length of the output.

4. If desired, type **.n**, where *n* is the maximum length of the output.

5. Type **s**, which stands for *string*.

✔ Tips

■ If *m* (in step 3) is greater than the number of characters in the input, extra spaces are added to obtain *m* characters.

■ If *n* (in step 4) is less than the number of characters in the input, the input is truncated to obtain *n* characters.

■ The alignment only makes a difference when padding is added (e.g., when *m* is greater than the number of characters in the input). In that case, the alignment determines on which side the spaces are added.

■ Zeros are never used to pad strings.

■ If *m* is greater than *n*, the string is first truncated to *n* characters and then spaces are added to obtain *m* characters.

■ Remember that extra spaces are generally ignored in HTML code.

Changing the Case

Perl has a number of functions that make it easy to change the characters in a string from upper- to lowercase or vice-versa.

To change the case:

1. Type **uc** if you want to convert all the characters in the string to uppercase.

    Or type **ucfirst** to convert only the first letter of the string to uppercase.

    Or type **lc** if you want to make all the characters in the string lowercase.

    Or type **lcfirst** to convert only the first letter of the string to lowercase.

2. Then type **($string)**, where *string* contains the characters whose case should be changed.

    Or type nothing to operate on the default variable ($_).

✔ Tips

■ The uc, ucfirst, lc, and lcfirst functions don't change the value of the operand. If you want to save the converted string, use, for example, $changed = uc($string);.

■ You can also change the case of a string with the tr function. For more details, consult *Changing Characters* on page 227.

```
1    #!/usr/local/bin/perl -wT
2    use strict;
3    use CGI ':standard';
4    my $name = param('name');
5
6    $name = ucfirst($name);
7
8    print "Content-type: text/html\n\n";
9    print "Hi, $name, how're you doing?";
```

6:   The ucfirst function capitalizes the first letter in the string contained in the $name variable. Then, we store the result back into the $name variable.

Figure 17.13 *The* ucfirst *function doesn't change the content on which it operates. You have to store the result somewhere unless you use it right away.*

Figure 17.14 *The visitor enters his name without bothering to capitalize the first letter.*

Figure 17.15 *The script capitalizes the visitor's name to avoid being rude.*

```
1   #!/usr/local/bin/perl -wT
2   use strict;
3   use CGI ':standard';
4
5   print "Content-type: text/html\n\n";
6
7   my $price = param('price');
8   my $tax = param('tax');
9   $tax =~ tr/,/./;
10  $tax = $tax/100;
11
12  my $salestax = $price * $tax;
13
14  my $formattax = sprintf("\%.2f",
        $salestax);
15
16  $formattax =~ tr/./,/;
17
18  print "In France, where they separate
        the whole number from its fractional
        part with commas, they'd say you have
        to pay <b>$formattax francs</b>";
```

9: If the visitor uses a comma in a fractional value for the VAT tax, the tr function converts it to a period so that Perl will recognize it. If there's no comma, nothing is changed.

10: Once the number is in the proper format, this line divides it by 100 (to get the percentage) and uses it in the salestax formula.

16: After the number is formatted with sprintf in line 14, the decimal period still needs to be converted into a decimal comma so that French visitors won't be confused.

Figure 17.16 *The* tr *function converts each element of the first list into the corresponding member of the second list.*

Figure 17.17 *The visitor has entered a VAT tax value with a comma. The* tr *function will change the comma to a decimal period so that Perl understands it.*

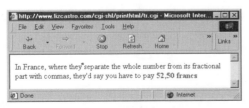

Figure 17.18 *The decimal period in the output is changed to a comma since that's the way they write fractional parts in France (and many other places).*

Changing Characters

Perl's tr function (which stands for *transliteration*, but is sometimes referred to as *translation*), lets you replace individual characters in a string with other characters.

To change characters:

1. Type **$scalar =~**, where *scalar* contains the string you want to manipulate.

   Or type nothing to manipulate the contents of the default variable ($_).

2. Type **tr/**.

3. Type one or more characters that you want to change.

4. Type **/**.

5. Then type the replacement characters into which the old characters, in order, should be changed.

6. Type **/** to finish the tr function.

7. Type **;** to finish the line.

✔ Tips

- You can use the hyphen to specify a range of characters in either the old or the new characters: tr/a-z/A-Z/.

- If there are more characters to change than replacement characters, the last replacement character is used for all the remaining old characters, by default.

- Assign the result of the tr function to a scalar variable to get the number of changes that were made: $count = $formattax =~ tr/./,/;.

- As alluded to in step 1, $_ =~ tr/a/A/; is equivalent to tr/a/A/; (and in both cases would change all the lowercase *a*'s in the default variable into uppercase *A*'s).

Finding the Length of a String

There are several ways to count the number of characters in a string. The `length` function is probably the most straightforward.

To find the length of a string:

1. Type **length**.

2. Type **($scalar)**, where *$scalar* contains the string whose characters you want to count.

   Or type nothing to count the characters in the default variable ($_).

✔ Tips

- You can assign the result to a scalar variable, as in `$number = length ($string);`.

- The `length` function counts all of the letters, symbols, and white space in a string. Escaped characters, like \n (the newline) are considered single characters.

- You can count particular characters—for example only the digits—in a string by assigning the results of the `tr` function to a scalar variable. Of course, you could use `tr` to count all of the characters as well. For more details, consult *Changing Characters* on page 227.

```perl
1   #!/usr/local/bin/perl -wT
2   use strict;
3   use CGI ':standard';
4
5   my ($string, $length);
6
7   $string = param ('story');
8   $length = length ($string);
9
10  print "Content-type: text/html\n\n";
11  print "This string:
        <blockquote>$string</blockquote> had
        $length characters in it.";
```

8: The `length` function gets the total number of characters (including symbols, numbers, and letters) in the `$string` variable and stores the result in `$length`.

Figure 17.19 *The* length *function can be handy for limiting the content of a particular field.*

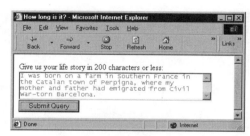

Figure 17.20 *It's just an example. I'm not from France.*

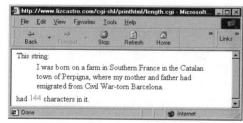

Figure 17.21 *The length of the string is output.*

```
1   #!/usr/local/bin/perl -wT
2   use strict;
3   use CGI ':standard';
4
5   my ($string, $chunk, $where);
6
7   $string = param ('story');
8   $chunk = param ('chunk');
9   $where = index($string, $chunk);
10
11  print "Content-type: text/html\n\n";
12  if ($where > -1) {
13    print qq(I found "$chunk" at position
         $where in your story.);
14  } else {
15    print qq(I couldn't find "$chunk" in
         your story);
16  }
```

9:    The index function looks in the $string variable and returns the position of the first occurrence (from the left) of the contents of $chunk.

12:   If the string is not found, the $where variable is set to -1 and an error is printed for our visitor. Otherwise, the position is displayed in the browser.

Figure 17.22 *If you don't specify where you want the search to start,* index *starts from the left (beginning).*

Figure 17.23 *The visitor types the string that they want to find.*

Figure 17.24 *Note that the "F" in "France" is actually the 34th character, which is precisely why its position is 33, since positions start at 0.*

Finding Where Something Is in a String

While a regular expression *(see Chapter 15)* can tell you whether a string exists in another string, it can't tell you exactly *where* it exists.

To find where something is in a string:

1. Type **$position =**, where *$position* is the scalar in which you'll store the position of the first occurrence of the first character of the string you're looking for.

2. Type **index (source,**, where *source* is the string in which you are looking.

3. Type **substring**, where *substring* is the string that you want to find in the source string from step 2.

4. If desired, type **, start**, where *start* identifies the position in the source string where you want to begin the search, other than the beginning, which is the default.

5. Type **);** to finish the line.

✔ Tips

■   The result of the index function is the numeric position of the first character of the first occurrence of the substring, starting from the beginning of the source string. As usual with Perl, positions start at 0 (not 1).

■   The rindex function has the same syntax as the index function, but instead of starting a search at the beginning of the source string, it starts from the end and returns the position of the *first* letter of the *last* occurrence of the substring.

Extracting One String from Another

If you want to not only find where a string occurs in another string but also get it, you'll need the substr function.

To extract one string from another:

1. Type **substr (** to begin the function.

2. Type **source,**, where *source* is the string that contains the string you want to get.

3. Type **start**, where *start* notes the position in the source where you want to start looking.

4. If desired, type **, number**, where *number* is the number of characters that you want to extract from the source string.

5. If desired, type **, replacement**, where *replacement* is the string with which you want to replace the extracted string.

6. Type **)** to complete the function.

7. Type **;** to complete the line.

✔ Tips

- Use a negative value for start to begin the search at the *end* of the source string.

- Omit the number argument to extract all the characters from the start position to the end of the source string. Use a negative number to extract up to that many characters at the end of the source string.

- Another way to replace the extracted string (or insert something new if the number is zero) is to assign new material to the substr function: substr (source, start, length) = "add_replace";.

- The replacement argument is not supported by MacPerl 5.2.0r4.

```
1  #!/usr/local/bin/perl -wT
2  use strict;
3  use CGI ':standard';
4  print "Content-type: text/html\n\n";
5  my ($string, $chunk, $replace);
6
7  $string = param ('story');
8  $chunk = param ('chunk');
9  $replace = param ('replace');
10
11 if (index($string, $chunk)>-1) {
12   substr($string, index($string,
        $chunk), length($chunk), $replace);
13
14   print "The new story goes:
        <blockquote>$string</blockquote>";
15   print qq(You replaced "$chunk" with
        "$replace".);
16 } else {
17   print "Sorry, I couldn't find $chunk
        in your story";}
```

12: I use the index function to get the position of the $chunk variable (where I'll start the extraction), and the length function to get the $chunk's length (to determine the number of characters to extract). Then I replace that chunk with the contents of the $replace variable.

Figure 17.25 *The string you extract and the string you replace it with can have different lengths.*

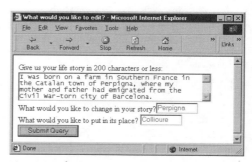

Figure 17.26 *The visitor types the story, the chunk that they want to remove* (Perpigna) *and the replacement text* (Collioure). *(Yes, it's true, in Catalan,* Perpignà *should have an accent.)*

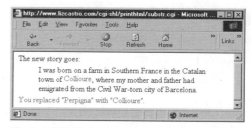

Figure 17.27 *The replacement text is now part of the story and the visitor gets a message about exactly what was removed and replaced.*

```
1   #!/usr/local/bin/perl -wT
2   use strict;
3   use CGI ':standard';
4   print "Content-type: text/html\n\n";
5
6   my $chunk =param ('chunk');
7
8   print qq(You started with "$chunk" );
9
10  my $gobble=chop($chunk);
11
12  print qq(and chopped off a "$gobble" );
13  print qq(and now you've got "$chunk");
```

10: The chop function permanently changes
    $chunk and stores the removed character in the
    $gobble variable.

Figure 17.28 *The* chop *function removes the last character from a string, no matter what it is.*

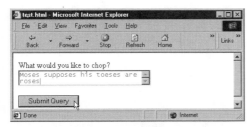

Figure 17.29 *The visitor types the string...*

Figure 17.30 *...and the last character is removed.*

Cleaning up the End of a String

When you input directly from visitors or from an external file, it's possible that the data will have extra spaces or returns tacked to the end of it (because visitors often type Enter or Return to have the program accept the input). You can use the chop and chomp functions to clean up the incoming data.

To clean up the end of a string:

1. Type **chop** to remove the final character, no matter what it is.

   Or type **chomp** to remove only a final newline, if there is one.

2. Type **($data)**, where *$data* is the variable that contains the data that needs to be truncated.

3. Type **;** to finish the statement.

✔ Tips

■ The chomp function returns the number of characters deleted (1, if it's just a newline). The chop function returns the actual character deleted. This is the main reason why $input = chop($input); gives possibly unexpected results; $input is set to the character that has been eliminated, not to the newly cleaned up input.

■ Another, perhaps better, way to get rid of extra white space at the end of a line is with $input =~s/\s+$//g;. For more details about substitution, consult *Finding and Replacing* on page 183.

■ Strictly speaking, chomp removes whatever is in the special $/ variable, which by default is the newline.

Cleaning up the End of a String

Formatting Output with HTML

You can print HTML tags with your script as you would any other constant.

To add HTML formatting to output:

1. Type **print**.

2. Type **qq (**.

3. Type **<TAG>**, where *TAG* is the name of the HTML tag and includes any desired attributes.

4. If desired, type **data**, where data is the output from the Perl script that you wish to output.

5. If necessary, type **</TAG>**, where */TAG* is the closing tag that corresponds to the tag used in step 3.

6. Type **)**.

7. Type **;** to complete the line.

✔ Tips

■ The qq function will interpolate any variables included in the string and will not complain if your HTML contains special symbols like double and single quotation marks, semicolons, the ampersand, and the sharp (#) symbol, as HTML code is wont to do. For more details about qq, see *Quoting without Quotes* on page 31.

■ Of course, you're welcome to use double quotes instead of the qq function to enclose strings with variables that need to be interpolated. In that case, however, you'll have to backslash any special symbols in the code.

■ You can use single quotes (or the q function—see page 31) for any strings that don't need to be interpolated.

```
1   #!/usr/local/bin/perl -wT
2   use strict;
3   my (@time,@days,@months,@catdays,
      @catmonths,$time,$days,$months,
      $catdays,$catmonths);
4
5   @time = localtime;
6
7   @days = qw(Sunday Monday Tuesday
      Wednesday Thursday Friday Saturday);
8   @months = qw(January February March
      April May June July August September
      October November December);
9
10  @catdays = qw(diumenge dilluns dimarts
      dimecres dijous divendres dissabte);
11  @catmonths = qw(Gener Febrer Mar&#231;
      Abril Maig Juny Juliol Agost Setembre
      Octubre Novembre Desembre);
12
13  print "Content-type: text/html\n\n";
14  print '<HTML><HEAD><TITLE>Get the
      date</TITLE></HEAD><BODY>';
15  print qq (Today is <B>$days[$time[6]],
      $months[$time[4]] $time[3]</B>);
16  print qq (<P>In Catalonia, they'd say:
      Avui &eacute;s <B>$catdays[$time[6]],
      $time[3] de
      $catmonths[$time[4]]</B>.);
17  print '</BODY></HTML>';
```

1: The Perl aspects of this script are explained in detail on page 143.

14: While most browsers won't complain if you leave out the HTML headers, it's probably a good idea to include them. Since this line contains no variables, I've used single quotes to enclose it.

15: The bold tags, <B>, around the date make the results more obvious in the browser.

16: The qq function saves us from having to backslash the & and ; symbols in the character entity that would otherwise be misinterpreted as part of the Perl code.

17: Finally, we print out the closing tags.

Figure 17.31 *Adding HTML to the results of a script is just like adding HTML anywhere else. Just insert the proper tags (and attributes) before and after the text you want to format.*

Figure 17.32 *The result is shown in the browser. Notice how the bold formatting helps highlight the important part of the result of the script.*

```
13  print "Content-type: text/html\n\n";
14  print qq(<HTML>\n<HEAD>\n<TITLE>Get the
      date</TITLE>\n</HEAD>\n<BODY>\n);
15  print qq (Today is <B>$days[$time[6]],
      $months[$time[4]] $time[3]</B>.);
16  print qq (\n<P>In Catalonia, they'd say:
      Avui &eacute;s <B>$catdays[$time[6]],
      $time[3] de $catmonths[$time[4]]</B>.);
17  print qq(\n</BODY>\n</HTML>);
```

1: Lines 1–12 are the same as in Figure 17.31.
14: I've added newlines (\n) to the string so the source code will be more legible. Since newlines need to be interpolated, I've used qq instead of single quotes.
16: Lines 16–17 also include a few extra newlines to keep the generated source code intelligible.

Figure 17.33 *While the newlines are completely optional—the result in the browser is identical—the newlines do help make the generated HTML code much more readable, and thus easier to correct.*

Figure 17.34 *The result is identical (cf Figure 17.32).*

Figure 17.35 *If you or your visitors choose View > Source in Internet Explorer (shown) or View > Page Source in Netscape, the HTML code (but not the CGI script) used to generate the page will be shown (see Figure 17.36).*

Figure 17.36 *The source code for the generated document is easy to read, thanks to the newlines. The browser doesn't care either way, but if you want to be able to decipher the generated code, newlines make it a lot easier.*

■ You can use one `print` statement for each HTML tag, or print several tags at once, as you prefer. Or use special `here` documents as described on page 234.

■ To create legible source code, add a newline character (\n) where you would like a return in the HTML code **(Figures 17.33, 17.34, and 17.36)**.

■ Remember that HTML and Perl treat newlines differently. A browser will not recognize any newlines inserted in the HTML code: to insert returns or line breaks between lines of text, you must use P or BR tags, respectively. On the other hand, Perl doesn't recognize HTML tags, so if you want the output to look recognizable when you're testing locally without a browser, you might want to add some newlines as well.

■ The popular CGI.pm module, available at *http://stein.cshl.org/WWW/software/CGI/*, written by Lincoln Stein, lets you use a whole system of predefined subroutines to add HTML formatting to Perl output.

■ If you want to learn more about HTML's formatting possibilities, check out my other book, *HTML 4 for the World Wide Web: Visual QuickStart Guide, Fourth Edition*, also published by Peachpit Press.

Formatting Output with HTML

Printing Several Lines at a Time

It can get downright tedious typing a lot of quotation marks and a million `print` statements to create all the HTML code that you may want to use. Perl has a nifty shortcut, cryptically called a `here` document, that can save you a lot of typing (and tedium).

To print several lines at a time:

1. Type **print <<"label";**, where *label* is the word or phrase that you will type to signal the end of the print statement.

2. Type all of the HTML codes and Perl content you want to print.

3. Begin a new line and type **label**, where *label* matches the label you chose in step 1, *exactly*. Then press the Return key. No semicolon is necessary at the end of this line. In fact, the line should contain nothing except the label itself.

✔ Tips

■ Don't forget the semicolon in the first line.

■ By default, the content of a `here` document is interpolated (*see page 30*). Enclose the label in single quotes if you'd rather the content not be interpolated.

■ As long as you're happy with interpolation—and your label doesn't contain any spaces—you can omit the double quotes.

■ You don't have to backslash special symbols (like & or ;) within a `here` document.

■ A `here` document is something similar to the PRE tag in HTML. Everything contained within will be printed just as it is.

■ The closing label of the `here` document must not be the last line in the script. (It's fine if the last line is empty.)

```
13  print "Content-type: text/html\n\n";
14
15  print <<"HTML code";
16
17  <HTML>
18  <HEAD>
19  <TITLE>Get the date</TITLE>
20  </HEAD>
21  <BODY>
22
23  Today is <B>$days[$time[6]],
        $months[$time[4]] $time[3]</B>.
24  <P>In Catalonia, they'd say: Avui
        &eacute;s <B>$catdays[$time[6]],
        $time[3] de $catmonths[$time[4]]</B>.
25
26  </BODY></HTML>
27
28  HTML code
29
```

1:   Again, lines 1–12 are the same as in Figure 17.31 on page 232.
15: This line begins the `here` document. The label I've chosen, "HTML code" contains a space so I've enclosed the whole thing in quotation marks. If the space weren't there, the quotation marks wouldn't be necessary. Lines 15–26 are equivalent to lines 14–17 in Figure 17.33 on page 233, but are a good deal easier to type.
28: This line contains the label from the opening `print` statement and nothing else—not even a leading or trailing space. It does however, end with a return.
29: The closing label of the `here` document must not be the last line in the script.

Figure 17.37 *This script is equivalent to the one shown in Figure 17.33 on page 233 but it was much easier to write.*

Figure 17.38 *The result is identical to that shown in Figure 17.34 on page 233. (The source would also look identical to that shown in Figure 17.36 on page 233.)*

```
1   #!/usr/local/bin/perl -wT
2   use strict;
3
4   print "Content-type: text/html\n\n";
5   print <<"HTML code";
6   <HTML><HEAD>
7   <TITLE>Using the BASE tag</TITLE>
8   <BASE HREF="http://www.cookwood.com/
    images/">
9   </HEAD><BODY>
10
11  <CENTER><H1>Saint George Tours</H1>
12  <P><IMG SRC="Santjord.gif">
13  <H2>Thanks for responding to our
    questionnaire.</H2></CENTER>
14  </BODY></HTML>
15
16  HTML code
17
```

8: This line (within the here document that begins on line 5) prints the BASE tag which defines the base URL with which all relative URLs in the generated page will be resolved. Since the BASE tag is within the here document, the double quotes surrounding the URL do not need to be backslashed.

12: The relative URL for the image will be resolved as *http://www.cookwood.com/images/Santjord.gif.*

Figure 17.39 *The BASE tag lets you define the URL for the generated document with which all the relative URLs for images, links, applets, and other referenced files will be resolved.*

Figure 17.40 *The actual location of this image is* http://www.cookwood.com/images/Santjord.gif. *Without the BASE tag, I would either have to use this absolute URL or figure out the relative location of the generated document (in the cgi-bin directory or somewhere else?) with respect to the image.*

Simplifying Paths to Images and Links

It's sometimes a little tricky to figure out what path to use to images and links that you want to reference from an HTML document that you've generated with a script. Unless you use absolute paths, you'll need to know what the relationship is between the location of the images and the location of the HTML page. But, where is a generated HTML document located? Depending on how your server is set up, your answer may vary. The easiest way to get around this problem is to avoid it altogether. You can use HTML's BASE tag to override the page's physical location and make the HTML document act as if it were in a particular directory of your choosing on the server. Then you can use that information to set up the links to images (and other files).

To simplify paths to images and links:

1. Decide which directory you want the generated page to act as if it were located in.

2. In the script, after printing the opening HEAD tag but before printing the closing HEAD tag, type **<BASE HREF="pretend. location.url">**, where *pretend.location.url* is the directory that you've chosen in step 1.

✔ Tip

■ If you print the BASE tag in a here document or with the print and qq functions, you won't need any extra backslashes. However, if you use double quotes to enclose the string, you'll have to backslash the double quotes that surround the URL (or use single quotes).

Outputting Data in a Table

One of the nice things about outputting Perl data using HTML tags is that you can add formatting that makes your data really stand out and get noticed. One great way to view data is to format it with a table.

To output data in a table:

1. Create the part of the script that generates the data that will be contained in the table.

2. Type **print "<TABLE>\n";** to begin the HTML table. Add any TABLE attributes (like BORDER, WIDTH, etc.) as desired.

3. If desired, **print "<TR><TH>Header1 </TH><TH>Header2</TH></TR>";** where *Header1* and *Header2* are the headers for the first and second columns of the table.

4. Create a foreach loop that takes an array or hash and prints a *single row* of the table each time through. The loop should, at the least, print out an initial **<TR>** tag, then begin each cell by printing **<TD>**, accessing the variable that contains that cell's contents, complete the cell by printing **</TD>** (and so on for each cell), and then finish the row by printing **</TR>**.

5. Type **}** to complete the foreach loop.

6. Outside the foreach loop, type **print "</TABLE>";** to complete the table definition.

✔ Tip

- You can create a list in a similar way, printing the opening and closing UL or OL tags outside of the foreach loop, and each LI element within the foreach loop itself.

```perl
1   #!/usr/local/bin/perl -wT
2   use strict;
3
4   my ($data, @data);
5
6   $data = 'Tiger,panthera tigris,4500,
    endangered:Florida Panther,Puma
    concolor coryi,50,endangered:Giant
    River Otter,Pteronura brasiliensis,
    1000,endangered';
7
8   @data = split (/:/ , $data);
9
10  print "Content-type: text/html\n\n";
11  print "<TABLE BORDER=1>\n<TR><TH
    align=left>Name</TH><TH
    align=left>Latin Name</TH> <TH
    align=left>Current Population</TH><TH
    align=left>Status </TH></TR>";
12
13  foreach (@data) {
14  my ($name, $latin_name, $pop, $status);
15  ($name, $latin_name, $pop, $status) =
    split (/,/);
16  print "<TR><TD>$name</TD>
    <TD>$latin_name </TD><TD>$pop</TD><TD>
    $status</TD></TR>";
17  }
18  print "</TABLE>";
```

1: This script (well, one very much like it) is explained in Figure 15.7 on page 185.
11: The initial TABLE tag must be printed outside of the foreach loop. This line also prints a row of headers.
13: The foreach loop goes through each member of an array and will create a table row for each one.
16: This line will be executed for each member of the array. It begins the row and creates individual cells to display the contents of each variable.
17: The curly bracket closes the foreach loop.
18: Create the closing TABLE tag outside the foreach loop.

Figure 17.41 *The only part of the table that should be within the* foreach *loop is the actual contents of each of the cells.*

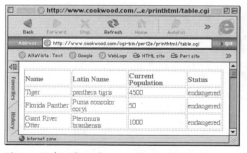

Figure 17.42 *The information is displayed neatly in a table.*

Outputting Data in a Table

SECURITY

In the introduction to this book, I raised the question of whether programming is dangerous. In fact, carelessly written CGI Perl scripts *can* make your server vulnerable to attack from outside forces.

In particular, before embarking on opening, creating, and deleting files (in Chapter 19), you should be fully versed in the techniques needed to keep your system safe. Please read this chapter carefully.

Beware! While I haven't found any particular problems, the CGI scripts in this book are not intended to be perfect from a security standpoint. They are intended to teach you specific, individual tasks without distracting you with other concepts, like security. Before publishing (using them for testing and personal study is probably fine) *any* CGI scripts that you have copied from this book, or indeed that you have copied from anywhere or written yourself, you must be sure that they pose no security risk to your system. You may want to consult your ISP about possible security risks and make sure to, at the very least, follow the tips outlined in this chapter. Remember that once you start writing your own scripts, or using scripts written by others (including the ones from this book), it is **your responsibility** to close all security loopholes that exist.

Security

Reading the Security FAQs

This chapter includes a few very basic strategies you can employ to reduce your risk. I also recommend reading as much about security as you can find out on the Web. Perhaps the most respected source of security information is Lincoln Stein's World Wide Web Security FAQ, which includes a section devoted to the problems with CGI scripts. You can find it at the World Wide Web Consortium's (W3C) site: *http://www.w3.org/Security/Faq/wwwsf4.html* **(Figure 18.1)**.

You might also want to check out Selena Sol's helpful article on *Security Issues When Installing and Customizing Pre-Built Web Scripts*. It can be found at *http://Stars.com/Authoring/Scripting/Security/* **(Figure 18.2)**.

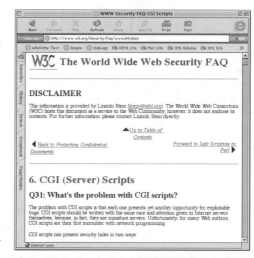

Figure 18.1 *Lincoln Stein's World Wide Web Security FAQ, and in particular, the section on CGI Scripts, should be required reading for all CGI Perl programmers.*

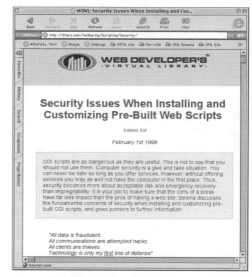

Figure 18.2 *Selena Sol's article on Security and CGI Scripts offers a lot of good tips on keeping your scripts and server safe.*

Reading the Security FAQs

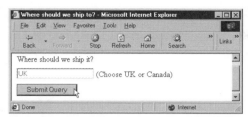

Figure 18.3 *In the first form, the visitor chooses the item they want to buy (not shown). Then the item information is stored in a hidden field and the visitor is invited to choose their country—with a text field. Unfortunately, besides our meek suggestion, there's nothing to keep the visitor from choosing some unsupported country.*

Figure 18.4 *As long as the input is what we expect, everything works well.*

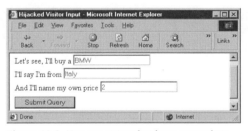

Figure 18.5 *Now our visitor decides to create their own form and chooses data we had not anticipated.*

Figure 18.6 *Unfortunately, our script has no safeguards against such unexpected data, and the output is, well, not quite right.*

The Problem with Visitor Input

The first rule of CGI security is that you should **never** trust your visitors to input what you think they're going to input. Even with the best of intentions, visitors sometimes don't understand what information you're asking for. And with downright bad intentions, visitors may be actively trying to trash—or spy on—your server's files.

Even if a visitor's choices seem limited by a menu or set of check boxes, or by hidden fields that you've generated yourself **(Figure 18.3)**, you're not safe. The problem is that there is no way to keep a visitor from calling your CGI script with their *own HTML form*. And that form can include any data they'd like **(Figure 18.5)**.

Your first line of defense begins with vigilantly checking a visitor's input to make sure it is in the form you expected. For example, if you're asking for a person's name, the data should look like one or two words without special symbols like <, !, or *, among others. Or you might want to ensure that filenames are comprised solely of alphanumerics and the underscore. You can use search patterns to verify incoming data and to filter out strange looking input *(see page 181)*. Make sure your conditionals cover all the possibilities, and not just the ones you've planned for by specifying *what you want* (and not what you don't want—since there's almost definitely something out there that you don't want but that you haven't thought of yet).

Protecting Calls to the System

Perl has several functions (system, pipe open, eval, and exec among them) that actually pass data directly to the operating system running behind Perl. Letting your visitors send data directly to the system with one of these functions through a CGI script is roughly akin to letting them sit down at your keyboard while you go off for a cup of coffee. It's not a great idea.

The truth is that system calls (as such functions are referred to) are a bit beyond the scope of this book. Only the pipe open function is discussed at all, and I've only shown you a way to use it safely *(see page 265)*. Still, the security concerns are so great, that it's a good idea to be aware of them.

There are two strategies for dealing with system calls. The first is to avoid them as much as possible. The second is to scrupulously and carefully check any data that you send to the system. This includes data that comes directly from visitors as well as environment variables.

To protect calls to the system:

1. Avoid system calls whenever possible.

2. Make sure any data that you send to the system looks exactly the way it should (using regular expressions, for example). Never use visitor input in a system call.

✔ Tips

■ It's not enough for the data to not look bad—it has to look right. You might not be sneaky enough to have thought of all the possible ways the data could be corrupt or corrupted.

■ You can use Perl's taint mode to check incoming data *(see page 244)*.

```
1   #!/usr/local/bin/perl -wT
2   use strict;
3   use CGI ':standard';
4   print "Content-type: text/html\n\n";
5
6   my $language = param('language');
7   my $filename;
8
9   if ($language=~/English/) {
10    $filename = "gatetseng.html";
11  } elsif ($language =~ /Catalan/) {
12    $filename = "gatetscat.html";
13  } else {
14    print "Sorry, you can only choose
         between English and Catalan.";
15  }
16
17  open (FILE, "/home/user4/lcastro/WWW/
        personal/$filename") ||
        &Error('open','file');
18  my @page = <FILE>;
19  close FILE;
20
21  foreach (@page) {
22      print;
23      }
```

9:    The `if` conditional looks at the input to see
      which file should be opened, but does not rely
      on the input for the filename itself.

Figure 18.7 *Using the filename itself as the value in the form and then appending that to the path in line 17 would be inviting disaster. You never know what input your visitor is going to give you.*

Figure 18.8 *Here, some bad visitor is trying to use my script to print out my server's password file.*

Figure 18.9 *My script is protected in two ways: first, I've checked the incoming data and only accept it if it looks like what I'm expecting. Second, I don't use the visitor's input directly to create the filename that I reference with the system command* (open)*.*

Limiting Access to Files

As I will show you in Chapter 19, *Files and Directories*, you can use Perl to open, create, rename, and even delete files and directories all over your server, in order to store and retrieve data in a more permanent way. While it can be useful to give your visitors access to particular files, perhaps so they can consult a database or write to a guestbook, it would be foolhardy to give them access to your entire server. One way to limit their access is to be very careful when specifying the name and path of the file to be used.

To limit access to files:

- Never use visitor input to directly choose which file to use.

- Let visitors choose from among several available, predefined filenames.

- Or, specify a portion of the filename yourself so that visitors are limited to creating filenames that match a certain pattern.

- Or, use regular expressions to ensure that the filename is one of a chosen few acceptable files in a particular directory.

✔ Tips

- Specifying the path and letting the visitor freely choose the filename is a faulty method since the visitor could add relative path information in their input which would lead them to other files outside the approved directory. You could conceivably use this system *if and only if* you use a regular expression to make sure the visitor's filename included only filename characters and no path information.

- Be careful to set permissions so that *only* authorized people or programs can access your files *(see page 291)*.

Limiting Access to Files

Using CGI.pm to Limit Incoming Data

Another way that mean and mischievous people can do bad things to your system is by trying to upload excessive quantities of data. While this is certainly easier when uploading actual files, they could also simply paste a huge amount of data into a text field and try to submit that. CGI.pm has a built-in function that prevents such attacks.

To use CGI.pm to limit incoming data:

Near the beginning of your script, before using the param function to access and parse incoming data, type **$CGI::POST_MAX = n;**, where *n* is the maximum number of bytes you allow each visitor to submit, including data submitted through regular form fields *and* uploaded files.

✔ Tips

- Remember, 1 byte is usually equal to one character. 1024 bytes are equal to 1K. 1,048,576 bytes are equal to 1Mb. Always specify the $POST_MAX value in bytes.

- If you have installed your own copy of CGI.pm in a private library, you can change the global value of the $POST_MAX variable in the CGI.pm module itself. You'll find it near the top of the CGI.pm module within a subroutine called initialize_globals.

- The default value for $POST_MAX is "unlimited" (represented by -1).

- The value of the $POST_MAX variable in a local script overrides the value in the CGI.pm module itself.

- You have to preface the $POST_MAX variable with $CGI:: in a local script so that Perl knows that it comes from the CGI.pm module.

```perl
1   #!/usr/local/bin/perl -wT
2   use strict;
3   use CGI ':standard';
4   $CGI::POST_MAX = 50;
5
6   my $comments = param ('comments');
7   print "Content-type: text/html\n\n";
8   print "<P>You said:
        <blockquote>$comments</blockquote>";
```

4: I've set the $POST_MAX variable to a ridiculously low level as an example. Visitors won't be able to submit more than 50 bytes of information with the form.

Figure 18.10 *You can use the* $POST_MAX *variable to set an outer limit for file uploads and submitted data.*

Figure 18.11 *The visitor enters their information as usual—although in this case it's more than the limit allows.*

Figure 18.12 *Surpassing the upload/submit limit creates an Internal Server Error. While this is much better than crashing your server, it's probably not the ideal solution for limiting the length of fields (which you could do more calmly with a regular expression).*

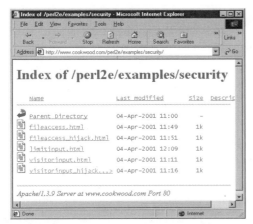

Figure 18.13 *Many servers automatically display a list of the files contained in a directory when only the directory—and no page—is specified in the URL. You may not want to give your visitors all this information.*

Figure 18.14 *Check with your Web host to see what name you need to give to a default page. Then use that name when saving the page—in the directory whose contents you wish to protect.*

Figure 18.15 *The URL in both this illustration and in Figure 18.13 are identical. The difference is that this directory now contains a default file that will be shown if no other page is specified.*

Keeping Information to Yourself

The less a cracker knows about your system, the harder it will be for them to infiltrate it. Many servers, for example, will show the contents of a directory if you jump to the URL of that directory and there is no other default HTML page available **(Figure 18.13)**. The easiest way to avoid this is to create a blank (or otherwise innocuous) default page for every directory on your system.

To create blank default pages:

1. Create a very basic HTML page.

2. Name it as a default page. On Unix servers, it's usually *index.html*. On Windows servers, it's usually *default.htm* **(Figure 18.14)**.

3. Save a copy of it to each directory on your system whose contents you wish to hide.

✔ Tips

- Of course, it's fine if your default page contains useful information that you'd like your visitors to receive. You only need this technique if the directory would otherwise not have a default page.

- Store any files that do not need to be accessed through the Web outside of the Web directory. This would include log files, database files, and any other files that a CGI script might need but that your visitors don't need direct access to.

- Hiding information is not a sufficient security method in itself. Crackers may be able to find out the desired information in other ways. While it's not a bad idea to be discrete about your information, it's not enough to keep your server secure. Make sure each and every script is safe, whether people know it's there or not.

Avoiding Tainted Data

Perl has a built-in system that tracks data that originates from outside the script and limits the way it can be used by your script. Such so-called *tainted* data, including visitor input and environment variables, can not be used to affect anything outside the script (like external log files) unless you clean or *untaint* it first.

To avoid tainted data:

At the end of the shebang line for your Perl script, type **-T**. If you use unverified outside data to modify a file, directory, or process, you'll get an error message.

✔ Tips

■ Use the -T switch in all your scripts, as we've done throughout this book.

■ If you use tainted data to create some other data, that new data is also tainted.

■ Specifically, you can't use tainted data in a system call *(see page 240)*, or when writing, renaming, or deleting files. More generally, you can't use tainted input to *modify* anything outside the script.

■ Note that you can use tainted data to specify the file that you want to open (as read only), since you're not actually modifying the external file. Therefore, you'll have to guard files from unauthorized eyes some other way *(see page 241)*.

■ Indeed, protecting yourself against tainted data is not the solution to all your problems. It only keeps you from using untested outside data to modify other outside data.

■ To check the syntax of a script that uses the -T switch, type **perl -cT filename.cgi**. For more information on checking a file's syntax, see page 40.

```
1   #!/usr/local/bin/perl -wT
2   use strict;
3   use CGI ':standard';
4   print "Content-type: text/html\n\n";
5
6   my $file=param('name');
7   my $comments=param('comments');
8
9   open (FILE,
        ">../../../../logs/public/$file") ||
        Error('open', 'file for writing');
10  print FILE "$comments";
11  close FILE;
12
13  print "You wrote <i>$comments</i> to
        <b>$file</b>";
```

1: The -T at the end of the shebang line turns on taint checking to keep you from unwittingly using outside (tainted) data to modify files, directories, or processes.

6: Line 6 contains tainted data, since it comes from visitor input. (Line 7 does too.)

9: This dangerous line tries to open a file whose name was given by the visitor. This is a very, very bad idea. (Don't do it!) Luckily, since we've got taint checking turned on, this script will produce an error and the file will not be written to.

Figure 18.16 *You may think setting the path to the file is secure enough, but it's not. The visitor could easily add relative path information to create the file in any directory she likes, overwriting what's already there.*

Figure 18.17 *Your visitor chooses the file by clicking a radio button. We've already seen, however, how they could use their own form to input any data they like (see page 241).*

Figure 18.18 *Perl doesn't let you use untested data from the visitor to choose which files to modify or create. This is one time where you should be happy the script generates an Internal Server Error.*

```
8   $file =~
      /^(comments\.txt|question\.txt)$/;
9   my $goodfilename=$1;
10
11  if ($goodfilename) {
12    open (FILE, ">../../../../logs/
      public/$goodfilename") ||
      Error('open', 'file for writing');
13    print FILE "$comments\n";
14    close FILE;
15    print "You wrote <i>$comments</i> to
      <b>$file</b>";
16  } else {
17    print 'Sorry, that filename is not
      allowed.';
18  }
```

1: Lines 1–7 are virtually the same as in Figure 18.16. (I added a $POST_MAX limit *(see page 242)*

8: This time we check to see if the filename is acceptable (in this case, it must be either *comments.txt* or *question.txt*, with nothing extra). Note that it was necessary to backslash the periods to remove their special wildcard meaning. The parentheses enclose the part of the data that will be gleaned from the incoming data and considered *untainted*.

9: The untainted data is stored in $goodfilename.

11: The conditional checks to see if there is anything in $goodfilename. If there is, the filename is acceptable and can be written to. If not, an error message is displayed.

Figure 18.19 *The test makes sure that the input data is what I want it to be: either* question.txt *or* comments.txt.

Figure 18.20 *The visitor chooses the desired file and writes their comments. Even if they use their own form, they won't be able to choose another file besides the ones I allow.*

Figure 18.21 *The newly untainted filename is accepted and used without problem. Any non-allowed filename, perhaps from a rogue form, generates an error.*

Cleaning and Using Outside Data

Of course, if you *want* to use outside input, you can. But first, you have to verify or *untaint* it. The only way to do that is to run it through a search pattern and then assign the matched part to a scalar variable. That scalar variable will no longer be tainted. The idea is that if you've checked it, it must be OK. It's your responsibility to ensure that your regular expression does a good job of ensuring that the data is what it should be.

To untaint data:

1. Type **$outside_data**, where *$outside_data* is the information coming from outside your script.

2. Type **=~ /regex/;**, where *regex* is a regular expression that only produces a match if the data is in the form you need. Use parentheses in the regular expression to enclose the chunk of matching data that you'd like to use in your script. Anything outside the parentheses is filtered out.

3. Type **$clean_data = $1;**. The scalar variable **$1** is automatically set to contain the parenthesized, matched expression from step 2 *(see page 202 for more details)*.

✔ Tips

- You can also assign the result of the first expression directly to a scalar variable: $clean_data = $outside_data =~ /regex/;.

- If there is more than one chunk of data that you want to get (and clean), use additional parentheses and then assign the results to $2, $3, and so on (or if you're using the first tip above, assign the results to a list instead of a scalar).

FILES AND DIRECTORIES

We've already talked about how to input data from a form and how to output data to the browser. You can also input and output data to and from a file on the server. This is handy when you want to store information for longer periods of time, or when you want to access that stored data. In Perl, you create a label for the file, called a *filehandle*, and then refer to the label when opening, closing, writing, or otherwise working with the files.

Working with external files raises additional security concerns. You don't want just anybody to be able to remove directories or overwrite your log files. Be sure and read Chapter 18, *Security*.

Opening a File

Before you can read or write to a file, you have to open a connection to it.

To open a file:

1. Type **open (**.

2. Type **LABEL,**, where *LABEL* is the file-handle. You'll use this label from this point on when referring to the file. Don't forget the comma.

3. Type **"**.

4. If you want to be able to write to the file, type **>**. Any existing contents in the file will be lost.

Or, to append data to the file, type **>>**. Existing data is left unchanged with new data following directly thereafter (with no spaces or returns separating them).

Or, to simply read or input data from the file, no extra symbol is required. (If you like being explicit, type **<**.)

5. Type **filename,** (directly after the symbol in step 4, if any) where *filename* is the actual name, including the path, of the file that you wish to open. You can also use a scalar variable or expression for the filename.

6. Type **"**.

7. Type **)** to complete the function.

8. Type **;** to complete the line.

✔ Tips

■ It's considered good style and Perl convention to use all uppercase letters for the filehandle.

■ You only need the full path of the file in step 5 if the file is not located in the working directory *(see page 261)*.

```
1   #!/usr/local/bin/perl -wT
2   use strict;
3   use CGI ':standard';
4   my $comments = param('comments');
5
6   open (LOG, ">>../../../../logs/
    logfile.txt") || Error('open', 'file');
7   print LOG "$comments\n";
8   close (LOG);
9
10  print "Content-type: text/html\n\n";
11  print "<P>You said: <I>$comments</I>\n";
12  print qq(<HR>Would you like to see all
    the <A HREF="http://www.cookwood.com/
    cgi-bin/perl2e/files/readfromlog.cgi">
    messages?</A>);
13
14  sub Error {
15    print "Content-type: text/html\n\n";
16    print "The server can't $_[0] the
      $_[1]: $! \n";
17    exit;
18  }
```

6: This lines assigns the filehandle LOG to the *log-file.txt* file and opens it for appending data (with the >>). Notice the quotation marks that enclose the greater-than signs, the path, *and* the filename. (We'll get to the second part of the line on the next page.)

Figure 19.1 *Before reading from or writing to a file, you must open it and assign it a label or filehandle. You can't really see the effect of the open function—it is a precursor to reading from or writing to an external file.*

Opening a File

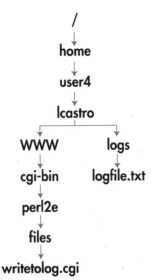

Figure 19.2 *Probably the trickiest part about the* open *function is getting the path names right. Here is a partial map of my directories. The script is called* writetolog.cgi *and is located in the* cgi-bin *directory. I want to open the* logfile.txt *file. To reference that file, I could either use an absolute file name like* "/home/ user4/lcastro/logs/logfile.txt" *or a relative name like* "../../../../logs/logfile.txt". *I chose the latter. For more about paths on Unix servers, consult* Dealing with Paths in Unix *on page 299. Also note that by putting the* log-file.txt *file outside my WWW directory, I make it impossible for folks to access it by typing its URL in their browser. It has no URL.*

- If Perl can't open the file, for whatever reason, you'll want to know about it. For more information, consult *Verifying File and Directory Operations* on page 250.

- If the script writes to an external file, you'll want to make sure it has exclusive access, so that several visitors don't use the script at once and leave you with a garbled file. For more information, consult *Getting Exclusive Access to a File* on page 252.

- It's important to close the file as soon as possible after opening it so that other visitors can use it. For details, consult *Closing a File* on page 254.

- If you try to open a file for writing or appending (that is with > or >>) that doesn't exist, Perl will create it for you— *as long as* the permissions of the directory in which the file is being created are amenable.

- If you try to open a new file in a directory that doesn't yet exist, you'll get an error.

- If you try to open a file for reading that doesn't exist (with < or nothing), Perl will ignore you. (Hey, it's hard to read nothing.) This is a good time to use an error subroutine *(see page 250).*

- You may want to specify the full path to the root directory explicitly so that you don't have to use all the .. and / that I use in my example. The environment variable $ENV{'DOCUMENT_ROOT'} should contain the full path to the directory that holds your Web files.

- While you can use / to specify directories on Windows and Unix, on Macintosh you need to use a : (colon). For more details, choose Help > Macintosh Specific Features in MacPerl.

Opening a File

Verifying File and Directory Operations

Unfortunately, Perl will continue running a script even if it hasn't been able to open the external file. Therefore, it's a good idea to create a manual alert system in case something goes wrong. You can create a subroutine that prints out an error message and then exits the script.

To verify file and directory operations:

1. Type the desired function (for example, the open function as described on page 248).

2. On the same line, type ||. This is a logical or operator. It requires that one of its two arguments be true. Therefore, if the open function fails, what follows the || will run (and therefore return true).

3. Continuing on the same line, type **Error(args)**, where *Error* is the name of the subroutine that takes *args* as its arguments, prints out an error message, and then exits the script.

4. Type **;** to finish the line.

5. Create the subroutine elsewhere in the script (or in an external file).

✔ Tips

■ For more information on the exit function and creating an error subroutine, see page 280. You might also want to consult Chapter 13, *Subroutines*.

■ The most common problems that trip up the open function are incorrectly set permissions (of either the file or the directory that contains the file) and erroneous path names. Check both carefully.

```perl
1   #!/usr/local/bin/perl -wT
2   use strict;
3   use CGI ':standard';
4   my $comments = param('comments');
5
6   open (LOG, ">>../../../../logs/
    logfile.txt") || Error('open', 'file');
7   print LOG "$comments\n";
8   close (LOG);
9
10  print "Content-type: text/html\n\n";
11  print "<P>You said: <I>$comments</I>\n";
12  print qq(<HR>Would you like to see all
    the <A HREF="http://www.cookwood.com/
    cgi-bin/perl2e/files/readfromlog.cgi">
    messages?</A>);
13
14  sub Error {
15    print "Content-type: text/html\n\n";
16    print "The server can't $_[0] the
      $_[1]: $! \n";
17    exit;
18  }
```

6: The || operator requires that either the open function return true (that is, be successful) or the Error subroutine be executed.

14 I've included the Error subroutine in the same script but you could easily move it to another file *(see page 164)*.

16: This message will be output to the browser if Perl can't open the file referenced in line 6. Note that the subroutine uses both the arguments passed to it in line 6 (by referencing $_[0] and $_[1]) as well as the $! variable, in order to make the error more specific and useful. For more details, see page 280.

17: Finally, the exit function aborts the entire script—if you can't open the log file, there's not much point in continuing.

Figure 19.3 *An error subroutine for the* open *function should include two parts: an error message that will advise the visitor of the problem and an* exit *line that will abort the script.*

Figure 19.4 *If the* open *function fails, instead of continuing merrily along, Perl will output this error message and abort the rest of the script.*

Verifying File and Directory Operations

```
1   #!/usr/local/bin/perl -wT
2   use strict;
3   use CGI ':standard';
4   my $comments = param('comments');
5
6   open (LOG, ">>../../../../logs/
       logfile.txt") || Error('open', 'file');
7   print LOG "$comments\n";
8   close (LOG);
9
10  print "Content-type: text/html\n\n";
11  print "<P>You said: <I>$comments</I>\n";
12  print qq(<HR>Would you like to see all
       the <A HREF="http://www.cookwood.com/
       cgi-bin/perl2e/files/readfromlog.cgi">
       messages?</A>);
```

6: The >> before the filename indicates that print statements will be *appended* to the file.

7: This line prints the contents of the variable $comments and a newline (\n) to the file referenced by the filehandle LOG (that is, *logfile.txt*).

10: Lines 10–12 create output for the browser. Without them, line 7 is still executed properly, but the visitor will get an error from the browser. (Browsers can't show "nothing".)

13: Lines 13–18 (the definition of the Error subroutine) are the same as in Figure 19.3 on page 250.

Figure 19.5 *The newline in line 7 ensures that each visitor's comments will be on a separate line and will thus be easier to read later.*

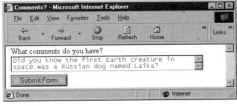

Figure 19.6 *The visitor enters comments and then clicks Submit Form to start the script.*

Figure 19.7 *The visitor's comments are written to the external file,* logfile.txt...

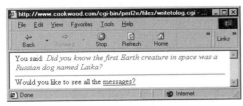

Figure 19.8 ...*and the browser displays the output you've sent its way (lines 10–12).*

Writing to an External File

Printing information to an external file is a way to save the data more permanently.

To write to an external file:

1. Open the file as described on page 248, using > or >> in step 4.

2. Type **print LABEL**, where *LABEL* is the filehandle from step 2 on page 248 that you used to refer to the file to which you want to print.

3. Type **content**, where *content* is a variable or constant that contains what you want to write to the open file.

4. Type **;** to finish the line.

5. Close the filehandle *(see page 254)*.

6. Create some output for the browser. Otherwise, the visitor will get an error.

✔ Tips

- Note that there is no comma after the filehandle (between steps 2 and 3).

- If you do print a string constant to a file, you should enclose the string in quotation marks. It's not necessary to enclose a variable within quotes.

- If you use the print function without a filehandle while the file is open, it simply goes to the browser (*standard output* in Perlspeak) as usual.

- Nothing extra is written or appended to the external file. If you want to separate a series of comments from each other, add a newline (\n) to the external file after each set of comments.

- You can only write to an external file if you've opened it with the > or >> symbols. See step 4 on page 248 for details.

Getting Exclusive Access to a File

If several visitors simultaneously try to use a CGI script that writes to an external file, you'll have a problem—and perhaps a damaged file. One solution is Perl's flock function, which advises other scripts not to use the file for the time necessary to write to it (by not letting them have a lock).

To get exclusive access to a file:

1. After opening the file, type **flock (LABEL,**, where *LABEL* is the filehandle for the file.

2. Type **2** to request exclusive access to the file (say, for writing). Or type **1** to request shared access to the file (for reading).

3. Type **)** to complete the function.

4. Verify that the flock function was successful *(see page 250)*.

5. Type **;** to end the line.

✔ Tips

■ Closing the file *(see page 254)*, or indeed opening it again, releases the lock on a file.

■ Since no other visitor can access the file while the file is flocked, you want to keep flock time to an absolute minimum. Make sure you prepare any necessary data before flocking the file, and then unflock it as soon as you're done with it.

■ Not all platforms support the flock function.

```
1   #!/usr/local/bin/perl -wT
2   use strict;
3   use CGI ':standard';
4   my $comments = param('comments');
5
6   open (LOG, ">>../../../../logs/
      logfile.txt")|| Error('open', 'file');
7   flock (LOG, 2) ||Error('lock', 'file');
8   print LOG "$comments\n";
9   close (LOG) || Error ('close', 'file');
10
11  print "Content-type: text/html\n\n";
12  print "<P>You said:
      <I>$comments</I>\n";
13  print qq(<HR>Would you like to see all
      the <A HREF="http://www.cookwood.com/
      cgi-bin/perl2e/files/readfromlog.cgi">
      messages?</A>);
```

7: Directly after opening the logfile in line 6, the flock function signals that the file referenced by the LOG filehandle is in use and that other scripts (or invocations of this same script) should not attempt to access it.

9: Closing the filehandle releases the lock so that other scripts can use the file.

Figure 19.9 *It's a good idea to flock a file before writing to it. This ensures that two visitors won't try to write to the script simultaneously, possibly damaging or garbling the file's contents.*

```
1   #!/usr/local/bin/perl -wT
2   use strict;
3
4   open (LOG, "<../../../../logs/
       logfile.txt")|| Error('open', 'file');
5   flock (LOG, 2) || Error ('lock', 'file');
6   my @logmessages = <LOG>;
7   close (LOG) || Error ('close', 'file');
8
9   print "Content-type: text/html\n\n";
10  my $n=1;
11  print "<b>Messages</b><ul>";
12  foreach (@logmessages) {
13    print "<LI>Message # $n was <i>$_</i>
         \n";
14    $n++;
15  }
16  print "</ul>";
```

4: The < before the filename indicates that it is being opened for reading.
6: Line 6 stores each line of the file referenced by the LOG filehandle as individual elements in the @logmessages array.
9: Lines 9–16 print out the contents of the array (which contains the contents of the external file).

Figure 19.10 *Notice that it was not necessary to call CGI.pm for this script since all the input comes from the external file and none comes directly from the visitor.*

Figure 19.11 *Here is the current contents of the* logfile.txt *file that will be read by the script and stored in the* @logmessages *array.*

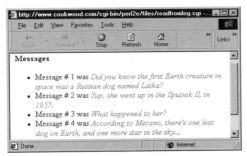

Figure 19.12 *The contents of the* @logmessages *array are printed using a* foreach *loop.*

Reading Data from an External File

You can use external files to hold accumulated data (like a log file for guestbook entries) or for templates for your Web pages, among many other possibilities. You can read in one or more lines from the external file as necessary.

To read all the data from an external file:

1. Open the file as described on page 248, paying special attention to step 4.

2. Type **@array**, where *array* is the name of the array that will contain each of the lines from the external file.

3. Type **=**.

4. Type **<LABEL>**, where *LABEL* corresponds to the filehandle for the file as used in step 2 on page 248.

5. Type **;** to finish the line.

6. Remember to close the external file (see page 254).

✔ Tips

■ Once the array contains the external file's contents (each line will be an individual element in the array), you can process the data as usual. For more information about arrays, Chapter 12, *Working with Arrays*.

■ To read and process one line at a time (instead of saving all the input to the array), use while <FILE> { #do such and such; } using the default variable, $_, to refer to each line of the external file. You might want to use this system if you're looking for a particular piece of data, and will stop reading in data once you've found it.

Reading Data from an External File

Closing a File

It's good practice to close filehandles manually when you are finished with them.

To close a file:

1. Type **close (LABEL);**, where *LABEL* is the filehandle for the file.

2. Verify that the filehandle was successfully closed *(see page 250)*.

✔ Tip

■ While some systems will close filehandles automatically when the script is finished, it's always a good idea to clean up after yourself.

```
1   #!/usr/local/bin/perl -wT
2   use strict;
3
4   open(LOG, "<../../../../logs/
      logfile.txt")|| Error('open', 'file');
5   flock (LOG, 2) || Error ('lock','file');
6   my @logmessages = <LOG>;
7   close (LOG) || Error ('close', 'file');
8
9   print "Content-type: text/html\n\n";
10  my $n=1;
11  print "<b>Messages</b><ul>";
12  foreach (@logmessages) {
13    print "<LI>Message # $n was <i>$_</i>
        \n";
14    $n++;
15  }
16  print "</ul>";
```

7: This line closes the file referenced by the LOG filehandle (which is *logfile.txt*).

Figure 19.13 *It's good practice to close a filehandle as quickly as possible after using the file's contents. (This is the same script as the one shown in Figure 19.10 on page 253).*

```
1   #!/usr/local/bin/perl -wT
2   use strict;
3
4   my ($mday,$mon,$year)=
        (localtime)[3,4,5];
5   $mon += 1;
6   $year += 1900;
7
8   my $date=sprintf('%04d%02d%02d', $year,
        $mon, $mday);
9   my $filename="logfile$date.txt";
10
11  rename("../../../../logs/logfile.txt",
        "../../../../logs/$filename") ||
        Error('rename', 'file');
12
13  print "Content-type: text/html\n\n";
14  print "The new name of the file is
        $filename";
```

4: Lines 4–9 get (a slice of) the date, format it, insert it between "logfile" and ".txt" and store the resulting name in `$filename`.

11: This line renames the *logfile.txt* file with the name stored in `$filename`. Notice I've appended the path name to the new filename. Otherwise, Perl would try to create the new file in the current working directory (usually cgi-bin) and would probably give a permissions error.

Figure 19.14 *Be especially careful with paths and filenames. They are often the culprit when something isn't working. For more help, consult* Dealing with Paths in Unix *on page 299.*

Figure 19.15 *The visitor clicks the Archive Log File button (which is the submit button) to rename the file.*

Figure 19.16 *Since the visitor can't access or see the contents of the logs directory, the output to the browser shows the new name that has been given to the log file. However, although it's nice to tell your visitor what's going on, it's essential to give the browser some output—otherwise, it will give you an error.*

Renaming a File

Sometimes it becomes necessary to change the name of a file. For example, you might want to periodically change the name of a log file with your guestbook entries so that it is not replaced with the new log file.

To rename a file:

1. Type **rename (name,**, where *name* is the current filename for the file, or a scalar variable that refers to the filename.

2. Type **newname**, where *newname* is the desired new name that you want the file to have. You may also use a scalar variable that contains the new name.

3. Type **)** to complete the function.

4. Type **;** to complete the sentence.

✔ Tips

- Either the file must be located in the working directory *(see page 261)* or you must provide the full path (either absolute or relative) to the file.

- You can use the `rename` function to move a file to a new location. Just make sure that the new name that you use in step 2 contains the correct new path. The file will no longer exist in the old location.

- As always, literal filenames (but not variables) should be enclosed in quotation marks.

- If a file already exists with the filename (and path) given in step 2, it will be overwritten by the file you're renaming.

Removing a File

You can eliminate a file from within your Perl script. This is handy if you've created temporary files that you're now ready to get rid of.

To remove a file:

1. Type **unlink (**.

2. Type **filename**, where *filename* is the constant or variable that references the filename (and path, if necessary) of the file that you want to delete. Separate multiple filenames with commas.

    Or type **@array**, where *array* is the name of the array that contains the filenames of the multiple files that you wish to eliminate.

3. Type **)**.

4. Verify that the file was successfully deleted *(see page 250)*.

5. Type **;** to complete the sentence.

✔ Tips

■ For security reasons, you should not let your visitors specify the name of the file to be deleted—at least without verifying the information first. For more details, see Chapter 18, *Security*.

■ You could also use an expression for the filename. Something like `$path . $filename` is not uncommon.

■ The path is necessary if you're eliminating a file that is not in the working directory *(see page 261)*.

```
1   #!/usr/local/bin/perl -wT
2   use strict;
3
4   my ($mday,$mon,$year)=
        (localtime)[3,4,5];
5   $mon += 1;
6   $year += 1900;
7
8   my $date=sprintf('%04d%02d%02d', $year,
        $mon, $mday);
9   my $filename="logfile$date.txt";
10
11  unlink ("../../../../logs/$filename")
        || Error('delete', 'file') ;
12
13  print "Content-type: text/html\n\n";
14  print "<P>$filename was deleted";
```

4: Lines 4–9 are the same as in Figure 19.14 on page 255 and get (a slice of) the current date, format it, slip it between "logfile" and ".txt" and save the result in the `$filename` variable.

11: The file referenced by `$filename` is eliminated. If it cannot be eliminated (perhaps because it doesn't exist, the permissions are wrong, or the path is incorrect), the `Error` subroutine *(see page 250)* is called.

Figure 19.17 *In this example, I don't let the visitors have any input with regard to the filename. That way, they cannot choose to delete files I don't want them to delete.*

Figure 19.18 *The visitor clicks the Delete Today's Log File button (a submit button) to activate the script that deletes the file.*

Figure 19.19 *The output to the browser shows the visitor exactly what's happened since they can't access or see the contents of the logs directory.*

```
1   #!/usr/local/bin/perl -wT
2   use strict;
3   use CGI ':standard';
4
5   print "Content-type: text/html\n\n";
6
7   my $year = param('year');
8   my $month = sprintf("%02d",
      param('month'));
9   my $day = sprintf("%02d", param('day'));
10
11  my $desired_file =
      "logfile$year$month$day.txt";
12
13  if (-e "../../../../logs/$desired_file"){
14    print qq(A log does exist for
      $month/$day/$year);
15    ... # see lines 4-16 in Figure 19.10

28  } else {
29    print "Sorry, the log for $month/$day/
      $year doesn't exist.";
30  }
```

7: Lines 7–11 create a filename based partially on the input from the visitor.

13: The condition checks to see if the file the visitor requested exists. If so, the visitor is notified (line 14) and the log is displayed (lines 15–27 are virtually identical to the hopefully now familiar lines 4–16 from Figure 19.10 on page 253). If not, the visitor is told that the log file doesn't exist (line 29).

Figure 19.20 *The visitor chooses part, but not all, of the filename. In addition, the file is only opened if the filename already exists, which keeps the visitor from being able to process extraneous or malicious commands.*

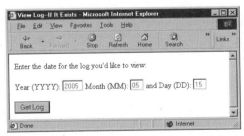

Figure 19.21 *The visitor enters the year, month, and day of the desired log file.*

Figure 19.22 *If the file doesn't exist, the script displays a simple error message to the visitor explaining what happened.*

Checking a File's Status

It's often useful to know whether a file already exists, if it's readable, writable, or executable, and so on. You can combine the use of a conditional with a special set of codes that test for certain file states.

To check a file's status:

1. Type **-e** to check if the file exists.

   Or type **-r** to check if its permissions are set such that it can be read.

   Or type **-x** to check if its permissions are set such that it can be executed.

   Or type **-w** to check if its permissions are set such that it can be written to.

   Or type **-d** to check if it's a directory.

2. Type the filename that you're interested in checking. You can use either a scalar variable or a constant. If you use a constant, enclose it in quotation marks.

✔ Tips

- There is a difference between a file being *able to be* read (it exists, has the proper permissions, and so on) and it being opened properly for reading or for writing *(see step 4 on page 248)*.

- If you prefer, you can use a filehandle LABEL instead of the filename in step 2.

- There are several other ways to check a file or directory. The full table can be found at *http://www.perl.com/pub/doc/manual/html/pod/perlfunc/_X.html*.

- In Unix, directories are considered nothing more than special kinds of files. Therefore, you can also check a directory's status using the steps outlined above.

Opening a Directory

Imagine saving each message in a guestbook in an individual file within a particular directory. It would be very useful to be able to look at the directory's contents from within the script to see the files it contains. The opendir function lets you do just that.

To access a directory:

1. Type **opendir (LABEL,**, where *LABEL* is the label you'll use to reference the directory throughout the script. Don't forget the comma after the label.

2. Type **"path/directory"**, where *path/directory* (with no trailing forward slash) is the path to the desired directory.

3. Type **)**.

4. Verify that the directory was opened successfully *(see page 250)*.

5. Type **;** to finish the statement.

✔ Tips

- Once you've accessed a directory with opendir, you can view its contents *(see page 259)*. Don't forget to close the directory when you're done *(see page 260)*.

- You can use "." to refer to the working directory and ".." to refer to the parent directory, that is, the directory that contains the working directory. For more information on constructing relative paths, consult *Absolute and relative paths* on page 300.

```perl
1  #!/usr/local/bin/perl -wT
2  use strict;
3  use CGI ':standard';
4
5  print "Content-type: text/html\n\n";
6
7  my $year = param('year');
8  my $month = sprintf("%02d",
     param('month'));
9  my $day = sprintf("%02d", param('day'));
10
11 my $desired_file =
     "logfile$year$month$day.txt";
12
13 if (-e "../../../../logs/
     $desired_file") {
14   print qq(A log does exist for
       $month/$day/$year);
15   open (LOG,
       "<../../../../logs/$desired_file")
       || Error('open', 'file');
16   flock (LOG, 2) || Error('lock','file');
17   my @logmessages = <LOG>;
18   close (LOG)|| Error('close', 'file');
19
20   my $n=1;
21   print "<P><b>Messages</b><ul>";
22   foreach (@logmessages) {
23     print "<LI>Message # $n was
         <i>$_</i>\n";
24     $n++;
25   }
26   print "</ul>";
27
28 } else {
29   print "Sorry, the log for
       $month/$day/$year doesn't exist.";
30
31   opendir (LOGDIR, "../../../../logs/")
       || Error ('open', 'directory');
32   my @logfiles = readdir (LOGDIR);
33   closedir(LOGDIR);
34   if (@logfiles) {
35     print "<P>You can choose from the
         following logs:<ul>";
36     foreach (sort @logfiles) {
37       print "<LI>$_" if /^logfile/;
38     }
39   print '</ul>';
40   }
41 }
```

1: Lines 1–29 are the same as in Figure 19.20.

31: This line opens the log directory and assigns it the directory handle LOGDIR. Note that if the script is unable to open the directory (perhaps the permissions don't allow it), it will return false. The || operator requires that one of the two halves of the statement return true, and thus will run the Error subroutine (not shown).

32: Lines 32–41 are described on pages 259–260.

Figure 19.23 *You must open a directory and assign it a filehandle before you can look at or access its contents.*

Opening a Directory

```
28  } else {
29    print "Sorry, the log for
        $month/$day/$year doesn't exist.";
30
31    opendir (LOGDIR, "../../../../logs/")
        || Error ('open', 'directory');
32    my @logfiles = readdir (LOGDIR);
33    closedir (LOGDIR);
34    if (@logfiles) {
35      print "<P>You can choose from the
          following logs:<ul>";
36      foreach (sort @logfiles) {
37        print "<LI>$_" if /^logfile/;
38      }
39      print '</ul>';
40    }
41  }
```

1: Lines 1–29 are the same as in Figure 19.23.
31: This line opens the logs directory and assigns it the filehandle LOGDIR (*see page 258*).
32: Line 32 stores the name of each file and directory contained in the directory referenced by the filehandle LOGDIR in the @logfiles array. We'll work with the data in lines 34–40.
33: Once we've stored the data, we can close the filehandle (*see page 260*).
34: Line 34 checks to see if there is anything in the directory referenced by LOGDIR. If there is, it prints out an explanatory message in line 35.
36: The foreach loop sorts the @logfiles array and outputs an HTML list item with each element of the array that starts with the word *logfile*.

Figure 19.24 *The* readdir *function is handy for looking inside a directory and working with the files and directories that it contains.*

Figure 19.25 *In this example, the visitor has entered a date for which there is no log.*

Figure 19.26 *This script looks inside the logs directory and lists its contents so that the visitor can see which log files do exist.*

Reading the Contents of a Directory

Once you've opened a directory, you can see which files it contains.

To see what's in the directory:

1. Open the directory as explained on page 258.

2. Type **@array**, where *array* is the name of the array that will contain the names of all the files (and directories) in the open directory.

   Or type **$scalar**, where *scalar* is the variable that will contain only the next single item in the directory.

3. Type **=**.

4. Type **readdir (LABEL)**, where *LABEL* corresponds to the label you gave the opened directory (*see step 1 on page 258*).

5. Type **;** to finish the statement.

✔ Tips

- It's a good idea to close the directory after reading its contents (*see page 260*).

- Each time you use $scalar_variable = readdir (LABEL);, you will get the *next* filename contained in the opened directory.

- You probably won't want to use everything you find in a directory. You can write a regular expression to choose only those contents that match a certain criteria. For example, in line 37 of Figure 19.24, I use an if statement with a regular expression to print only those files whose names begin with *logfile*. (This filters out . and .. and the files and directories I'm not interested in.)

Reading the Contents of a Directory

Closing a Directory

Once you've finished looking at a directory's contents, you should close the directory.

To close a directory:

1. Type **closedir (LABEL)**, where *LABEL* corresponds to the directory handle you used when opening the directory in step 1 on page 258.

2. Type **;** to finish the line.

```
28  } else {
29      print "Sorry, the log for $month/$day/
           $year doesn't exist.";
30
31      opendir (LOGDIR, "../../../../logs/")
           || Error ('open', 'directory');
32      my @logfiles = readdir (LOGDIR);
33      closedir (LOGDIR);
34      if (@logfiles) {
35          print "<P>You can choose from the
               following logs:<ul>";
36          foreach (sort @logfiles) {
37              print "<LI>$_" if /^logfile/;
38          }
39          print '</ul>';
40      }
41  }
```

1: Again, lines 1–29 are the same as in Figure 19.23 on page 258. (In fact, the entire script is the same as the one in Figure 19.23. We're just focusing on the closedir function here.)

31: Line 31 is described on page 258.

32: Line 32 is described on page 259.

33: This line closes the directory referenced by the directory handle, LOGDIR (which was opened in line 31 and read in line 32).

34: Lines 34–40 are also described on page 259.

Figure 19.27 *If you don't use the* closedir *function, the directory is automatically closed when the script is completed or just before the directory is reopened.*

```
1   #!/usr/local/bin/perl -wT
2   use strict;
3   use CGI ':standard';
4
5   print "Content-type: text/html\n\n";
6
7   my $year = param('year');
8   my $month = sprintf("%02d",
      param('month'));
9   my $day = sprintf("%02d", param('day'));
10
11  my $desired_file =
      "logfile$year$month$day.txt";
12
13  chdir ("../../../../logs") || Error
      ('change', 'directory');
14
15  if (-e $desired_file) {
16    print qq(A log does exist for
        $month/$day/$year);
17    open (LOG, "<$desired_file")
        || Error ('open', 'file');
18    flock (LOG, 2) || Error('lock','file');
19    my @logmessages = <LOG>;
20    close (LOG) || Error ('close','file');
21
22    my $n=1;
23    print "<P><b>Messages</b><ul>";
24      foreach (@logmessages) {
25        print "<LI>Message # $n was
          <i>$_</i>\n";
26        $n++;
27      }
28    print "</ul>";
29
30  } else {
31    print "Sorry, the log for
        $month/$day/$year doesn't exist.";
32
33    opendir (LOGDIR, ".")
        || Error ('open', 'directory');
34    my @logfiles = readdir (LOGDIR);
35    closedir (LOGDIR);
36    if (@logfiles) {
37      print "<P>You can choose from the
          following logs:<ul>";
38      foreach (sort @logfiles) {
39      print "<LI>$_" if /^logfile/;
40      }
41      print '</ul>';
42    }
43  }
```

13: This line changes the working directory to the one that contains the log files. This means that in lines 15 and 17 you don't have to specify the path to `$desired_file`—as long as it resides in the current directory specified with `chdir`.

33: I use the period to denote the current working directory (the one referenced by `chdir`).

Figure 19.28 *This script is equivalent to the one described on pages 258–260. The only difference is that the* `chdir` *function has saved us some typing.*

Changing the Working Directory

The default working directory is the one that contains the script itself. If you want to work with another file (or directory) in that same directory, you don't need to specify any path information. However, if you want to work with a file in some other directory, you either have to specify the absolute or relative path that indicates the file's location, or you have to change the working directory to the directory that contains the file, and then just use the filename. If you'll be using several files within a directory, the second option is often quicker.

To change the working directory:

1. Type **chdir (**.

2. Type **directory**, where *directory* is the absolute or relative path that identifies the new working directory.

3. Type **)** to complete the function.

4. Verify that the directory was changed properly *(see page 250)*.

5. Type **;** to finish the line.

✔ Tips

- You can use a scalar variable (or even an expression) that references the directory, if desired.

- You can use an absolute or a relative path name to indicate the location of the new working directory. For more information, consult *Absolute and relative paths* on page 300.

Changing the Working Directory

Creating a Directory

You can use a script to create a new directory that will accommodate new files.

To create a new directory:

1. Type **mkdir (**.

2. Type **directory**, where *directory* is the name (and path, if necessary) of the new directory.

3. Type **0oge**, where *0* is a zero, and *oge* indicates the directory's initial permissions, before the umask takes effect. Generally, you'll want to use **0777**, which, with the standard umask of 22, will result in a directory with 755 permissions *(see page 292)*.

4. Type **)** to complete the function.

5. Type **;** to finish the sentence.

✔ **Tips**

- The directory will be created within the working directory *(see page 261)* unless you specify its full path, from the root. For more information on absolute and relative paths in Unix, consult *Absolute and relative paths* on page 300.

- On Unix, when you create a directory with a script, the script is considered the directory's owner, with respect to permissions. This may make it difficult for you to change permissions manually from within Unix. For details, consult *Who's the Owner?* on page 294.

- For more information on umask, consult *Default Permissions* on page 293.

- You can create a script that changes the permissions of a directory *(see page 263)*.

```
1   #!/usr/local/bin/perl -wT
2   use strict;
3
4   print "Content-type: text/html\n\n";
5   my ($mday,$mon,$year)=(localtime)[3,4,5];
6   $mon += 1;
7   $year += 1900;
8
9   my $date=sprintf ('%04d%02d%02d',
        $year, $mon, $mday);
10  my $filename="logfile$date.txt";
11
12  chdir ("../../../../logs")
        || Error ('change','directory');
13
14  if (-e "public/archives") {
15    print "<P>The archives directory does
        exist.";
16  } else {
17    print "<P>The archives directory does
        not exist.";
18    mkdir ("public/archives", 0777) ||
        Error ('make', 'directory');
19    print "<P>The archives directory has
        been created.";
20  }
21  rename ("logfile.txt",
        "public/archives/$filename")
        || Error ('rename', 'file');
22
23  print "<p>The new name of the file is
        $filename";
```

14: First, the script checks to see if the directory already exists. If so, it won't be necessary to create it.

18: As long as the condition in line 14 is false, that is, the directory does not exist, this line creates the directory with 777 permissions. Note that with a standard umask of 22, the directory will have 755 permissions, with the script as owner.

Figure 19.29 *This script differs from the one shown in Figure 19.14 only with respect to the new directory. Instead of renaming the file in the same directory, in this script, the renamed file is placed in the new directory.*

Figure 19.30 *It's always a good idea to tell your visitor what's happening, especially since they cannot see inside your directories themselves.*

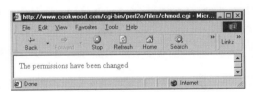

Figure 19.31 *Since I'm not the owner, I can't delete the archives directory nor change any of its files—even though they're in my space on the server.*

```
1   #!/usr/local/bin/perl -wT
2   use strict;
3   print "Content-type: text/html\n\n";
4
5   chdir ("../../../../logs")
       || Error ('change','directory');
6
7   if (-e "public/archives") {
8     chmod (0777, "public/archives") ||
         Error ('change', 'permissions');
9     print "<P>The permissions have been
           changed";
10  } else {
11  print "that file/directory doesn't
         exist";
12  }
```

8:   This line gives everyone (including me!) full permissions to the archives directory. If for some reason the chmod function cannot change the permissions, the Error subroutine (not shown) will run.

9:   This line is not fluff! Without it, the browser would have nothing to do and would complain.

Figure 19.32 *You might want to keep a script like this handy in case you need to change the permissions of a directory created by a script.*

Figure 19.33 *When the script runs, the browser confirms the permission change—and is happy because it's outputting something.*

Figure 19.34 *After the script runs, you can go back to the server and delete the directory and its contents (or rename them or whatever) at will.*

Changing Permissions from within a Script

On Unix, whether a file can be accessed—by you, your script, or your visitors—depends on the file's permissions *(see page 291)*. You can change a file or directory's permissions either from the Unix prompt *(see page 296)* or from within your script, as described here.

To change a file or directory's permissions:

1. Type **chmod (**.

2. Type **0oge,**, where *0* is a zero, *o* is the number that indicates the *o*wner permissions, *g* is the number that indicates the owner's *g*roup's permissions, and *e* is the number that indicates *e*veryone else's permissions *(see page 292)*.

3. Type the name of the file or directory whose permissions you want to change.

4. Repeat step 3 as desired, separating each element with a comma.

5. Type **)** to complete the function.

6. Verify that the permissions were changed properly *(see page 250)*.

7. Type **;** to complete the sentence.

✔ Tips

■ Permissions are generally only an issue on Unix machines, not Windows or Macs.

■ Since you are not the owner of files and directories created with a script, it is sometimes essential to use a script like this one to get the permissions you need.

■ For more information about permissions, see Appendix C, *Permissions on Unix*.

■ You may use scalar variables or an array in the chmod function.

Changing Permissions from within a Script

Removing a Directory

You can eliminate any directory—as long as it is empty—from within the Perl script.

To remove a directory:

1. Type **rmdir (**.

2. Type **directory**, where *directory* is the name (and path, if necessary) of the directory that you wish to eliminate.

3. Type **)** to complete the function.

4. Verify that the directory was properly removed *(see page 250)*.

5. Type **;** to finish the sentence.

✔ Tips

■ If the directory is not empty, you'll have to remove its contents before deleting it. For more information on deleting files, consult *Removing a File* on page 256.

■ The data from filehandles and directory handles is automatically tainted. You'll have to untaint any filenames that come from either source before performing a system call (like deleting) on them. For more information about tainted data, consult *Avoiding Tainted Data* on page 244. For more information about cleaning tainted data, consult *Cleaning and Using Outside Data* on page 245.

■ Depending on your Web host, and the permissions they have set up for your directories, the rmdir function may not work properly on Windows systems.

```
1   #!/usr/local/bin/perl -wT
2   use strict;
3   print "Content-type: text/html\n\n";
4   chdir ("../../../../logs")
       || Error ('change', 'directory');
5
6   if (-e "public/archives") {
7     chdir ("public/archives")
         || Error ('change', 'directory');
8     opendir (ARCHIVES, ".")
         || Error ('open', 'directory');
9     my @archives = readdir (ARCHIVES);
10    closedir (ARCHIVES);
11
12    if (@archives) {
13      foreach (@archives) {
14        if (m/^(logfile\d{8}\.txt)/) {
15          my $file = $1;
16          print "<P>looking at file $file";
17          unlink $file
             || Error('unlink','file');
18          print "<P>$file was deleted";
19      }}
20    } else {
21        print "<P>The archives directory
             was empty";
22    }
23    rmdir ("../archives")
         || Error ('remove', 'directory');
24    print '<P>The directory has been
           removed';
25  } else {
26    print '<P>The directory could not be
           found';
27  }
```

6: This line checks to see if the directory exists.

7: Lines 7–22 open the directory and delete its contents, if any *(see page 256)*. Since directory handles are automatically tainted, the logfile names must be untainted (lines 14–15) before being deleted *(see page 245)*.

23: This line removes the directory. If the rmdir function has a problem, the Error subroutine runs.

24: Confirmation is printed for the visitor's benefit and also so the browser won't complain about having nothing to output.

Figure 19.35 *The series of conditional statements makes this script more flexible. It is able to deal with several different situations (Does the directory exist? Is it empty? and so on) without sending out a server error.*

Figure 19.36 *Once the directory is empty, it can be deleted.*

```
1   #!/usr/local/bin/perl -wT
2   use strict;
3   use CGI ':standard';
4   my ($to, $from, $subject, $contents);
5
6   print "Content-type:text/html\n\n";
7
8   $to = param('to');
9   $from = param('from');
10
11  $subject = param('subject');
12  $contents = param('contents');
13
14  open(MAIL, "|/usr/lib/sendmail -t")
        || Error ('open', 'mail program');
15
16  print MAIL "To: $to \nFrom: $from\n";
17  print MAIL "Subject: $subject\n";
18  print MAIL "$contents\n";
19
20  close(MAIL);
21
22  print "Thanks for your comments.";
23
24  sub Error {
25    print "The server can't $_[0] the
        $_[1]: $! \n";
26    exit;
27  }
```

14: Here I've opened a connection to the sendmail
    program on the server, and called it MAIL for
    future reference. The -t flag ensures that the
    sendmail program will look in the incoming
    data for the mail headers like *To:*, *From:* and
    Subject:. Notice that both the vertical line (the
    pipe symbol, which means the connection is to
    a program) and the path to that program are
    enclosed in quotation marks. Finally, if there is a
    problem opening the connection, the Error
    subroutine will run.

16: Lines 16–18 are explained on page 266.

20: Close the filehandle as usual *(see page 254)*.

22: Don't forget to send some output to the
    browser. Otherwise it will complain. (Feel free
    to send it something better than this.)

Figure 19.37 *Opening a connection to a program like
sendmail is similar to opening a file or directory. The
main syntactical difference is the vertical line preceding the path to the program.*

Getting Ready to E-mail Output

Most Unix systems include an e-mail program
called *sendmail* that you can use to send the
output from a form via e-mail.

To prepare sendmail to receive output:

1. Type **open (MAIL**, where *MAIL* is the label
   you'll use to reference your mail program.

2. Type **"**.

3. Type **|**. This is called the pipe symbol and
   is necessary when you want to send data
   to a separate program (like sendmail).

4. Type **/usr/lib/sendmail**, where */usr/lib/
   sendmail* is the path to the sendmail program on your Unix server. You can also
   use a variable that contains such a path.

5. Type a space and then **-t** to have sendmail
   get the addressee, sender, and subject
   from the To:, From: and Subject: lines.

6. Type **"** to complete the piped in data.

7. Type **)** to complete the open function.

8. Verify the filehandle was successfully
   opened *(see page 250)*.

9. Type **;** to finish the line.

✔ Tips

- If you don't know where the sendmail
  program is on your Unix server, try
  /usr/lib/sendmail, /usr/sbin/sendmail or
  try typing **whereis sendmail** at the
  prompt (with telnet). Or just ask your ISP!

- The sendmail program is so common on
  Unix systems that its absence is almost
  always intentional. In other words, if it's
  not there, it's probably because your ISP
  doesn't want you to send mail. Ask them.

Sending Output via E-mail

Once you've set up sendmail to receive the output, you're ready to actually send it.

To send output via e-mail:

1. Complete steps 1–9 on page 265.

2. Type **print MAIL "To:**, where *MAIL* is the same label that you used in step 1 on page 265.

3. Type the address (or scalar variable that contains the address) to which the message should be sent.

4. Type **\n** to create a newline between the To: and From: lines.

5. Type **From:** .

6. Type the address (or scalar variable that contains the address) that should appear in the message's From line.

7. Type **\n** to create a newline between the From: and Subject: lines.

8. Type **Subject:** .

9. Type the text (or the scalar variable that contains the text) that should appear in the Subject line of the e-mail message.

10. Type **\n** to separate the Subject line from the contents.

11. Type the contents (or the scalar variable that contains the contents) of the e-mail message.

12. Type **";**.

13. Close the connection to the mail program by typing **close (MAIL);**, where *MAIL* is the same label that you used in step 1 on page 265.

```
1   #!/usr/local/bin/perl -wT
2   use strict;
3   use CGI ':standard';
4   my ($to, $from, $subject, $contents);
5
6   print "Content-type:text/html\n\n";
7
8   $to = param('to');
9   $from = param('from');
10
11  $subject = param('subject');
12  $contents = param('contents');
13
14  open(MAIL, "|/usr/lib/sendmail -t")
        || Error ('open', 'mail program');
15
16  print MAIL "To: $to \nFrom: $from\n";
17  print MAIL "Subject: $subject\n";
18  print MAIL "$contents\n";
19
20  close(MAIL);
21
22  print "Thanks for your comments.";
23
24  sub Error {
25    print "The server can't $_[0] the
          $_[1]: $! \n";
26    exit;
27  }
```

1: Lines 1–12 get the data for the message from the Web page.
14: See page 265.
16: Once the connection to the sendmail program is opened, lines 16–18 send data there with the print function and the filehandle (MAIL). Notice there are no commas or parentheses.
20: It's always a good idea to close your filehandles.

Figure 19.38 *I've used three* print *statements to send the data to the sendmail program, but you could just as easily use a single* print *statement, as long as there are newlines between each of the e-mail fields.*

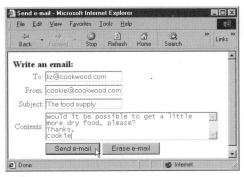

Figure 19.39 *The visitor enters the data on the Web form. The contents of each field will be used to send the e-mail message.*

Figure 19.40 *Once again, it's not only helpful for your visitor to get confirmation that everything's going ok, it's also important that the browser have something to output. Otherwise, it'll will output an error.*

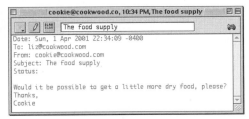

Figure 19.41 *Here's the message once it's been received in Eudora. (Eudora is my e-mail program, but any e-mail program would work just fine.)*

✔ Tips

■ You may specify any part of the message with a variable. For example, you might use `print MAIL "To: $recipient\n From: $sender\nSubject:New Web Site\n $body";`.

■ If you prefer, you can split up the contents of the message into various lines. You can use an individual `print` function for each header, or combine all the headers into one `print` function. The most important thing is that you separate each header from the next with newlines (\n).

■ If you type the addresses as constants (that is, not with a scalar variable), you must precede each @ in the address with a backslash so that Perl doesn't think it's an array. For example, you might use `print MAIL "To: liz\@cookwood. com\n";`. Of course, if the constant is single quoted, no backslash is required: `print MAIL 'To: liz@cookwood.com';`. For more on quotes and backslashing, see page 30.

■ You can use this syntax of the `open` function to send output to other Unix programs besides sendmail, like grep or cat.

■ While the sendmail program is available for Windows (*http://www.indigostar.com/sendmail.htm*), it's much, much more prevalent on Unix systems. If you're on a Windows server, you'll have to ask your Web host about the program that they recommend for sending e-mail.

Sending Output via E-mail

UPLOADING FILES

The form elements that we've talked about so far let you process text that your visitors enter in fields. If, however, you want to allow your visitors to upload complete files to your site, you have to follow an entirely different process.

One of the advantages of using CGI.pm is that it makes it relatively easy to allow people to upload files to your server. While this chapter covers the basic technique, you should also be familiar with the processes discussed in Chapter 19, *Files and Directories*, before going on here.

Letting your visitors upload files also creates a variety of security risks. Be sure to read Chapter 18, *Security* thoroughly.

Creating a Form for Uploading Files

There is a special HTML code for creating the parts of a form in which the visitor can choose the file they'd like to upload to your site.

To create a form for uploading files:

1. In your HTML document, create the FORM tag, complete with the ACTION and METHOD attributes, as usual *(see page 86)*.

2. Within the FORM tag, add **ENCTYPE = "multipart/form-data"** so that the server knows what sort of data is coming.

3. Create an explanatory message inviting visitors to upload a file.

4. Type **<INPUT TYPE="file"** to create the box in which the visitor can specify the file they wish to upload.

5. Type **NAME="upload"**, where *upload* is the label that will identify the incoming file.

6. If desired, type **SIZE="n"**, where *n* is the *box's* physical size, in characters. (It has absolutely nothing to do with the size of the file itself!)

7. Type **>** to complete the upload box.

8. Create a Submit button as usual *(see page 93)*.

9. Type **</FORM>** to complete the form.

✔ Tips

- For more details about creating forms, Chapter 7, *Getting Data from Visitors*.

- To have visitors upload more than one file at a time, simply repeat steps 3–7.

```
<html><head><title>Uploading Files</title>
</head><body>

<form action="http://www.cookwood.com/cgi-
bin/perl2e/uploading/uploading.cgi"
method="post" enctype="multipart/form-data">

What file would you like to upload?
<input type="file" name="uploadfile" size="30">
<input type="submit">

</form></body></html>
```

Figure 20.1 *Be sure to add the* ENCTYPE *attribute to the opening* FORM *tag and then create the upload box.*

Figure 20.2 *Here's what a file upload field looks like with Internet Explorer for Windows (top) and Macintosh (bottom).*

```
1   #!/usr/local/bin/perl -wT
2   use strict;
3   use CGI ':standard';
4
5   print "Content-type: text/html\n\n";
6
7   my $file= param('uploadfile');
8
9   if ($file) {
10    print "<p>You want to upload
        <b>$file</b>";
11
12  } else {
13    print "No file was chosen";
14  }
```

7: We use the `param` function on the name of the upload file field (*uploadfile* in this case, see Figure 20.1 on page 270) and then store the result in a scalar variable (called `$file`) in order to get the uploaded file's name.

9: It's a good idea to check to see if a file has actually been chosen. In this case, the condition will be true if `$file` contains anything and false if it is empty or undefined.

10: If a file was designated, its name will be printed out.

13: If no file was selected, the script outputs an error message.

Figure 20.3 *Use the* `param` *function on the field's* NAME *attribute to get the uploaded file's name, as specified by the visitor.*

Figure 20.4 *The visitor either types in the file name or uses the Browse button to select a file.*

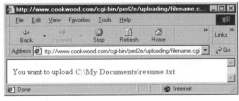

Figure 20.5 *This simple script does nothing more than tell the visitor which file they've chosen. It does not yet actually upload the file. But we'll get there.*

Getting the Name of the Uploaded File

Your first step in processing an uploaded file is to identify it by finding out what the visitor called it on his or her system. CGI.pm's `param` function, when used as a scalar, returns the name of the uploaded file.

To get the name of the uploaded file:

1. In your CGI script for processing uploaded files, type **$file =**, where *$file* is the variable that will contain the uploaded file's name.

2. Next type **param ('fieldname')**, where *fieldname* matches the contents of the NAME attribute for the file uploading box you created with HTML in step 5 on page 270.

✔ Tips

- The contents of the `$file` variable will match the file name that the visitor enters in the File Uploading box. If the visitor uses the Browse button to choose the file, the entire path from the root directory is included for Windows machines but only the filename is used on Macintosh systems. If the visitor types in the name manually, that's what will be stored in the `$file` variable.

- The file isn't uploaded yet. We've only got its name. Keep reading!

- CGI.pm offers a new `upload` function in version 2.47 and later which checks to make sure that the visitor has selected a proper file to be uploaded. You'd want to add `my $fh = upload ('fieldname');` where *$fh* is the filehandle for the file to be uploaded. And then use `$fh` as the condition of the `if` statement in line 9 to make sure it has a defined (and valid) value.

Finding out a File's MIME Type

The next bit of information you can find out about a file that a visitor wishes to upload is its MIME type. You can save this information for later reference or even use it as a condition for uploading the actual file.

To find out an uploaded file's MIME type:

1. Once you've used `param` on the file upload field's name *(see page 271)*, type **$info = uploadInfo($file);**, where *$info* is the name of a scalar variable that will contain information about the MIME type and *$file* matches the name of the scalar variable you used in step 1 on page 271.

2. Next, type **$type= $info->{'Content-Type'};** to pull the MIME type out of the `$info` variable you created in step 1 and store it in the *$type* variable.

3. If desired, create an `if` statement that allows the file upload if the MIME type matches a certain string *(text/html, image/jpeg,* etc.).

✔ Tips

■ The `uploadInfo` function creates a *reference* to a hash, and not the hash itself. That's why you need the `->` (arrow) operator when accessing the hash's information: to dereference the hash and get the value that corresponds to the *Content-Type* key. If this all sounds too confusing, don't worry about it. Just type it as is.

■ Note that *Content-Type* is case sensitive. If you type a little *t* for *type*, it won't work.

```
1   #!/usr/local/bin/perl -wT
2   use strict;
3   use CGI ':standard';
4
5   print "Content-type: text/html\n\n";
6
7   my $file= param('uploadfile');
8
9   if ($file) {
10    my $info = uploadInfo($file);
11    my $type= $info->{'Content-Type'};
12
13    print "<p>You want to upload
        <b>$file</b> with a MIME type of
        <b>$type</b>";
14
15  } else {
16    print "No file was chosen";
17  }
```

10: First we use the `uploadInfo` function (from CGI.pm) to store information about the file in the `$info` variable.

11: Next, we extract the MIME type from the `$info` variable by dereferencing the hash and then accessing the value that corresponds to the *Content-Type* key. Don't sweat the details here.

Figure 20.6 *CGI.pm's* `uploadInfo` *function helps you find out what sort of file is being uploaded.*

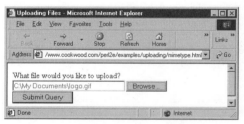

Figure 20.7 *As before, the visitor specifies the file they wish to upload.*

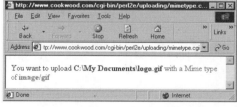

Figure 20.8 *Now, the script knows (and can output) the MIME type of the file to be uploaded.*

```
1    #!/usr/local/bin/perl -wT
2    use strict;
3    use CGI ':standard';
4
5    print "Content-type: text/html\n\n";
6
7    my $file = param ('uploadfile');
8    my $info = uploadInfo ($file);
9    my $type = $info -> {'Content-Type'};
10
11   if ($file) {
12     open (UPLOAD, ">../../../tmp/
          uploadfile") || Error ();
13
14     my ($data, $length, $chunk);
15       while ($chunk = read ($file, $data,
            1024)) {
16         print UPLOAD $data;
17
18         $length += $chunk;
19           if ($length > 51200) {
20             print "That file is too big. The
               limit is 50K.";
21             exit;
22           }
23       }
24     close (UPLOAD);
25
26     print "<p>You uploaded <b>$file</b>
          which had a MIME type of
          <b>$type</b>.";
27
28   } else {
29     print "No file was chosen.";
30   }
31
32   sub Error {
33     print "Couldn't open temporary file:
          $!";
34     exit;
35   }
```

12: Line 12 specifies that the uploaded file will be
     stored with the filename *uploadfile* in the *tmp*
     directory (within a bunch of other directories).
     We'll be able to write to this space by using the
     filehandle UPLOAD.

Figure 20.9 *The first step in processing an uploaded file is to decide where it should be saved. I'll describe the rest of this script on the following pages.*

Specifying Where the File Should Be Saved

Uploaded files need to be uploaded to a particular location on your server. You can specify such a location by opening a filehandle and assigning it a path and filename. (You've already learned all about filehandles in Chapter 19, *Files and Directories*, but I'll give you a quick refresher here.)

To specify where the uploaded file should be saved:

1. Type **open (UPLOAD,**, where *UPLOAD* is the filehandle or label for the location on the server where the file is to be uploaded.

2. Then type **">uploadfile")**, where *uploadfile* is the path and file name where the uploaded file will be stored on your server.

3. Verify that the filehandle was opened correctly *(see page 250)*.

4. Type **;** to complete the line.

✔ Tips

■ For security reasons, make sure you, and not your visitor, create the filename in step 2. For more details, see Chapter 18, *Security*.

■ You have to change a directory's permissions in order for it to accept uploaded files from a script. For more information about permissions, see Appendix C, *Permissions on Unix*.

Reading in and Limiting Uploaded Files

Curiously enough, when you treat the $file variable as a scalar, it returns the name of the file to be uploaded. However, if you treat it like a filehandle, you get access to the data to be uploaded itself.

It's important to limit the size of uploaded files as you read them in. Otherwise, malicious or unwitting visitors may choke your server with huge files.

To read in and limit the size of an uploaded file:

1. Type **my ($data, $length, $chunk);**, where *$data* will temporarily hold each chunk of data from the incoming file, *$length* is the variable that will monitor the file's size in bytes, and *$chunk* is the actual amount of data that is read in.

2. Type **while ($chunk = read ($file, $data, 1024)) {** to assign successive chunks of 1024 bytes of the uploaded file specified by $file (from step 1 on page 271) to the $data variable (from step 1 above) and store the actual number of bytes read in in $chunk (also from step 1 above).

3. Type **print UPLOAD $data;** to copy each successive chunk of data (that was temporarily stored in the $data variable) to the *UPLOAD* filehandle you opened on page 273.

4. Type **$length+=$chunk;** to store the current size of the output file in the $length variable declared in step 1.

5. Type **if ($length > upload_limit) {**, where *upload_limit* specifies the maximum number of bytes that you want your visitors to be able to upload.

```perl
1   #!/usr/local/bin/perl -wT
2   use strict;
3   use CGI ':standard';
4
5   print "Content-type: text/html\n\n";
6
7   my $file = param ('uploadfile');
8   my $info = uploadInfo ($file);
9   my $type = $info -> {'Content-Type'};
10
11  if ($file) {
12    open (UPLOAD, ">../../../tmp/
        uploadfile") || Error ();
13
14    my ($data, $length, $chunk);
15      while ($chunk = read ($file, $data,
          1024)) {
16      print UPLOAD $data;
17
18      $length += $chunk;
19        if ($length > 51200) {
20        print "That file is too big. The
            limit is 50K.";
21        exit;
22        }
23      }
24    close (UPLOAD);
25
26    print "<p>You uploaded <b>$file</b>
        which had a MIME type of
        <b>$type</b>.";
27
28  } else {
29    print "No file was chosen.";
30  }
31
32  sub Error {
33    print "Couldn't open temporary file:
        $!";
34    exit;
35  }
```

15: Read in successive chunks of 1024 bytes from the $file variable (that contains the data to be uploaded and was created in line 7), storing them temporarily in the $data variable.

16: Write the contents of the $data variable to the specified location on the server identified with the UPLOAD filehandle (in line 12).

18: Lines 18–22 update the $length variable with the current number of bytes that have been uploaded and makes sure the upper limit is not breached. If it is, an error is output and the script is aborted.

24: Once the file is completely uploaded, the filehandle can be closed.

26: The visitor receives confirmation of the upload.

Figure 20.10 *The uploaded file is written to the space designated on the server in successive chunks of 1024 bytes.*

Figure 20.11 *The visitor selects the file to be uploaded and presses the Submit Query button.*

Figure 20.12 *As long as the file is properly uploaded, the visitor receives confirmation of such.*

Figure 20.13 *If the file to be uploaded exceeds the maximum size, the visitor gets an error message and the upload is aborted.*

6. Type **print "That file is too big. The limit is upload_limit";** which will be output if the amount of uploaded data exceeds the limit you've set in step 5.

7. Type **exit;** to stop uploading data if the file is too big (that is, the condition in step 5 becomes true).

8. Type **}** to complete the conditional that tests the file size.

9. Type **close (UPLOAD);** to close the file-handle that you opened on page 273.

✔ **Tips**

■ You may also wish to notify the visitor if the file is successfully uploaded. At any rate, you will have to create some output for the browser.

■ You may want to change the name and location of the file once it's properly uploaded and then delete the temporary file. For more details, consult *Renaming a File* on page 255 and *Removing a File* on page 256.

■ It may also be a good idea to create either a log file or e-mail with information about uploaded files. These too are discussed in Chapter 19, *Files and Directories.*

■ If a file is too large, the allowed portion will still be uploaded. It's probably a good idea to immediately remove a temporary file if a file has exceeded the limit and has not been fully uploaded. Again, see *Removing a File* on page 256.

■ The value of the $chunk variable will only differ from 1024 when the last bit of the file is read in—assuming the size isn't equally divisible by 1024.

Reading in and Limiting Uploaded Files

DEBUGGING

Debugging is one of those scary programming words with a simple meaning: reviewing your script and getting out all the kinks (or *bugs*, as programmers call them). Strangely enough, the most common bugs have nothing to do with Perl and all to do with typing. If you type *pirnt* instead of *print*, Perl will spit out an error. On the next two pages, I point you in the direction of many of these simpler, but still frustratingly elusive, bugs.

You can also create an error subroutine, and then use it in your main script to output specific information (detailed by you) when something happens that shouldn't. Notice, I didn't say "unexpected". Part of your job is to anticipate what might go wrong, or at least test that things go right, and then provide alternatives for when they don't.

A good way to debug your programs is to get rid of all the fluff. If you've got a lot of HTML formatting, get rid of it. If you've got a whole branch of the program that only runs in extreme cases, lose it. You can test bits and pieces of your program by temporarily commenting out the parts you don't want to look at. For more details, consult *Isolating the Problem* on page 283.

Checking the Easy Stuff

Perhaps the biggest mistake that folks make when debugging a script is to look at the most complicated parts first, thinking that that's where an error would be most likely to crop up. The problem is that the complicated parts are complicated to fix but no more likely to contain errors than the simple sections. My advice is to start with the simple stuff and work your way up.

To check the easy stuff:

- Are you running the Perl CGI script through a server? You can't (generally) run CGI scripts from the command line. For more details, see Chapter 3, *About Servers, Perl, and CGI.pm.*

- If you're creating and editing scripts on a local computer (say, a Mac or PC), did you actually upload the new version to the server or just save the changes locally? (I've done this a million times!) For more details on uploading files, consult *Uploading Your Script* on page 53.

- Does the ACTION attribute in the FORM tag of the HTML page that calls the script actually point to the right place—including the file name and path?

- Did you use the Perl interpreter to check your script's syntax? It might be able to help pinpoint the problem *(see page 40).*

- Does your script have a shebang line? Does that shebang line correctly point to the Perl interpreter on your server? For more details, consult *The Shebang Line* on page 35.

- Did you set the proper permissions for the script and any other external files and directories that it uses, creates, reads from, or writes to? For more details, consult Appendix C, *Permissions on Unix.*

- Does your script produce output for the browser? Just processing input is not enough. Something, no matter how small, must go to the browser or else your visitor will get an error.

- Did you insert the MIME content line before any output that goes to the browser? For more details, consult *Creating Output for a Browser* on page 38.

- Have you spelled everything right, including function names, names and values that must match their counterparts on the HTML form, subroutine names, and others. Watch out for extra spaces, upper- and lowercase letters, and special symbols.

- Does every line in your script end with a semicolon? (OK, except the first and last lines of conditional blocks, the shebang line, and comments.)

- Have you preceded quotation marks in HTML coding with backslashes so that Perl doesn't think the quotation marks are meant for it? Have you backslashed other special characters that you want Perl to ignore?

- Are you using the right variable symbol: $ for scalars, @ for arrays and % for hashes?

- Are you using parentheses instead of curly brackets or vice versa? (Try using a large font for displaying your code.)

- Do your external files that contain subroutines contain a last line of 1;? If they don't you won't be able to require them successfully *(see page 164)*.

- Are you mixed up about a function's return value versus its immediate result? Consult *Result vs. return value* on page 29 for more details.

Creating an Error Subroutine

If you're sick of the plain vanilla errors produced by your browser in conjunction with the server, you can create a special error subroutine that may be able to give you more information during testing.

To create an error subroutine:

1. Type **sub Error {**, where *Error* is the name of the subroutine that will output the information about the error.

2. Type **print "Content-type: text/html\n\n";**. This line will only be necessary if the error is called before the MIME content line in your main script *(see page 38)*.

3. Create a `print` statement that includes arguments passed to the subroutine in the main program that identify the origin of the error and/or the special `$!` variable that contains the last system error string.

4. If desired, type **exit;**. The `exit` function immediately stops the script. You'll want to abort the script if, for example, you haven't been able to open a required external file.

5. Type **}** to complete the subroutine definition.

6. If this is an external subroutine, the last line in the file should be **1;** so that requiring it returns true *(see page 165)*.

✔ Tips

- This subroutine will be particularly helpful if you pass detailed information as the argument to the subroutine in the main script.

- The more standard Perl `die` function is described on page 281.

```
22   open (FILE, "nofile.txt") ||
         Error('open', 'file');
23
24   sub Error {
25   print "Content-type: text/html\n\n";
26   print "The server can't $_[0] the $_[1]:
         $! \n";
27       exit;
28   }
```

22: On this line (which could be practically any line in a larger script), I attempt to open a non-existent file (for demonstration purposes). If it fails (and I know it will), the `Error` subroutine is called with the arguments *'open'* and *'file'*.

24: This line defines the name of the subroutine.

25: This line prints the MIME content line for the error output.

26: This line prints an error message, customized with the two arguments that come from the main script. It ends by printing out the contents of the special `$!` variable, which contains the most recent system error string.

27: The `exit` function aborts the entire script.

28: The curly bracket completes the definition of the subroutine.

Figure A.1 *You can add a subroutine within the main script itself as in this example, or create a separate file in which to store it.*

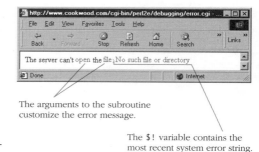

The arguments to the subroutine customize the error message.

The `$!` variable contains the most recent system error string.

Figure A.2 *If the error message is for your visitors, you might want to add some HTML formatting to jazz it up (see page 232).*

```
1  #!/usr/local/bin/perl -wT
2  use strict;
3  use CGI::Carp qw(fatalsToBrowser);
4
5  open (FILE, "nofile.txt")
     || die ("Can't open file: $!");
6
7  print "Content-type: text/html\n\n";
8  print "Due to some miracle, I was able
     to open the file!";
```

3: Use this line to output fatal errors to the browser, so that they're more accessible. (Without it, the errors will only be stored in the system error log.)

5: I try to open a non-existent file (for demonstration purposes). When the open function fails, the die function will output my custom error message, the contents of the $! variable, the full path to the script, and the line number where the error occurred.

Figure A.3 *You can add a subroutine within the main script itself as in this example, or create a separate file in which to store it.*

Figure A.4 *The CGI::Carp module outputs the information from die to the browser. In order, we have (1) the personalized error message specified as the argument to the die function, including the (2) contents of the $! variable, followed by the (3) full path to the script—and the line number within that script—where the error occurred.*

Using Perl's Error Reporting

When your program creates an error, Perl stores a message about that error in a special variable called $!. Perl's die function captures that error message, specifies the script and line number where it occurred, and lets you add personalized information before sending the whole thing to the system error log. Finally, the CGI::Carp module can make the die information more accessible by sending it directly to the browser.

To capture and customize errors with die:

1. After an operation that you want to test, type **|| die**.

2. Then type **("Error message: $!")**, where *Error message* is a personalized message that describes what you were trying to do. Perl sets the $! variable automatically to the system error message.

To output system error information to the browser:

Near the top of your script, type **use CGI::Carp qw(fatalsToBrowser);**. This ensures that the error messages captured and created with the die function are output to the browser and not just to the less accessible system error log.

✔ Tips

■ The die function is a more standard, *Perlish*, way of capturing and displaying error messages and then exiting from a script. The Error subroutine described on page 280 is a less-powerful, homegrown, but perhaps simpler alternative.

■ The ! in $! is supposed to be a mnemonic for "BANG!, What happened?".

■ Without CGI::Carp, die only sends data to the system error log *(see page 282)*.

Viewing the System Error Log

The errors generated by your Perl CGI script (and all the other Perl CGI scripts and Web pages on a server) are gathered and stored in a system error log. Unix system users can look at the end of the error log while a script is running to see what happened.

To read the system error log:

1. Telnet to the Unix server *(see page 296)* and type **tail -f /path/to/errorlog**. The last few error messages will be displayed and, perhaps more importantly, new errors will be displayed as they occur.

2. Leaving the Telnet window open in the background, go to your browser and run the script that's creating the problems.

3. Watch the Telnet window to see the information about the error.

4. When you've finished looking at the system error log, type Control C.

✔ Tips

- You'll have to ask your Web host where your error log is *(see page 46)*.

- The error log will probably contain errors from many different domains (the ones that are served by your server). That's why it's better to use the `tail` function to see just the last few (and the ones happening as you run your script) instead of downloading and sifting through the entire, usually very large, system error log.

- You can also type **tail -f /path/to/errorlog | grep search_pattern** to view only those errors that have the *search_pattern* (like your domain name, for instance) in them.

- It's usually simpler to use the CGI::Carp module as described on page 281 to view the system error information.

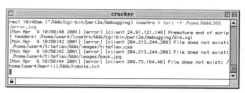

Figure A.5 *Type* **tail -f path/to/errorlog** *in the Telnet window and leave the window open in the background. The last messages from the error log are displayed.*

Figure A.6 *Run your script as usual. Don't worry that you don't get much information in the browser.*

Figure A.7 *Switch back to the Telnet window to see the information being added to the error log. (This is the same information as that which is shown in Figure A.4 on page 281.) When you're done, type Control C to stop viewing the error log.*

```
1   #!/usr/local/bin/perl -wT
2   use strict;
3
4   print "Content-type: text/html\n\n";
5   print "<HTML><HEAD><TITLE>Showing off
      in either
      browser</TITLE></HEAD><BODY>";
6
7   my $browser = $ENV{'HTTP_USER_AGENT'};
8
9   if ($browser =~ /Mozilla/) {
10    print "You're using Netscape";
11    print "You can show off in Netscape
        with the <BLINK>Blink</BLINK> tag";
12  }
13  #else {
14    #print "You're not using Netscape,
        which means you're probably using
        Explorer";
15    #print "In Internet Explorer, a cool
        tag is the <MARQUEE BEHAVIOR=
        "scroll"> Marquee tag</MARQUEE>";
16  #}
```

13: After getting an Internal Server Error, I decided to comment out lines 13 through 16 by preceding them with a #. Now, when I check the script, there is no error and I know the error must be in lines 13–16. Can you see it? (You could also catch this error by using the -c flag on your server—see page 40.)

15: Those quotation marks around *scroll* are messing Perl up. One solution would be to use qq instead of double quotes to delimit the string. Or, since *scroll* contains no spaces or symbols, the quotation marks are not required and I can delete them. Or, if I'm determined to quote with double quotes, I can backslash the quotes surrounding *scroll* to take away their special meaning for Perl *(see page 232)*.

Figure A.8 *There are actually two problems with this script. By isolating part of the script, we can find the problem with the quotation marks. The second problem is solved on page 284.*

Isolating the Problem

If you've written a long or complicated script, it's often hard to figure out where the problem is. One solution is to create specific error messages, using the subroutine described on page 280. Another solution is to comment out parts of the script so you can test one section at a time. Commenting out is a quick and easy way to temporarily hide troublesome parts of the script without having to remove them from the file completely.

To isolate the problem:

Type a **#** in front of each line in the Perl script that you want to hide. When you run the script, Perl will act as if those lines did not exist.

✔ Tips

- For more information on commenting, consult *Documenting Your Script* on page 39.

- To make the lines active again, simply remove the # symbol.

- Be careful that you don't comment out parts of the script that you need in the uncommented sections.

- Sometimes I end up commenting practically everything except the shebang line, the MIME content line, and a single print statement. That's OK. Maybe the problem is with uploading the file, or the extension, or the permissions. Peel away the layers until it works and then gradually put them back until it breaks. That should help pinpoint the problem.

Following a Variable's Progress

Another way to test what's going in your script is to use the print function exhaustively to watch each variable's progress. Once you figure out where the problem is, you can get rid of the extra printing.

To follow a variable's progress:

Add a print statement after each change to the variable. When you run the script, you'll be able to see what the variable is doing and compare it with what you expected.

✔ Tips

■ For testing arrays and hashes, you might want to add a foreach loop before the print statement in order to print out each element in the array or hash.

■ You can add the information within HTML comments so that it's not immediately visible to visitors, as in print qq(<!--browser is $browser-->);.

Figure A.9 *The script "works", but clearly doesn't work very well. This is Explorer, and yet the script is telling me it's Netscape. What's the deal?*

```
1    #!/usr/local/bin/perl -wT
2    use strict;
3
4    print "Content-type: text/html\n\n";
5    print '<HTML><HEAD><TITLE>Showing off in
         either browser</TITLE></HEAD><BODY>';
6
7    my $browser = $ENV{'HTTP_USER_AGENT'};
8    print "browser is $browser";
9
10   if ($browser =~ /Mozilla/) {
11     print "You're using Netscape";
12     print '<P>You can show off in Netscape
           with the <BLINK>Blink
           </BLINK> tag';
13
14   } else {
15     print "You're not using Netscape,
           which means you're probably using
           Explorer";
16     print '<P>In Internet Explorer, a cool
           tag is the <MARQUEE
           BEHAVIOR=scroll>Marquee
           tag</MARQUEE>';
17   }
```

8: This line prints the contents of the $browser variable so I can see where the problem is.

Figure A.10 *Printing variables as you operate on them can help you pinpoint where things start to go wrong.*

Figure A.11 *By printing out the $browser variable, I can see that for some strange reason, Internet Explorer identifies itself as Mozilla, Netscape's code name. I'll have to think of another way to distinguish between the two—perhaps searching on MSIE.*

Using Other Folks' Scripts

One of the nice things about Perl and CGI is that they've been around for a while and most of the things that you'll want to do on your Web site have already been done. Instead of reinventing the wheel, many people will let you copy their wheel and use it on your own site.

The most common kinds of Perl scripts are access counters, guestbooks, Web-based bulletin boards, randomizers, and, of course, shopping carts. Nevertheless, you can find other kinds of programs available, including an Engineering Units Conversion Calculator, games like chess, hangman, and concentration, and a program called WebHints that lets you create a Joke (or Hint) of the Day page for your visitors, among many others.

Where to find scripts?

While you can do a search at Google or AltaVista, I've listed a couple of my favorite sites in Appendix E, *Perl and CGI Resources*.

Using Other Folks' Scripts

As you might expect, installing someone else's script is not so different from installing your own. You simply save the step of writing the script itself. Since I've already explained how to install your own scripts Chapters 4, 5, and 6 (depending on the server), I will simply reference the pertinent sections here instead of repeating them. The rest of this chapter is devoted to the specific steps that deal with borrowed scripts.

To use other people's scripts:

1. Find the script you want to use and download it *(see page 287)*.

2. Expand the script if it's compressed *(see page 288)*.

3. Read through the script to get an idea how it works.

4. Make sure the script is secure *(see Chapter 18)*. Does it use -w and use strict? How about -T and taint checking?

5. Configure the script for your server and needs *(see page 289)*. It may be necessary to adjust the shebang line and any paths.

6. Customize the script, if desired *(see page 290)*.

7. Upload the script to the server paying attention to any special instructions in the documentation.

8. For Unix servers, adjust the permissions as necessary *(see page 56)*.

9. Check the syntax *(see page 40)* to make sure the script still works after your changes to it.

Using Other Folks' Scripts

Figure B.1 *This is the home page for The WebScripts Archive, by Darryl Burgdorf. I've clicked on WebBBS to show you the download page for his excellent bulletin board system.*

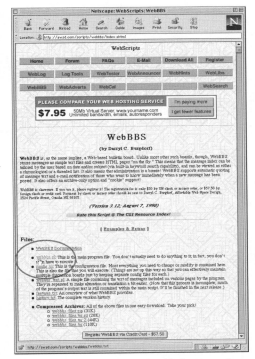

Figure B.2 *Click on the download links to copy the script to your computer. If you download the uncompressed form (as shown here), be aware that you may need to change the extension once the file is downloaded.*

Getting Other People's Scripts

In your search for already-written scripts, you should keep in mind that some programmers offer scripts—and very decent scripts at that—for free, while others charge. Some offer documentation, limited technical support, and other services, and others don't. And some let you make changes to their scripts, while some ask that you refrain from doing so.

To get other people's scripts:

1. Use your browser to jump to a site that lists or offers scripts. (For my list of favorites, consult *Other Folks' Scripts* on page 312.)

2. Browse around the site until you find the script you need.

3. Click the Download link.

✔ Tips

■ You can (of course) do a search at Google *(http://www.google.com)*, AltaVista *(http://altavista.digital.com)*, or some other search engine for your own sources of CGI scripts.

■ Make sure the script you're interested in is compatible with your server. There are slight differences between Perl scripts on different platforms.

■ Don't forget to download the documentation and configuration files. You'll need them to figure out how to install, configure, and customize the script. If there is no documentation, don't despair. You may find information in the form of commented lines within the script itself. If even that is not available, I'd recommend finding a different script.

Expanding Compressed Scripts

Scripts are text files and can therefore be opened and looked at on practically any kind of platform, including Macs, PCs, and Unix machines. However, scripts are often compressed in order to save downloading time, and the particular compression format is often platform-specific.

Aladdin Systems *(http://www.aladdinsys.com)* offers a range of excellent freeware and shareware programs for both Macs and PCs that can decompress the most common compression schemes used on all platforms. For Macintosh, StuffIt Expander plus the Expander Enhancement plug-ins can expand .zip, .tar, .tar.gz files and others, as well as the Macintosh .sit, .sea, .hqx., and .bin files. Aladdin Expander for Windows is a freeware program that expands all the above formats for Windows users. To use these programs, simply drag the compressed file over the icon of the expander program.

If you download files compressed in a Unix format, you can upload them to your server and then decompress them with the programs available on your Unix server. For more details, consult *Decompressing Tar and Zipped Files* on page 307.

Finally, you can simply download the uncompressed version. This might take slightly longer in the short run, but save you time overall by avoiding the need for compression software. In this case, be aware that sometimes the extension of the file will be changed from .cgi or .pl to .txt so that you can download the file instead of executing it. You'll have to change the extension back once you've uploaded it to your server.

It may be necessary to change a script's line endings depending on the platform it was written for. (StuffIt is a good tool for this.)

Figure B.3 *Aladdin Systems offers a range of decompression products for Macs and Windows machines.*

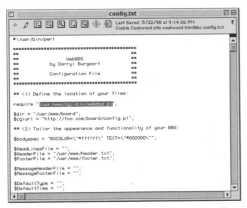

Figure B.4 *Open the configuration file, or the script if applicable, and select the setting that you need to change.*

Figure B.5 *Replace the example text with the actual path or data that you will need to make the script work. Consult the script's documentation as necessary.*

Configuring Borrowed Scripts

Depending on its complexity, there are several elements in the script which may need to be configured for your system. For example, if the script generates a log, you'll have to tell the script where on your server it should create and write the log file. Or, if it sends you the data collected from forms via e-mail, you'll want to give it your e-mail address.

Some Perl programmers create a separate configuration file that contains all the data that needs to be personalized **(Figures B.4 and B.5)** while others sprinkle the configurable elements throughout their scripts, making it a bit harder to find what needs to be changed.

To configure a borrowed script:

1. Read the documentation that hopefully explains what needs to be configured.

2. Open the script in your text editor.

3. Make sure the shebang line reflects the location of the Perl interpreter on your server.

4. Make sure the paths are correct and point to directories and files on your server.

5. Change the variables that need to reflect the circumstances of your particular server.

6. Save the file as text-only with the proper line endings. (This option is often available through the Save As box.)

✔ Tip

■ If you edit a script for a Unix server locally on a Mac or PC be sure to save it in text-only format and then upload it with Text or ASCII (and not binary). Or, you can use one of the special text editors that save in Unix format *(see page 310).*

Customizing Borrowed Scripts

If you're not crazy about the way a borrowed script outputs data, you can often change the script so that it better suits your taste. For example, if the programmer doesn't know much about HTML, or is more interested in processing data than making it look pretty, you might want to add some extra formatting touches to wow your visitors' eyes as well as their brains.

To customize borrowed scripts:

1. Open the script and analyze what it does. Figure out where you would like to make changes.

2. Edit away. Now that you know how to program in Perl, you can use the script as a base and go from there.

3. Save the file as text only with the appropriate line endings for your server.

✔ Tips

- Make sure the script's author permits you to make changes to the script. You'll often find a copyright and warning at the beginning of the script. Just because a script is offered free of charge does not always give you permission to make changes to it.

- Keep a copy of the unedited file, just in case you somehow corrupt the script and need to go back.

- Some programmers are interested in the changes you make to their scripts. If you feel so inclined, drop them a note— certainly a thank you is *always* in order.

- For more details on adding HTML formatting to output, see page 232.

Figure B.6 *I love Darryl Burgdorf's WebBBS script (see page 312), but I wanted to make it fit in with the look of the rest of my site.*

Figure B.7 *One of the purely cosmetic changes I made was to comment out (with a #) the two lines that print the name of the bulletin board (so that these lines would be ignored—see page 39). That way, I could use my own titling system, without it looking strangely repeated.*

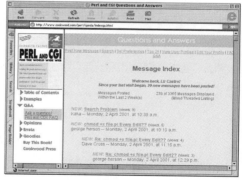

Figure B.8 *While the guts of the script are virtually identical, the outward appearance is quite different, all due to three or four minor edits to the HTML coding within the script. I've also shoehorned the whole thing into one of my framesets on my site.*

PERMISSIONS ON UNIX

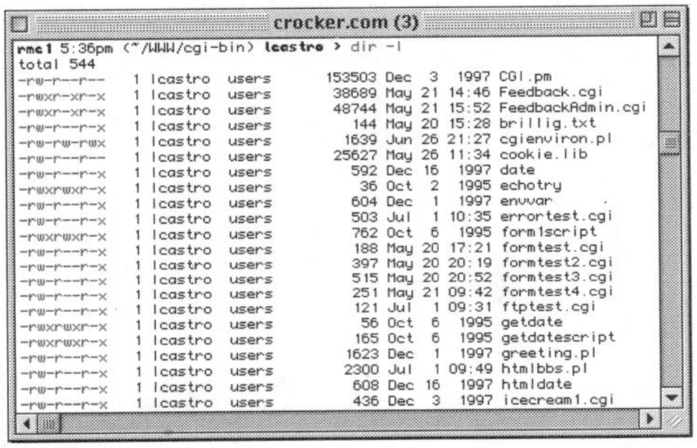

Figure C.1 *The* ls -l *function (and switch) produces a list of the directory's contents, together with the permissions of each file.*

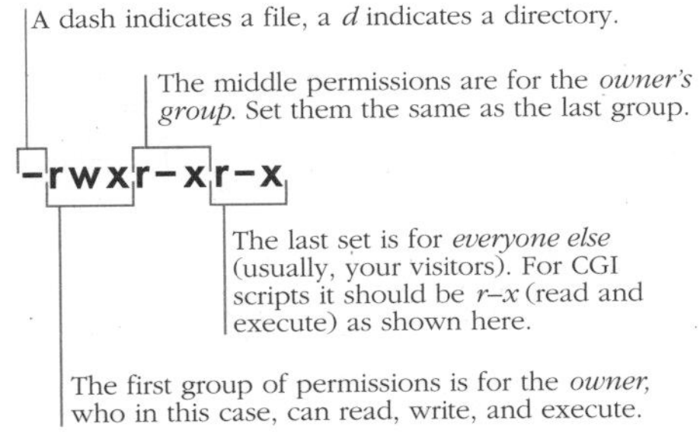

A dash indicates a file, a *d* indicates a directory.

The middle permissions are for the *owner's group*. Set them the same as the last group.

`-rwxr-xr-x`

The last set is for *everyone else* (usually, your visitors). For CGI scripts it should be *r–x* (read and execute) as shown here.

The first group of permissions is for the *owner*, who in this case, can read, write, and execute.

Figure C.2 *You can tell what permissions a file or directory has by looking at the weird string of characters to the left of its name when you use* ls -l *(Figure C.1).*

Every file and directory on a Unix server has a set of permissions that determine who can use that file or directory and just what they can do with it. It's essential to set enough permissions so that your scripts will work properly while at the same time restricting permissions enough to secure your scripts from invaders.

There are three kinds of permission: read, write, and execute. The creator or *owner* of the file or directory can bestow any or all of these privileges on each of three groups: the owner, the owner's group (a Unix thing that you probably don't need to worry about), and everyone else.

The meaning of permissions varies slightly for files and directories. A file that is read protected cannot be read or opened. For a directory, read protection means its contents cannot be listed. A file that is write protected cannot be written to (that is, changed). Similarly, you cannot create, move, rename, copy, or delete the contents of a write-protected directory. A file—particularly a CGI script—without execute permissions cannot be run. A directory without execute permissions will not let you read, write, or execute the files that it contains.

To view a file or directory's permissions:

Type **ls -l** at the Unix prompt. Permissions are displayed in a Unix server with a series of letters: *r* for read, *w* for write, and *x* for executable, in each of three columns which represent the owner, the owner's group, and everyone else **(Figures C.1 and C.2)**.

Figuring out the Permissions Code

There are two ways to change the permissions of a file or directory—either by telnetting to the Unix server *(see page 296)* or by using a script that contains the Perl commands for changing permissions *(see page 263)*. In either case, you'll use a four-digit numerical code that determines the new permissions.

To figure out the permissions code:

1. Determine which permissions you want to bestow on which groups.

2. Assign a value of 4 for read permission, 2 for write permission, and 1 for execute permission.

3. Add the values of the permissions together for each individual group.

4. Type **0oge**, where *0* is just zero, *o* is the sum of the values for the *owner's* permissions, *g* is the sum of the values for the *group's* permissions, and *e* is the sum of the values for *everyone* else's permissions.

✔ Tips

- You can usually omit the initial 0 when changing the permissions on the Unix server itself. Perl, on the other hand, requires it.

- Also see *Default Permissions* on page 293.

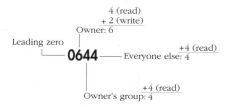

Figure C.3 *Use the 0644 permissions code for any non-executable file, including configuration files, preferences files, log files, and others.*

Figure C.4 *Use the 0755 permissions code for any executable files (including CGI scripts). Directories created by a script that contain files that will need to be changed, renamed, or deleted should also have 0755 permissions.*

Figure C.5 *Use the 0777 permissions code for any directory that you yourself create on the Unix server directly in which you'll want a script to be able to create, rename, delete, or otherwise change files.*

Figure C.6 *Here I've changed the permissions of the logs directory to 777. The new permissions (777=rwxrwxrwx) are displayed in the listing.*

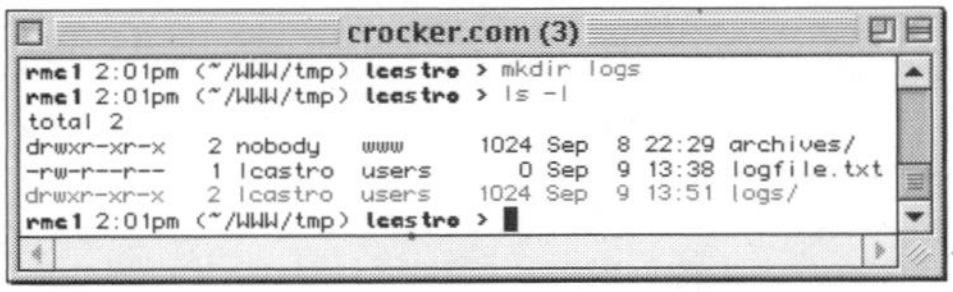

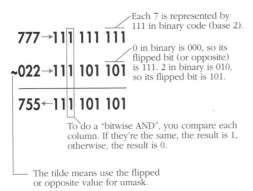

Figure C.7 *When you create a directory in Unix, it automatically is assigned 777 permissions, restricted by the value of umask. On my system, umask is 22, which leaves me with a directory with 755 permissions. If I wanted to let scripts create, rename, or delete files in this directory I'd have to change the permissions to 777 with* chmod *(see page 56).*

Figure C.8 *The* umask *command (with no arguments) lets you see how the umask has been set for your system.*

Each 7 is represented by 111 in binary code (base 2).

777→111 111 111

0 in binary is 000, so its flipped bit (or opposite) is 111. 2 in binary is 010, so its flipped bit is 101.

~022→111 101 101

755←111 101 101

To do a "bitwise AND", you compare each column. If they're the same, the result is 1, otherwise, the result is 0.

— The tilde means use the flipped or opposite value for umask.

Figure C.9 *The* umask *setting is not subtracted from the permissions but instead a rather complicated process called a "bitwise AND" is executed.*

Default Permissions

When you create a file or directory on a Unix server, its permissions are set and restricted automatically. Files start with 666, while directories start with 777. The restrictions are determined by the value of the *umask*, which is usually set at 022, although you can change it if you like.

For example, if you create a file on a Unix system with a umask of 022, the file's permissions are set at 644—anyone can read the file, only the owner can write to it, and nobody can execute it. If the file is a script, you'll have to change the permissions to at least 755, so that the owner can read, write, and execute, and everyone else can read and execute. On the other hand, if the file is just a logfile or other non-executable file, 644 will be fine.

If you create a directory on a Unix system with a umask of 022, the directory's permissions are set at 755. In order to let scripts (which are considered "everyone else") create, rename, and delete files, among other things, in that directory, you'll have to change its permissions to 777.

To see the value of the umask:

Type **umask** at the Unix prompt. Its current setting will be displayed **(Figure C.8)**.

To change the value of the umask:

Type **umask oge**, where the *oge* corresponds to the new restrictions you want to apply automatically.

✔ Tip

The umask value is not simply subtracted from the old permissions. Instead the bitwise representation of the old permissions are compared with the flipped bitwise representation of the umask to get the new permissions **(Figure C.9)**. Don't worry too much about it, though. Use the settings given above.

Default Permissions

Who's the Owner?

When you upload or create a file or directory on your Unix server, *you* are set as its owner. That means that the first number in the permissions code refers to you while the third number refers to everyone else, including your visitors.

If one of your scripts creates a file or directory, on most servers, you are *not* the owner. On my Web host for example, the owner is set to "nobody" since the script was run from an external site. That means you will only have the permissions granted by the third number, as part of "everyone else" while your scripts, executed by your visitors, will have the owner's permissions.

To see who the owner is:

1. Telnet to the directory that contains the file or directory in question.

2. Type **ls -l**. (Those are letter *l*'s.) The contents of the directory is displayed with expanded information. The third column shows the owner of the file or directory **(Figure C.10)**. On some servers, the fourth column will show the owner's group.

✔ Tip

■ The second number in the permissions code refers to the user's group, which has more meaning if you work together with a group of people on a Unix system. The easiest way to deal with the user group is to assign it the same privileges as everyone else—that is, set the second and third numbers the same.

Figure C.10 *The* ls -l *function (and switch) display the contents of the current directory. Notice that the first entry (for the* archives *directory) is owned by "nobody". It was created by a script. Even though it's in my space on the server, I can't open it or delete it. The second entry (for the* logfile.txt *file) was created by "lcastro"— that's me—which means that I created or uploaded it myself and that the owner's permissions apply to me.*

Why does it matter?

In order to create, delete, or rename files in a directory, a script has to have full permissions for that directory (7).

If *you* create a directory in Unix, the 7 in the default 755 permissions applies to *you* and you can do whatever you want with the file or directory. Meanwhile, your scripts will be restricted from creating, renaming, or deleting the directory's contents.

If you create a directory through a script, your *script* is the owner of the directory and the 7 in the default 755 permissions applies to your scripts (and now *you* are restricted from adding or deleting the directory's contents—bizarre but true).

So, if you need to give a script full permissions to a directory, you either have to create it yourself with 777 permissions or have the script create the directory with 755 permissions.

Unix Essentials

It seems crazy, but one of the biggest obstacles to writing and using Perl CGI scripts has nothing at all to do with Perl or CGI. If your Web site is hosted by a Unix server, you'll have to deal with Unix, an operating system that you may have little experience with. While some of Unix can be sleuthed out, other parts are only ridiculously simple to those folks who have worked with the system for some time.

If you've never worked with Unix, this chapter will serve as a "basic phrase book" for your journey. You'll get enough information to make yourself understood without a barrage of the details and complexities of the entire operating system. If you *have* worked with Unix, you can use this chapter as a quick reference for those commands whose syntax you may have forgotten.

Telnetting to Your Unix Server

While you may use a Mac or Windows machine to write your scripts (and indeed the rest of your Web site), you will need access to your Unix server in order to complete the configuration of those scripts. Instead of getting in your car and driving to your Web host's offices and using the Unix server in person, you can use Telnet to create a remote connection that works the same as if you were there in the flesh.

To Telnet to your Unix server:

1. Open the Telnet client on your Mac or PC. (I use BetterTelnet on a Mac and Microsoft Telnet on Windows. Both are free. For more details, see page 311.)

2. Choose the Connect command (however it's called in your program).

3. Type your Web host's name or IP address in the Host Name field.

4. Then click Connect **(Figure D.1)**. A window should appear asking you for your login name **(Figure D.2)**.

5. Type your login name and then press Return. (Ask your Web host if you're not sure what to use; usually it's the same as your e-mail before the @ sign.)

6. Type your password and then press return. You should see your home directory on the Unix server. Depending on the Unix server's settings, it might also tell you whether or not you have e-mail waiting.

✔ Tip

■ The techniques in the rest of this chapter assume that you have first opened a Telnet connection with your Unix server.

Figure D.1 *Whether you use BetterTelnet for Mac (top) or Microsoft Telnet for Windows, you'll need to type your server name and click Connect to open a Telnet connection to your server.*

Figure D.2 *The connection window shows you just what you'd see if you were at a real Unix terminal. Whether you use a Mac (top) or Windows, the contents of the Telnet window looks pretty much the same. Type your login (mine's lcastro) and your password. Your server (as mine does) may alert you about new mail received, tell you the time, give you your present location (here it's my home directory, indicated by the tilde), your user name, and the prompt. Now you're ready to go.*

Figure D.3 *To close the connection with the server, type* **logout** *or* **exit** *and then press Return or Enter. Shown here again are BetterTelnet for Macintosh (top) and Microsoft Telnet for Windows.*

Logging out ensures that nobody else can get access to your space on the Unix server if you happen to leave your machine for some period of time.

To close a Telnet connection:

1. Type **logout** or **exit** at the Unix prompt and then press Return or Enter.

2. If desired, quit your Telnet program.

✔ Tips

■ If you try to quit your Telnet program before you've officially logged out, it will ask you if you really want to close the connection. Say yes.

■ If your modem disconnects before you've officially logged out, your Telnet program will give you an error. It's not the end of the world, but it's definitely better to logout correctly and then disconnect your modem.

Telnetting to Your Unix Server

Executing Commands in Unix

If you're used to a graphical interface, getting things done in Unix can be a test of your patience and of your typing skills. Instead of double clicking programs and files, you tell Unix what you want it to do by typing commands at the prompt.

The Unix prompt

The Unix prompt, which takes different forms depending on the kind of Unix that is installed on your server and the way that your system administrator has configured it, is Unix's way of telling you it's listening and ready to do your bidding. It might look like a %, $ or, in my case, a >, and it may be accompanied by other data including the date or time, the name of the server, your user name, and the current working directory. Its most important function, however, is to indicate that it's ready for you to type a command.

Typing commands

To get Unix to do something, you have to type out a command at the prompt and then press Return or Enter. All commands (and filenames and paths) are case sensitive. Capital and small letters do matter! Some commands have special options that you can use to customize the command's results. Some commands need an object or *parameter* (like a filename or path to a directory) on which to work. In the rest of this chapter, you'll learn how to use the few basic Unix commands (together with the necessary options and parameters) that are necessary for installing and configuring Perl scripts.

Unix's response

Often when you type a command, Unix's only response is another prompt. You can generally assume that no news is good news.

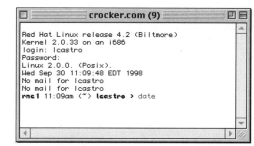

Figure D.4 *On my server, the prompt line shows the server name (rmc1), the time (11:09am), the current working directory (~, which stands for the home directory), and my user name (lcastro), followed by a >, which is the prompt that tells me that Unix is ready for a command. I've typed the command* date *and pressed Return.*

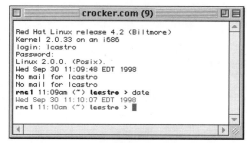

Figure D.5 *Unix displays its response to my command (that is, today's date and time), and then gives me a new prompt line indicating that it is ready for a new command.*

Executing Commands in Unix

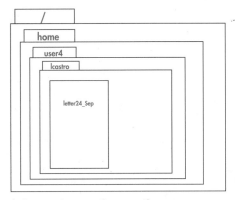

/home/user4/lcastro/letter24_Sep

Figure D.6 *The file* letter24_Sep *is located in the* lcastro *directory which is in the* user 4 *directory which is in the* home *directory which is in the root directory. You represent the root directory with a forward slash (/). You also use a forward slash to separate each successive directory from the next.*

Figure D.7 *On some servers (like mine, shown), when you log in, your home directory is the first directory you see (that is, it's your working directory—see page 302). My server shows the current directory within parentheses before the user name on the prompt line. The tilde is an abbreviation for the home directory.*

Dealing with Paths in Unix

On a Mac or Windows machine, when you want to refer to a specific file, you usually just give it a special name—like *letter24_Sep*, or whatever. On Unix, a file is referenced by its complete location on the server, starting from the top or *root* directory (represented with /). It might look something like this: */home /user4/lcastro/letter24_Sep.*

So how do you figure out what a file's complete path is? First, you should know that the top directory on all Unix servers is called *root* and is represented by a forward slash (/) to save typing. Then each directory within the root directory is given a name. Directories within other directories are separated by additional slashes. So if a file called *letter24_Sep* is in the *lcastro* directory inside the *user4* directory inside the *home* directory inside the *root* directory, it would have a full path like the one at the end of the last paragraph.

Your home directory

There is one directory on the server that has special significance for you: your *home* directory. (Your home directory is the directory you see when you first connect to the server via Telnet or an FTP program.) This is your little corner of the server where you have full access and in which you can create, upload, edit, and delete files and directories. Nobody else (except your system administrator) has access to your home directory or its contents.

Although most Unix servers recognize the tilde (~) as an abbreviation for your home directory, you generally should not use this abbreviation when specifying full path names for files, directories, or scripts in CGI scripts.

Dealing with Paths in Unix

Absolute and relative paths

Paths can be either absolute or relative. An absolute path shows every directory from the root to the actual file. An absolute path is analogous to a complete street address, including name, street, and number, city, state, and zip code, and country. No matter where a letter is sent from, the post office will be able to find the recipient. In terms of absolute paths, this means that no matter where the script that contains the path is located on your server, it will be able to find the designated file.

To give you directions to my neighbor's house, instead of giving her complete address, I might just say "it's three doors down on the right". This is a *relative* address—where it points to depends on where the information is given from. With the same information in a different city, you'd never find my neighbor.

In the same way, a *relative path* describes the location of the desired file with reference to the location of the script that contains the reference to that file. Since most scripts are contained in the cgi-bin directory, the original point of reference is often the same.

The relative path for a file that is in the same directory as the script that references it is simply the file name and extension **(Figure D.9)**. The path for a file in a subdirectory of the current directory is the name of the subdirectory followed by a forward slash and then the name and extension of the desired file **(Figure D.10)**.

Dealing with Paths in Unix

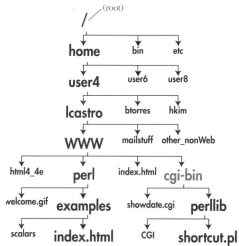

Figure D.8 *Here's a look at just some of the directories and files on my Unix server. It's something like a family tree—each directory may or may not have children (subdirectories) and those children may or may not have children of their own. The trick to creating relative paths is to figure out the relationships between each branch of the family.*

Inside the current directory, there's a file called *showdate.cgi*

"showdate.cgi"

Figure D.9 *Let's assume the script we're writing resides in the cgi-bin directory shown in Figure D.8. To reference another script in the same directory, all you need for a relative path is the name of the script itself.*

Inside the current directory there's a directory called *perllib*...

"perllib/shortcut.pl"

...that contains... ...a script called *shortcut.pl*

Figure D.10 *Again, we're writing a script that will be located in the cgi-bin directory. This time, we want to reference a subroutine that is contained within the libraries directory which is in the cgi-bin directory (see Figure D.8).*

The directory that contains the current directory...
...contains... ...a directory called *perl2e*...

"../perl/welcome.gif"

...that contains... ...a file called *welcome.gif*

Figure D.11 *This image, as you can see in Figure D.8 is in a directory (cookwood) that is inside the directory (WWW) that contains the directory (cgi-bin) that contains the script in which this path will appear—whew! In this case, we use two periods and a forward slash to go up a level, and then note the subdirectory, followed by a forward slash, followed by the filename.*

/home/user4/lcastro/WWW/
perl/examples/index.html

../perl/examples/index.html

http://www.cookwood.com/
perl/examples/index.html

Figure D.12 *Always assuming that this path will appear in a script that resides in the cgi-bin directory, at top we have an absolute path to the palette.zip file, in the middle there's a relative path to that same file, and at bottom the corresponding URL for the file is displayed.*

To reference a file in a directory at a *higher* level of the file hierarchy, use two periods and a forward slash **(Figure D.11)**. You can combine and repeat the two periods and forward slash to reference any file on the server that you have access to.

Relative paths can sometimes be useful but they're not nearly as prevalent as relative URLs in an HTML document. One problem is that it's not always clear where the script is located that contains the reference to the file. For example, even though I store CGI scripts in a cgi-bin directory, my server considers those scripts as residing within a virtual lcastro directory *inside* the cgi-bin directory. Obviously, this would affect all my relative paths. Absolute paths are always the same, regardless of the location of the script that contains them.

URLs vs. paths

While URLs often look something like paths, or use paths, they are not identical. A URL starts with a protocol, like *http:* and is then followed by the server name or IP address as it is identified out on the Web. Depending on how your server is set up, the path that comes after the server name starts with your *Web directory* which generally is somewhere within your home directory (but not equal to it).

For example, the URL of my home page is *http://www.cookwood.com/index.html.* My server is set up so that my Web directory is */home/user4/lcastro/WWW/.* Therefore, the path on the server of the *index.html* file referred to by that URL is */home/user4/lcastro/WWW/index.html.* It would be very unusual for the root directory of the server and the Web directory to be the same.

Dealing with Paths in Unix

Changing the Working Directory

While you can visualize several folders or directories at a time on your Mac or PC, in Unix you look at one directory at a time. The directory you happen to be looking at is called the *working directory*. Any commands that you type without filenames will affect the contents of the working directory and any relative paths or filenames that you reference will be with respect to the working directory.

By default, when you Telnet (or FTP) to the server, the initial working directory is your home directory. You can change the working directory as needed to save time typing complicated relative paths (or long absolute ones).

To change the working directory:

1. Type **cd** (which stands for *c*hange *d*irectory).

2. Type **path**, where *path* is the absolute or relative path that describes the location of the directory that you want to designate as the new working directory.

3. Press Return or Enter.

✔ Tips

■ To make your home directory the current working directory, don't type a path after cd (just press Return or Enter).

■ For more information on constructing absolute and relative paths, consult *Absolute and relative paths* on page 300.

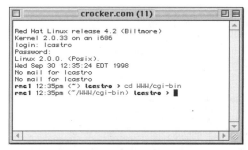

Figure D.13 *Type* cd *followed by the relative path (with respect to the current working directory) of the directory that you want to designate as the new working directory. Notice how the new location (in parentheses on the prompt line) reflects the change).*

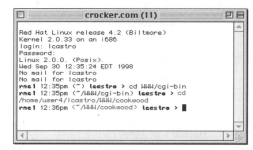

Figure D.14 *You can also use an absolute path name with the* cd *command. Again, the new working directory is displayed on the prompt line. Your server may not show the current working directory at every prompt line, but it will still change it with* cd.

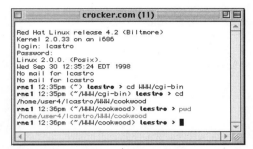

```
crocker.com (11)

Red Hat Linux release 4.2 (Biltmore)
Kernel 2.0.33 on an i686
login: lcastro
Password:
Linux 2.0.0. (Posix).
Wed Sep 30 12:35:24 EDT 1998
No mail for lcastro
No mail for lcastro
rme1 12:35pm ("~") lcastro > cd WWW/cgi-bin
rme1 12:35pm ("~/WWW/cgi-bin) lcastro > cd
/home/user4/lcastro/WWW/cookwood
rme1 12:36pm ("~/WWW/cookwood) lcastro > pwd
/home/user4/lcastro/WWW/cookwood
rme1 12:36pm ("~/WWW/cookwood) lcastro > █
```

Figure D.15 *If your server doesn't tell you where you are at all times (like mine), you can use the* pwd *function to see the full path of the current working directory.*

Finding out Where You Are

Depending on how your server is configured, it's not always obvious what the working directory is currently set to. You can use the pwd (*print working directory*) command to find out.

To find out where you are:

Type **pwd**. The full path of the current working directory is displayed.

Finding out Where You Are

Listing Directory Contents

To see what is in the working directory, you can list its contents.

To list a directory's contents:

1. Navigate to the directory whose contents you wish to see. (In other words, make the desired directory the working directory—see page 302.)

2. Type **ls** (that's a letter *l* and an *s*).

3. If desired, type **-l** (that's a letter *l* too) to view the permissions, modification date, user group, and other data about the directory's contents.

✔ Tip

■ Type **ls -ltr** to list the most recently changed files at the bottom (so you can find them easily).

■ There are other adjustments you can make to the listing command, including sorting the contents by modification date (-t), listing the contents on a single line (-m), and others. For a full listing, type **man ls** *(see page 308)*. When using more than one setting, you can combine them together: `ls -lt` is perfectly legitimate, although you can use `ls -l -t` if you like that better.

Figure D.16 *Type* ls *to list the contents of the current working directory.*

Figure D.17 *Type* ls -l *to list the contents of the current working directory together with information about the permissions, modification dates, and more.*

Figure D.18 *Type* ls -lt *to list the contents of the current working directory with extra information, and sorted by modification date.*

Listing Directory Contents

Figure D.19 *Type* **rm filename** *to delete a file. Depending on your server, you might get a warning like the one shown here asking if you really want to delete the file. Type* **y** *if so, or anything else, if not.*

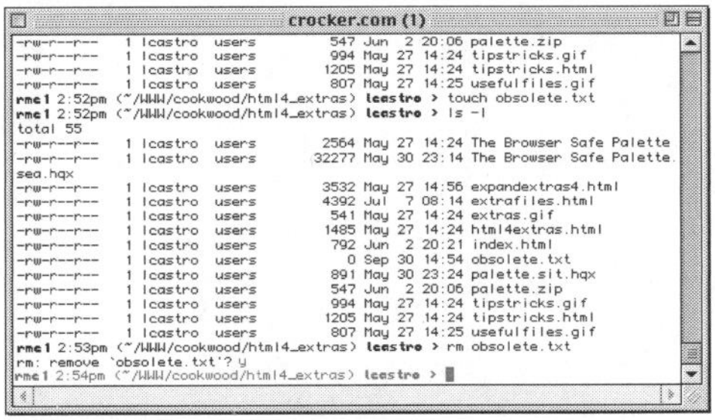

Figure D.20 *Generally, Unix won't confirm that the file has been deleted. It just gives you another prompt.*

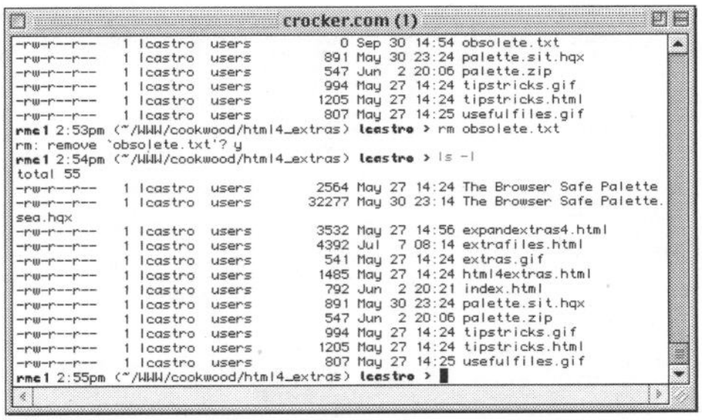

Figure D.21 *If you want to make sure that the file has been eliminated, type* **ls -l** *to check the contents of the directory from which it should have disappeared (see page 304).*

Eliminating Files

Getting rid of old and obsolete files is an essential part of keeping your Unix space organized and effective. In addition, since your Web host probably limits the amount of space that you have at your disposal, you'll want to make sure you're not wasting any of that space on files you no longer need.

To eliminate files:

1. If desired, navigate to the directory that contains the file you want to eliminate (that is, change the working directory to the directory that contains the file in question).

2. Type **rm filename**, where *filename* is either the complete filename with the full path starting from the root directory or includes a relative path with respect to the current working directory.

✔ Tips

- The letters *rm* are an abbreviation for *remove*.

- Depending on your server's configuration, you may or may not get an alert asking if you really want to remove the file. (Type *y* or *Y* to confirm the deletion, or anything else to cancel it.) At any rate, once you remove it, it's gone forever. There's no getting it back.

- How do you *create* a file—say, for a log? You can create an empty text file with pico, or with your local text editor and then upload it (*also see the fourth tip on page 249*). You can also use Unix' touch command to create a new file.

Eliminating Files

Creating and Eliminating Directories

You have full control over the contents of your home directory, including any files and directories contained within the home directory. As with your personal computer, it's often helpful to create additional subdirectories within the home directory so that you can organize your files better.

To create a directory:

1. If desired, navigate to the directory in which you want to create a new directory (that is, change the working directory to the directory that should contain the new directory).

2. Type **mkdir path**, where *path* is the absolute or relative (with respect to the working directory) path of the new directory.

To eliminate a directory:

1. If desired, navigate to the directory that contains the directory you want to delete (that is, change the working directory to the directory that contains the obsolete directory).

2. Make sure the directory to be deleted is empty. For more information on removing files, see page 305.

3. Type **rmdir path**, where *path* is the absolute or relative (with respect to the working directory) path of the obsolete directory.

✔ Tips

■ There is no "undo". Once you remove a directory, it's gone for good.

■ You can often use your FTP program to add and remove directories as well.

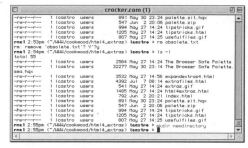

Figure D.22 *Type* **mkdir** *followed by the name of the new directory (including its path, if desired) to create the new directory. Again, Unix offers no response except for a new prompt.*

Figure D.23 *The nervous (and skeptical) among you can type* **ls -l** *to make sure that the new directory has been created. (I always do.)*

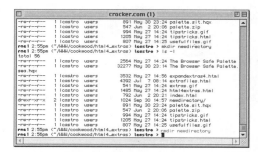

Figure D.24 *You can only remove a directory if it's empty.*

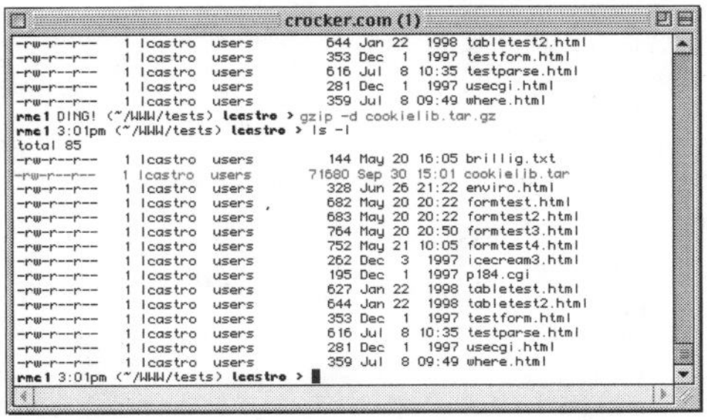

Figure D.25 *Type* **gzip -d** *and then the name of the tarred and zipped file that you want to decompress. The original file disappears and in its place you'll find an uncompressed tarred file.*

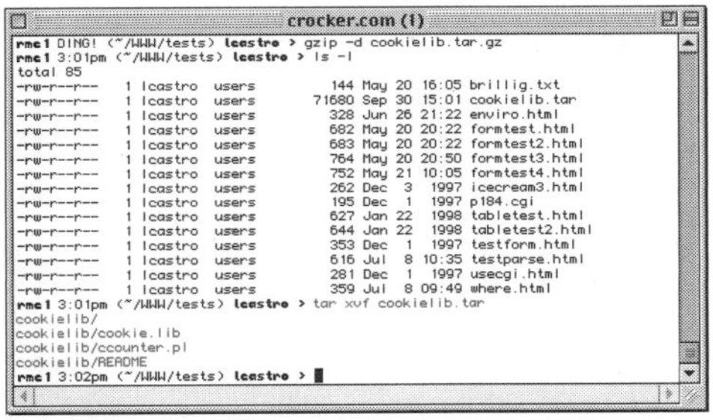

Figure D.26 *Type* **tar xvf** *followed by the name of the uncompressed tar file to extract the files it contains. Unix will display which files and directories it has created.*

Decompressing Tar and Zipped Files

Unix files are often compressed in tar (tape archive) and zip formats. Once you upload the files to your server you can use Unix commands to extract the scripts.

To decompress files on the Unix server:

1. Download the compressed scripts—with extensions like .tar, .tar.gz, .tar.Z, etc.—from the Web site to your hard disk *(see page 287)*.

2. Then upload the compressed scripts from your hard disk to your server.

3. Telnet to the Unix server *(see page 296)*.

4. Navigate to the directory that contains the file you want to decompress *(see page 302)*.

5. Type **gzip -d filename.tar.gz**, where *filename.tar.gz* is the name of the file (and its extensions) that contains the compressed script.

6. Press Return or Enter. You should now have a file that ends in .tar in your directory **(Figure D.25)**.

7. Type **tar xvf filename.tar** to extract the script from the tar file created in steps 5–6.

8. Press Return or Enter. Unix displays the extracted files **(Figure D.26)**.

✔ Tip

■ You can type **gzip -h** at the prompt to get more details about using gzip.

Getting Help with Unix

You can always find a little bit more help about a Unix command by looking at the manual page that is stored on the server itself. While these manual pages tend to be brief and cryptic, usually they'll give you enough clues to get a general idea of what the command does.

To get help with Unix:

1. Type **man**.

2. Type **command**, where *command* is the Unix function that you want help with **(Figure D.27)**.

3. Press Return or Enter. A screenful of information appears about the desired command **(Figure D.28)**.

4. Press space to see the next screenful of information **(Figure D.29)**.

   Or press **q** to quit out of the online manual and return to the Unix prompt.

✔ Tip

■ You can get information about the online manual itself by typing **man man**.

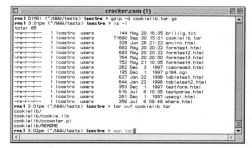

Figure D.27 *Type* **man** *and then the name of the command that you want to learn more about. Then press Return or Enter.*

Figure D.28 *The first page of the online manual for the command you have chosen is displayed. Press space to see the following page.*

Figure D.29 *Keep pressing space to pass from page to page or press* **q** *to leave the online manual and return to the Unix prompt.*

Getting Help with Unix

PERL AND CGI RESOURCES

Besides this book, you don't need much to write a Perl CGI script. Nevertheless, there are a few tools and extra sources of information that can make your job a lot easier.

Two caveats: First, printed material about the Web is often notoriously out of date. Feel free to check the updated lists of links on my Web site *(see page 22)*. Second, the lists on the following pages are by no means exhaustive. The Web is a huge and ever-changing collection of bits and bytes. If you don't find what you're looking for on these pages, jump to any search service on the Web (e.g., Google *http://www.google.com*) and look for *Perl, CGI, scripts*, or whatever it is you need.

Text Editors

You can use *any* text editor to write Perl scripts, including SimpleText on the Macintosh, WordPad for Windows, or vi or pico in Unix systems. As long as you save the file as text-only and upload it to the Unix server with ASCII or text (but not Binary), you'll be fine.

Nevertheless, there are several specialized text editors that offer a few extra features specially for Perl (and HTML) programmers.

BBEdit for Macintosh

In my opinion, the best text editor for the Mac is BBEdit, published by Bare Bones Software. Version 6 lets you edit, run, and save Perl scripts as if you were in MacPerl itself, and still take advantage of BBEdit's own strong search and replace features, excellent HTML editor and validator (if you need it), and ability to save files with Unix line endings so you don't have to worry if you've uploaded the file in Text or Binary format. You can find more information about both the shareware and commercial versions of the program at *http://web.barebones.com* **(Figure E.1)**.

UltraEdit for Windows

The best text editor for Windows that I've come across is UltraEdit. Again, it lets you create text files with Unix line endings, use regular expressions to search and replace, indent blocks of text in Perl programming style, and much more. You can download an evaluation copy at *http://www.ultraedit.com* **(Figure E.2)**.

If you're not convinced by UltraEdit, Elizabeth Knuth has a useful review site for Windows text editors—though it's slightly outdated. It's at *http://www.users.csbsju.edu/ ~eknuth/obcomp/htmled16.html*.

Figure E.1 *BBEdit's home page lists its myriad features and lets you download an evaluation copy or order a full version ($119).*

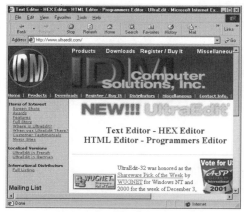

Figure E.2 *UltraEdit, developed by IDM Computer Solutions, has an extensive home page that explains its features and offers a 45-day evaluation period before requesting the $30 shareware fee.*

Figure E.3 *This is BetterTelnet's Web site, where you can get more information and download the program.*

Telnet Programs

While text editors *(see page 310)* can get very fancy, Telnet programs are still pretty basic looking. What can you expect from a program that tries to emulate a Unix terminal? While I'm sure there are many more options out there, here are the Telnet programs that I recommend.

BetterTelnet for Macintosh

The standard for Telnet programs for many years in the Macintosh community was NCSA Telnet, developed by the same folks who created Mosaic, an early and now almost obsolete browser. BetterTelnet **(Figure E.3)** is based on NCSA Telnet but has a much cleaner interface and fewer bugs. It's at *http://www.cstone.net/~rbraun/mac/telnet/*.

Microsoft Telnet for Windows

The easy solution for telnetting on Windows machines is using Microsoft Telnet which comes with the system software. It's nothing special, but it gets the job done. You can find it in your Windows directory. It's filename is *telnet.exe.* (To start it up, try choosing Start > Run and then typing *c:\Windows\telnet.exe.*)

Telnet Programs

Other Folks' Scripts

There are hundreds of scripts already written that you can download and use on your site. Some of these scripts are free, others require some sort of compensation to the programmer. While you can find scripts all over the Web, there are three particularly good places to look.

Be wary of scripts you find out on the Web. While there are many gems, you can also find lots of sloppily written security nightmares out there. Make sure the script is secure, that it uses use strict and the -w and -T switches. It's probably also a good idea to make sure it uses CGI.pm.

The CGI Resource Index

The CGI Resource Index, published by Matt's Script Archive, Inc., lists hundreds of links to Perl CGI scripts, documentation, books, magazine articles, programmers, and jobs. While the huge quantity of information is sometimes a bit overwhelming, it is a great place to get a sense for what's out there. It's at *http://www.cgi-resources.com* (**Fig. E.4**).

Extropia.com

Another famous source for free Perl CGI scripts is Extropia.com, created by Selena Sol and Gunther Birznieks. Though recently sporting a more commercial look, Extropia offers many useful scripts that its authors have generously released to the public domain. They now offer support for those scripts—for a fee. You can find them at *http://www.extropia.com.*

The WebScripts Archive

While not the biggest nor the most popular, Darryl Burgdorf's site houses what I consider to be the best documented and easiest to implement collection of Perl CGI scripts, including my favorite, WebBBS. You'll find them at: *http://www.awsd.com/scripts.*

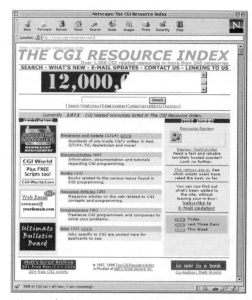

Figure E.4 *The CGI Resource Index is a helpful collection of links to CGI-related information on the Web, including hundreds of Perl scripts that you can download for your own use.*

Figure E.5 *The* www.perldoc.com *site is the place to go for Perl-related documentation*

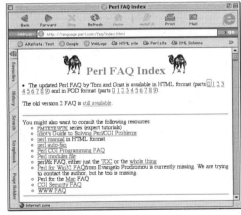

Figure E.6 *There are several helpful FAQ files about Perl. You can find a full list of them at* http://language.perl.com/faq/index.html.

Learning More

While this book has hopefully been a good start, there are many resources that you can tap to further your studies and improve your scripts.

www.perldoc.com

This site is a great repository of documentation about Perl, as well as links to other popular Perl sites. **(Figure E.5)**.

FAQs

There are several important FAQs about Perl and CGI. While some of these FAQs are annoyingly condescending, they also offer a wealth of information. You should read all of them before posting anything to any of the newsgroups listed below. Otherwise, you'll most likely be flamed. You can find a list of Perl related FAQs at *http://language.perl.com/faq/index.html* **(Figure E.6)**.

Newsgroups

There are two especially important newsgroups for folks writing Perl CGI scripts, one for Perl questions and one for CGI related questions. Although the folks on both newsgroups are very knowledgeable and more than willing to share their experience, they are not so happy about fielding questions that are answered in the FAQs or that fall outside the scope of each particular newsgroup. With that in mind, post questions specifically about Perl programming to *comp.lang.perl.misc* **(Figure E.7)**. Posts about using Perl to write CGI scripts are more welcome on *comp.infosystems.www.authoring.cgi* **(Figure E.8)**.

Learning More

Online documentation

Perl's complete documentation can be found online. In fact, it's often identical to what you'll find in *Programming Perl* (see below). You can find the online manual at: *http://language.perl.com/info/documentation.html*.

You can also type **perldoc CGI** at any command line (like MS-DOS Prompt or konsole).

Other books

In this book, you'll learn about creating Perl CGI scripts—specifically for getting, processing, and returning information through your Web pages. If you are interested in non-Web related applications for Perl scripts, try *Learning Perl* (affectionately known as the *Llama* book), by Randal Schwartz and Tom Christiansen or *Programming Perl* (the *Camel* book), by Larry Wall, Christiansen, and Jon Orwant. Both are geared towards experienced programmers interested in learning Perl.

For more information about CGI.pm, I recommend Lincoln Stein's *Official Guide to Programming with CGI.pm*.

Companion Web sites

This book has two companion Web sites that can both help you with the information contained herein as well as point you to other valuable resources. For more information, consult *The Perl and CGI VQS Guide Web Site* on page 22.

Figure E.7 *Post Perl-specific questions to the Perl programming newsgroup:* comp.lang.perl.misc. *This newsgroup is not very fond of fielding CGI-related questions.*

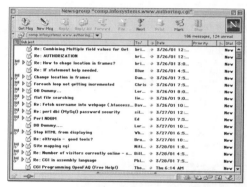

Figure E.8 *Post CGI-related questions (even about Perl) to the* comp.infosystems.www.authoring.cgi *newsgroup.*

Learning More

INDEX

Symbols

& (ampersand)
  and HTML 232
  and subroutines 159
  inputting data 97
  && (logical and operator) 125
* (asterisk)
  multiplication operator 112
  quantifier in search patterns 198
  ** (exponential powers operator) 114
@ (at sign)
  and hashes 171
  arrays 26, 139–155
  backslashing in interpolated strings 30
  escaping in e-mail addresses 267
  @_ (underscore array)
    and pop function 148
    and shift function 149
    and subroutines 160
\ (backslash)
  and character escapes 30
  escaping @ in e-mail addresses 267
  in search patterns 188
  removing special meaning from
    symbol 30
[] (brackets)
  and character classes 190, 191
  for individual elements of array 139, 142
^ (caret)
  limiting location of search patterns 193
  negating character classes 191
, (comma)
  and cookies 212
  for separating hash elements 27, 168
  for separating operands 28
{} (curly brackets)
  and blocks 32, 121
  and hashes 169, 170, 171
  closing 136
  in search patterns 199
$ (dollar sign)
  as Unix prompt 298
  for individual elements
    of arrays 142
    of hashes 169
  limiting location of search patterns 193

scalar variables 26
$&, and found data 184
$', and found data 184
$n, with regular expressions
  for cleaning tainted data 245
$n, with regular expressions 202
$`, and found data 184
$_ (default variable)
  and length function 228
  and matching patterns 182
  and mathematical functions 115
  and split function 185
  and string functions 226
  and substitutions 183
  and tr function 227
  loading 131, 253
  with simple scalar operations 109
$! (error string) 280, 281
$/ (line separator variable) 231
= (equals sign)
  assignment operator 25
  combined with other operators 119
  inputting arrays 140
  inputting hashes 168
  inputting scalar data 110
  storing data from environment
    variables 102
  =~ (binding operator)
    and finding 182
    and substituting 183
    and tr function 227
  => (corresponds to operator), and
    hashes 27, 168
  == (equal to comparison operator) 122
! (exclamation point) 35
  != (not equal to), comparison
    operator 122
/ (forward slash) 187
  for division 112
  for search patterns 187
> (greater than)
  and writing to files 248
  as Unix prompt 298
  comparison operator 122
  >>, appending files 248
  >= (greater than or equal to), comparison
    operator 122

Index

Index

8163

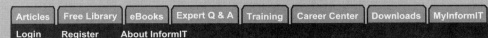